The Diaries of
LORD LOUIS MOUNTBATTEN
1920–1922

THE DIARIES OF
LORD LOUIS
MOUNTBATTEN
1920–1922

───◄≪≪≫≫►───

Tours with the Prince of Wales

Edited by
Philip Ziegler

COLLINS
8 Grafton Street, London W1
1987

William Collins Sons & Co. Ltd
London · Glasgow · Sydney · Auckland
Toronto · Johannesburg

BRITISH LIBRARY CATALOGUING IN PUBLICATION DATA

Mountbatten, Louis Mountbatten, *Earl*
The diaries of Lord Louis Mountbatten
1920–1922: tours with the Prince of Wales.
1. Mountbatten, Louis Mountbatten, *Earl*
2. Great Britain, *Royal Navy* – Biography
3. Viceroys – India – Biography
I. Title   II. Ziegler, Philip
941.082′092′4   DA89.1.M59

ISBN 0-00-217608-4

First published 1987
Text © Emberdove Ltd 1987
Selection, Introduction and editorial matter
© P. S. & M. C. Ziegler & Co. 1987

Photoset in Linotron Sabon by
Rowland Phototypesetting Ltd
Bury St Edmunds, Suffolk
Printed in Great Britain by
St Edmundsbury Press Ltd, Bury St Edmunds, Suffolk

CONTENTS

MAPS AND ILLUSTRATIONS

Maps

Illustrations

(All photographs come from the Broadlands Archives.)

PREFACE

In March 1920 Sub-Lieutenant Lord Louis Mountbatten was nineteen years old. He had served for the best part of a year as the junior of the two officers on P 31, a small vessel used for escort and anti-submarine work, and had subsequently been sent by the Royal Navy to spend a year at Christ's College, Cambridge. He was considered by his superiors to be capable and hard-working but not particularly brilliant; indeed, he had the reputation of being something of a plodder. He himself had less doubt about his capabilities, but though he would subsequently claim that his determination to rise to the position of First Sea Lord stemmed from the way in which his father was unjustly driven from that post at the end of 1914 on the grounds of his German origins, it is unlikely that his ambitions were so clearly defined at this early stage of his career. He was determined to get on, but was also out to have a good time and to see the world.

The Prince of Wales was some six years older than his cousin. His charm, frail good looks and genuine wish to do well by his future people had earned him public esteem as a paragon among princes. Those who knew him better were well aware of his moodiness, egotism and frivolity, but believed that there was nothing wrong which time and the love of a good woman would not cure. The good woman was on the scene, but not in the form that they envisaged; the Prince was besottedly in love with Freda Dudley Ward, who was wise, resolute and an excellent influence on him, but married and, for that as well as other reasons, inconceivable as a future Queen.

In 1919 King George V decided that it would further both the education of his son and the unity of the Empire if the Prince were to pay a series of visits to dominions, colonies and certain friendly countries. In August 1919 came a lengthy tour of Canada and the United States. Somewhat to the King's surprise, the visit was a triumphant success; the Prince's informality and determination to meet the people even at the price of breaching protocol, won the hearts of

9

his hosts, though it seemed less meritorious in Buckingham Palace. It was decided that two further tours should follow: the first to Australia, New Zealand, the colonies of the Pacific and the West Indies; the second to India, Burma and Japan. The Prince of Wales, whose relationship with his parents was at best formal and often acrimonious, viewed with equanimity the coming separation from his family but was in despair at being parted from Mrs Dudley Ward.

Mountbatten heard about his cousin's forthcoming visit to Australia seven or eight months before it took place. At once he began to pull every string that might secure him a place in the party. He persuaded his father that the experience he would gain on the trip could only be beneficial to his career, and enlisted Prince Albert (future Duke of York and King George VI) to plead his cause. His efforts bore fruit when, at a dance in December 1919, the Prince of Wales invited him to join the tour. 'Of course, I nearly jumped out of my skin for joy,' wrote Mountbatten.

His appointment was not to be to the Prince of Wales but as Flag Lieutenant to Rear-Admiral Sir Lionel Halsey, the Prince's Chief of Staff. This, Mountbatten explained rather obscurely to his mother, Lady Milford Haven, meant that 'when the Admiral is ashore . . . he will not require my services and David [the Prince of Wales] will take me inland as his guest'. Whatever his title, his role was to provide a companion and confidant for the Prince, and to jolly him along whenever his cousin became particularly moody or ill-tempered.

An official diary of the tour was kept by one of the equerries but, wrote Mountbatten, 'I have been instructed by the Admiral to keep an unofficial one which is going to be printed on board and kept for our own amusement.' Unlike his diary for the tour of India and Japan, which was written only for himself and his closest family, this diary was designed for an inner circle of courtiers and officials. It was indiscreet and light-hearted, but not particularly revealing about the relationships between the various members of the royal party. Its extremely frank comments about certain aspects of the tour would, however, have caused a furore if made public – a remote possibility which became alarmingly real when the ship's doctor absconded with one of the twenty copies produced on the printing press of H.M.S. *Renown*. The culprit was eventually tracked down to Kettner's restaurant, where he was bargaining with an American journalist, the diary on the table in front of him. The asking price was £5000.

Admiral Halsey, who commissioned this extravaganza, was forty-seven years old and had been Jellicoe's Captain of the Fleet. Bluff, hearty, imperturbable, far shrewder than his manner suggested, he contrived to retain the confidence and affection of both the Prince of Wales and the King. His principal assistant was Lieutenant-Colonel E. W. M. Grigg (later to become Lord Altrincham), the Prince's Private Secretary and political adviser, a highly intelligent Grenadier who had served mainly on the staff during the war, had edited the journal *The Round Table*, and had many connections in Australia. Personal Secretary was Sir Godfrey Thomas, aged thirty-one and tenth baronet, seconded from the Foreign Office and destined to remain with the Prince until the abdication. 'Godfrey Thomas is my best friend among the non-naval men,' wrote Mountbatten. 'He's so very much more interesting than the equerries, who are both honest, unintelligent, good souls.' The 'good souls' were Captain Lord Claud Hamilton and Captain the Hon. Piers 'Joey' Legh, both also of the Grenadier Guards. Hamilton was described by the *Herald* as 'clear-skinned, fair-haired, courteous, devoted to his task', embodying 'the highest ideals of the British aristocracy', but to most Australians he seemed stuffy and unapproachable – 'the least likeable of the crowd around the Prince', commented the *Bulletin*. Legh had been on the staff of the Duke of Connaught when he was Governor-General in Canada, had been appointed to the Prince's staff specifically for the Canadian expedition, and like Thomas stuck to him thereafter. Halsey's staff consisted of Mountbatten and his Secretary, Paymaster Lieutenant-Commander Arthur Janion, a robustly cheerful character who soon established a reputation for deep drinking and late nights, and is usually referred to in this diary as 'the Secretary'. Extra Equerry was Captain (later Admiral Sir Dudley) North, who acted as itinerant Master of the Household. The other most regular attender on the Prince was Surgeon-Commander A. C. W. Newport, referred to in the diary as 'the PMO' (Principal Medical Officer).

Mountbatten's diary gives the impression that the Prince's staff consisted of a band of merry comrades, united in loyalty to their master and resolved to enjoy themselves as well as to make the tour a success. This was by no means false, but concealed the fact that at first at least his presence was resented. Most members of the party had already accompanied the Prince on his visit to Canada, and they were not best pleased at the arrival of this youthful interloper, described by the Australian journalist, Keith Murdoch, as the 'Prince's special chum'. They made their resentment evident, particularly if Mountbatten was paid undue attention by journalists or their foreign hosts. 'At the bottom of it all is jealousy,' Mountbatten told his mother, 'that David should happen to like me more than they consider he ought to like a distant cousin.'

Mountbatten did his best to disarm such criticism by playing an unobtrusive role. It was not in his nature, however, to lie low for long. Dudley North objected to his habit of bursting into the Prince's cabin and shouting, 'Hurry up, David!' – 'In this ship, in company, please remember that he is our future King.' Even the Prince found it necessary to repress him from time to time: 'I have had to sit on him slightly once or twice,' he told Mountbatten's mother, 'but only in the spirit of being his best friend and he has appreciated that and is grateful.' But though his cockiness sometimes irritated his colleagues, and his intimacy with the Prince seemed threatening to at least the junior members of the entourage, the royal party was on the whole harmonious. Mountbatten's value in keeping his cousin in some sort of order was too obvious to ignore, and long before the tour was over he had been accepted as a trusted and welcome member of the team.

The diary is very much a young man's production. Though generally good-natured and as likely to make fun of the author as of anybody else, it takes little account of the embarrassment and alarm felt by those who confronted the Prince of Wales for the first time. Mountbatten's account of events would have been markedly different twenty, or even ten, years later.

H.M.S. *Renown*, the ship chosen to carry the royal party, was a battle cruiser of the same class as H.M.S. *Repulse* and had been launched in 1916. She was extremely fast but too lightly armoured to deserve a place in the battle line, and no further ships of this class were ordered. Her speed and glamorous appearance equipped her admirably for her present task, while her lack of armour was no disadvantage.

EDITOR'S NOTE

The original text of this diary was almost half as long again as the present version. I have eliminated many of the statistics in which Mountbatten delighted, such as the exact distance travelled each day, and lists of names of little interest to the general reader, as of those courtiers who accompanied the Prince to his functions. The largest cuts, however, have been made in the repetitious descriptions of the innumerable inspections, receptions, openings and suchlike 'stunts' (to use the phrase current at the time) which were the day-to-day business of the tour. By removing such detail I realize that I run the risk of giving a false impression of what was going on: I have tried to leave enough to suggest the often tedious and invariably gruelling hard work which composed the average day of the royal party, without subjecting the reader to too much of the same burden. Nothing has been removed on the grounds of discretion or confidentiality, and the sense of what remains has never been changed by the omissions. I have not, therefore, normally indicated by the traditional dots where sentences or paragraphs have been removed.

I

New Zealand, Australia, and the Colonies in The Atlantic and Pacific

16 March 1920 to 11 October 1920

Foreword

Everyone who looks through any page of this Diary will realize that it is frankly frivolous and not official in any sense. Cynics may jump to the conclusion that it contains an unusual measure of truth. It does not. On the contrary, its strongest point is its imaginative handling of facts. This holds particularly of its personal remarks.

Why, then, was it written, and how? Lincoln spoke of government 'of the people, by the people, for the people'. This is a Diary 'of the Staff, by the Staff, for the Staff'. It sprung in the first place from a desire to record the purely personal side of H.R.H.'s programme. Everyone knows how something of no account which happened this morning, or more likely never happened at all, becomes a highly coloured legend by tonight. That is how this Diary grew up. It has a painstaking basis in fact. Compare it with the official records, and you will find that its framework is laboriously correct. The rest, however, is legend, composed by many hands, and often by several at once. It is therefore a coat of many colours, with many patches of harmless libel and some patches of sheer romance. Not a word in it can be taken seriously. It is often most misleading when its tone is most correct.

There is of necessity much routine and repetition in an official tour; but for those who take part in it there is always a lighter side, which loses nothing in retrospect. We look to this Diary to remind us of that side, when history is sifting and solemnizing the really important facts.

LOUIS MOUNTBATTEN

The Journey Out

———————

TUESDAY, 16 MARCH 1920 His Royal Highness was inoculated against influenza during the forenoon.

The route to Victoria Station was lined with enthusiastic crowds. On the platform there were present Their Majesties The King, Queen and Queen Mother, and most of the other Members of the Royal Family. A few minutes before the train left, the crowd, headed by some Australian soldiers, broke through and cheered vigorously.

After the train had departed, with Prince Albert[1] and Prince Henry[2] on board, the former offered to post any letters on his return to London. The result of this was that half the occupants of the saloon car proceeded to write letters on weird-shaped pieces of paper.

A diversion was caused near Horsham by some hundreds of Blue Coat boys drawn up near the line. His Royal Highness waved a copy of the London *Mail* at them, which, however, only produced more uproar.

At Portsmouth, great crowds were collected on the Town Pier. After the visitors had left the ship, that is about 5.45 p.m., *Renown* cast off her wires and proceeded to Spithead, and thence shaped course down Channel.

WEDNESDAY, 17 MARCH The wind was still fresh but there was little motion on the ship, and, beyond a slight contretemps during the Midshipmen's instruction in the forenoon, no ill effects were felt until one of the Staff Clerks found the ciphering of a telegram too much for him. Colonel Grigg turned on the wrong tap in the bathroom and flooded Sir Godfrey Thomas out of his cabin before breakfast. This was considered such a good joke that Sir Godfrey was again flooded out before dinner.

---

[1] Prince Albert was to become Duke of York three months later, and eventually succeeded as King George VI.

[2] Prince Henry became Duke of Gloucester in 1928.

THURSDAY, 18 MARCH   The wind died down, but a marked swell remained. By some oversight no one turned on the wrong tap in the bathroom and Sir Godfrey came into breakfast quite dry. Quite early in the day a queue lined up outside the squash court with rackets and balls and the court was occupied until nightfall, when the lights suddenly went out.

Deck hockey and medicine ball were also played, in both of which games H.R.H. joined vigorously.

FRIDAY, 19 MARCH   A breeze had sprung up again during the night and the weather was noticeably warmer. A large number of officers, including H.R.H., had shots at clay pigeons during the dog watches. A small number of officers occasionally hit a pigeon. H.R.H.'s Secretary saw the light of a steamer overtaking us after dinner. On closer inspection this proved to be our own stern light.

SATURDAY, 20 MARCH   Lord Claud was punctual for breakfast this morning. On investigation it appeared that a fair friend of his resided in 'Flores in the Azores', and that he had turned out especially early to see the first sign of land. It was rather misty, and though we passed within ten miles of Flores the mountain peaks were lost in the clouds. It blew considerably.

In the dog watches H.R.H. constituted a record by running 45 minutes without stopping. Many people ran with him for short distances, but none stayed the course. Lord Claud produced a 'ball bearing' skipping rope after this, but the 'balls' wouldn't work. The Admiral's Secretary and his Clerk were inoculated before dinner.

SUNDAY, 21 MARCH   H.R.H. turned out immediately after breakfast and started dressing as he was going to inspect the ship's company at Divisions. The Captain decided shortly before Divisions that, as the Quarter Deck was still washing down, it would be better for H.R.H. to go round next Sunday. H.R.H. then turned in again. The gentlemen of the press, however, attended in top hats. Owing to risk of infection in confined quarters, H.R.H. and the Staff were forbidden to attend Divine Service. This came as a heavy blow to many of them.

MONDAY, 22 MARCH   With the exception of the soldiers the entire ship's company burst forth into whites. All 'the lads of the village' headed by H.R.H. 'sported' white socks, but were rebuked by the Admiral.

The Mess has now become divided into two sections: those who have read *Susan Lenox*[1] and those who have not. Those who have are definitely setting out to spoil the book for those who have not by openly discussing the most embarrassing situations in the book, at all hours of the day and night.

WEDNESDAY, 24 MARCH   At 3.00 p.m. a young Gunner, R.M.A., fell overboard. Both buoys were let go immediately and lifeboat was lowered. The man was, unfortunately, not recovered, and a funeral service was held over the spot. The dinner party was put off and the band did not play owing to the death.

Total distance made good at noon – 3189 miles.

THURSDAY, 25 MARCH   We anchored in Carlisle Bay, Barbados, at 5.00 p.m. An American schooner hoisted 'Welcome to Her Royal Highness the Princess of Wales'.

The Governor, Sir Charles O'Brien, and Members of the Executive Council paid their Official Visit at 6.00 p.m. At 8.00 p.m., the Governor, Lady O'Brien, the Bishop, and other leading residents came off to dinner. The Bishop partook of a glass of sherry, several whiskies and sodas, three glasses of port, and two of liqueur brandy. The Bishop enjoyed his evening.

At 9.45 p.m., 180 further guests arrived and were marched past H.R.H. in single rank. The Admiral's Personal Staff stood at the top of the superstructure ladder directing the young and beautiful maidens to the Reception Deck for dancing, and the others back to the Quarter Deck to sit out.

FRIDAY, 26 MARCH   At 9.50 a.m. H.R.H. landed officially, accompanied by the entire Staff. Crowds of niggers[2], who had lined the shore since daybreak, cheered and yelled as the barge drew near. H.R.H., Governor and respective Staffs embarked in ten motor cars and drove through town and then went for a 30-mile inland drive,

---

[1] *Susan Lenox. Her Fall and Rise* was the interminable story, written by D. G. Phillips, of a girl who 'learnt to live, but paid the price'. It had been published in 1917 but presumably had taken some time to filter through into royal circles.
[2] A curious instance of the vagaries of linguistic fashion. Twenty-four years later Mountbatten would have summarily dismissed anyone who used this epithet.

stopping at one or two places. Amazing crowds lined the route and shrieked remarks such as – 'Tank de Lord I'se seen my King', 'God bless de King', 'Sairtenly Sair'. One fat old woman was so excited that, although her mouth was open and her arms were waving, she produced no sound.

Before dinner, H.R.H.'s Personal Staff prepared to perspire by donning 'household coats', which, however, looked most effective. H.E. The Governor proposed H.R.H.'s health at the end of the official dinner, to which H.R.H. replied with a very popular speech and proposed the Governor's health. The Governor then made another speech which he prefaced with 'Your Excellency'!

SATURDAY, 27 MARCH A new 'White City' joy was added in the form of a large canvas bath filled with sea water.

H.R.H., the Admiral and some of the Staff slept on deck.

TUESDAY, 30 MARCH *Renown* and *Calcutta* arrived at Colon at 7.00 a.m. Six aeroplanes escorted the ships in, making such a noise that no 'pipes' could be heard on board.

Ships arrived at Gatun Locks at 8.00 a.m. The President of the Panamanian Republic[1] came on board while the ship was in the lower dock. The Director of Music, who had only received one copy of the Panamanian national anthem when the Military Attaché arrived, had written out parts for the band, which produced a very good imitation of the real thing.

H.R.H. then visited the control house and spill-way, eventually returning to the ship in the upper of the three locks. The ship was now on the lake level, 85 feet above sea level, and well over 6,000,000,000 foot pounds of work had been expended in raising her to this height.

The Marine Superintendent informed the Admiral of a 50-ton rock, only discovered that morning, right in the channel by the Culebra land-slide, which they were trying to haul away or blow up. The ship accordingly reduced speed to give the dredging party time, but eventually *Renown* had to secure up for an hour waiting for this rock to be cleared. The pilot worked the ship past the slide admirably, but even so one of her propellers hit a rock in passing.

After passing through the Mira Flores locks the ships eventually berthed alongside a very clean coaling wharf at Balboa. H.R.H. im-

[1] Señor Belisario Porras, now embarking on his second term of office.

mediately landed and drove to Panama. He dined with the British Minister at the Hotel Tivoli, where a reception and dance was afterwards given.[1]

WEDNESDAY, 31 MARCH   H.R.H., accompanied by Colonel Grigg, motored into the town, where they bought Panama hats.

After this, they obtained permission from the Military Barrack to visit forts and defences. They then proceeded to the islands of Naos and Flamenco and inspected the Canal defences, the big guns and howitzers. H.R.H. then sent car back and led a drooping Staff for a 3-mile walk back along the causeway, refusing numerous offers of help with scorn.

Work started again at 3.15 p.m., when deputations representing the White British Colony, Coloured West Indians, and Bombay Merchants came on board. All three insisted on reading addresses, though the last named somewhat mitigated this by presenting H.R.H. with a fine elephant tusk.

After this, H.R.H. and some of the Staff set out in motors to pay an official call on the President. After driving a few miles the cars were stopped opposite Señor Alfaro's house.[2] There was a dense, compressed crowd pressing round making a noise like the parrot house in the zoo, and the fact of H.R.H. shaking hands with coloured men, a thing an American would never have done, roused them to still further enthusiasm.

The party then entered two carriages, the leather seats of which were unpleasantly hot and, proved later, to have been very dirty, and drove on through Panama.

The streets were thronged with niggers, many of whom ran for long distances by the side of the carriage, in spite of the efforts of the Panamanian police to keep the road clear. At the approaches to the Presidencia, truncheons were used freely, and the local fire brigade, in red shirts and patent leather hats, were dealing blows right and left with bugles in their attempt to stem the rush.

S. Lefevre[3] received H.R.H. in a big yellow room plastered with portraits of the 40-odd Presidents which the Republic has had since it

---

[1] The Prince danced for the most part with an attractive girl who turned out to work at a local drugstore. This disturbed some of the stuffier local dignitaries. 'Well, it must be a jolly good drugstore,' was the Prince's comment.

[2] The Prime Minister, Señor Ricardo Alfaro.

[3] The Foreign Secretary, Señor Ernesto Lefevre.

came into existence, 17 years ago. Champagne was handed round, and, after the local cinematographer had taken pictures, H.R.H. and party left in motors and returned to Balboa Docks by the same route.

In the evening the President gave a State Banquet, which, to the undoing of many, was not dry, to H.R.H. at the Union Club, where the ball afterwards was also held.

THURSDAY, 1 APRIL   Captain Legh received an urgent message from the Admiral to come and watch some fine sharks chasing a whale, from the foc'sle. With his characteristic unselfishness, the Honourable Piers divulged this priceless information to Lord Claud, who dutifully woke H.R.H. and told him. As it was only about 9.30 a.m., H.R.H. couldn't quite understand what Lord Claud meant and went to sleep again. The Flag Lieutenant, however, joined the party and all rushed to the foc'sle. Seeing no signs of sharks they asked a Petty Officer, whose reply was ''e 'adn't seen no sharks but 'e 'ad seen the calendar'.

The trio returned to find, to their great consolation, that there was a regular stampede amongst the newspaper correspondents to see these sharks.

TUESDAY, 6 APRIL   It was much cooler. An offer was received from Los Angeles to send 8 aeroplanes to take H.R.H. and Staff to see a movie film being made, but this was refused.[1]

WEDNESDAY, 7 APRIL   The rig was 'half whites'. Shortly after 9.00 a.m. six American destroyers picked us up and escorted us into San Diego. The usual crowd of American aeroplanes buzzed round, drowning all 'pipes' as before.

We fired a 21-gun salute, which was answered by the shore batteries. The U.S.S. *New Mexico* (Flagship) then saluted the standard with 21 guns.

H.R.H. lunched in the *New Mexico* with Vice-Admiral Williams, the Acting C.-in-C.

At 2.30 p.m. H.R.H. left the ship in the barge, and, after 40 minutes steaming at full speed, arrived at the 'municipal' landing pier. On the pontoon the party was met by high officials, who behaved perfectly naturally, but no sooner did the party attempt to get on 'dry'(!) land

[1] Because the Prince of Wales was at that date not allowed to fly.

than the crowd rushed them, and apparently did their best to push them all back into the barge.

Amid a seething, screeching mass of humanity H.R.H. succeeded in shaking hands with about 120 returned British soldiers. The Staff then formed a 'rugger scrum' and forced their way towards the cars. There were about 20 cars waiting, and these drove the party at a reckless speed through the town to the stadium.

The procession, with H.R.H. standing up in the leading car, drove right round the enormous stadium and up to the box. The Spokesman of the Reception Committee, the Governor of California and the Mayor of San Diego made speeches, followed finally by H.R.H.

By means of two 'Magnavox' loud-speaking telephones the odd twenty thousand people in the audience were able to hear every word spoken. In the box there were four ladies present. These were the Governor's daughter, the Mayor's wife, the Mayor's daughter, and Mrs Charlie Chaplin.[1]

The entire party then drove to Coronado, crossing by the ferry, and arriving eventually at the Coronada Hotel, where H.R.H. changed into plain clothes.

'Bill' Nye[2] started to 'get busy' about this time on the 'phone, having Mrs Charlie (who called herself by her maiden name – Mildred Harris) cut out of the photograph taken at the Hotel Grant, San Diego. He reckoned that it must have cost her about $5000 for that piece of advertisement!

A 'dry' dinner party followed, during which Miss Lucile Wilde (whose 'coming out' party it incidentally was) presented H.R.H. with a key, officially belonging to the City Gates, but rumoured to fit the Mayor's wine cellar.[3]

After dinner H.R.H. excused himself for a few minutes, stating that he wished to put on his dancing rig. This opportunity was used by the *Sun* reporter to pretend that Sir Godfrey Thomas had arranged an interview for him with H.R.H., an account of which (a masterpiece of fabrication!) duly appeared in the following day's edition of the *Sun*.

THURSDAY, 8 APRIL   At 10.00 a.m., H.R.H. and the Staff landed in

---

[1] Mrs Chaplin was at the time engaged in divorcing her husband Charlie.
[2] Bill Nye was the U.S. Special Agent charged with the Prince's security during the visit to San Diego.
[3] Miss Wilde was the daughter of the Mayor of San Diego.

plain clothes, being conveyed to the shore in U.S. Submarine *Chaser*
299. They were met by Bill Nye and driven to the golf course, where
all played golf. Luckily, photographers and reporters were not allowed
on the course, but on the first and last greens the number of cameras
was overwhelming.

There was great speculation on board whether Mrs Charlie would
come off to the reception, in order to get her full $5000 worth, although
she had no invitation. Largely owing to the efforts of Bill Nye, she
remembered a pressing engagement in Los Angeles just before the
party.

Much difficulty was experienced in getting the guests out of the
ship, as ladies were found stowed away in the Gun Room at the very
last minute, and one R.A.F. Officer missed his passage altogether.

FRIDAY, 9 APRIL A new game has come into vogue in the Mess. After
meals everyone has to write down as many states of the U.S. or counties
of England, etc., as they can remember in a given time. The 'star turn'
at this is Sir Godfrey.

SATURDAY, 10 APRIL Warrants have been issued by H.M. King
Neptune summoning those who have not crossed the line before to his
Court next Saturday.

SUNDAY, 11 APRIL H.R.H. dined in the Gun Room. The evening was
an entire if somewhat noisy success, H.R.H. and nearly all the Staff
taking it in turns to hit the drum. Perhaps Captain North enjoyed his
evening the most, for rumour has it that he never noticed when H.R.H.
and others took their departure, but remained in the Gun Room quietly
beating the drum. By so doing he missed the best part of the evening,
for H.R.H. and Staff proceeded to play leap-frog on the Quarter Deck,
quite seriously, and all by themselves. Lord Claud, in trying to jump
over the Admiral, upset both himself and the Admiral. When Lord
Claud came to, he found H.R.H. sitting on his head, the Admiral
unbuttoning his braces, and the remainder of the Staff busily employed
in removing his boots, socks, trousers and, horrible to relate, even the
rest of his nethergarments. Nevertheless, he behaved as a soldier
should, and as he pattered past the sentry, orderly, and the two
messengers, in his bare legs, he found time for a pleasant word with
each of them.

MONDAY, 12 APRIL The Episcopal Member of the Staff annoyed H.M. King Neptune and his Private Secretary considerably by pointing out to the Archbishop of Canterbury that the warrants which had been issued by H.M. bore the date of the Christian era. Naturally, His Grace wished to know if the King had become a Christian, and, if so, whether he had been baptized.

The information that the bath was to contain 80 tons of water did not reach the ears of the Episcopal Member before he sent this message.

TUESDAY, 13 APRIL The ship was met by 12 U.S. destroyers, led by the U.S.S. *Birmingham*, at 6.00 a.m. and escorted in by them. The usual squadron of aeroplanes buzzed round the ship and attempted to drop leis (Hawaiian Flower Wreaths) on the ship. They also took some photographs of the ship, which they had developed and dropped on board within two or three hours of taking them.

The ship anchored outside Honolulu Harbour at 7.00 a.m., and the escorting flotilla steamed past into the harbour.

At 11.20 a.m., H.R.H. landed officially. The trip in was short and the crowd did not press round on arrival, which was a pleasant change. H.R.H. shook hands with returned British soldiers and nurses and American 'Veterans of the Great War'. After this, some fat and elderly Hawaiian ladies apparently took him for a Christmas tree, for they each hung a 'lei' round his neck till he almost disappeared from view. Meanwhile, a group of Hawaiian minstrels were busily playing on eukaleles and steel guitars, producing plangent notes.

After lunch H.R.H. changed into plain clothes and landed unofficially in the barge. A new set of Hawaiian ladies were lying in wait and pounced on him with many smiles as they presented a large calabash full of native fruit. Having escaped from the Hawaiian beauties, the party drove inland a short way to Rocky Hill, when they left the cars and entered the Royal Enclosure, one of the Hawaiian Princesses, with an unpronounceable name, who had the good sense to call herself, for short, Princess David, met H.R.H. in the enclosure. The crowd then rose and sang 'God Save'.

After this, the Centennial Pageant, which was given to celebrate the landing of the first missionaries in 1820, continued, and H.R.H. and the Staff witnessed 'Pictures II and III' of the Pageant. The Pageant took place on the opposite bank of the small valley and was very effective, the colours of the costumes being particularly brilliant and attractive. Picture II was perhaps the most thrilling, as a number of idols were carried in the train of King Liholiho. The King's mother then ate a banana, which being tabu, was apparently a dreadful thing to do. To save his mother the King gave a sign and all the idols were shattered with a great noise and eventually burnt. In Picture III, the fourteen missionaries were seen arriving and being greeted by Kaahumanu, the Queen Regent. The natives never having seen long skirts before lifted them up, to the consternation of the ladies and joy of the audience, to peep underneath.

H.R.H. and the Admiral then divided, the three Equerries and the Flag Lieutenant following H.R.H. down to the beach. H.R.H.'s party, having got into bathing suits with 'Moana' written on them, embarked in a large surf canoe and paddled out to where the surf was breaking. Duke Kanáhamaku, the world's champion swimmer, was the coxswain, and when the canoe reached the turning point another Hawaiian entered the craft. The canoe was then turned shorewards, and when Duke saw a big wave approaching he ordered 'Paddle', and everyone paddled for all they were worth. The stern of the canoe was lifted up by the wave as it caught up with her, and the canoe with its great outrigger appeared to be racing down hill into a non-existent valley in the water, which it never reached, at a speed which must have been over 20 knots. H.R.H., who was sitting right in the stern sheets, had the crest of the wave all round him nearly as high as his head. The canoe was then turned, and this performance repeated three times. After the third ride H.R.H. dived overboard and tried a surf board. He had hardly mounted when he slipped off again. However, he was soon on and had one or two successful rides. The others then all dived overboard and swam about, most of them trying surf boards also. The great danger was, that if one was just swimming alone, it was exceedingly difficult to keep out of the way of all the canoes and surf boards that came racing down on top of one. All this while, two cinema men kept abreast of the party in a canoe taking a film of them.

At 11.00 p.m., H.R.H. motored out eleven miles to a country house near Pearl Harbor. Here were gathered all the Highest Hawaiians, including the two Princesses. The party first of all witnessed the unearthing of four pigs which had been roasted whole in a small pit by means of hot stones. There were also some fish in this hole, and overall there were ti leaves. Everyone then sat down on the ground to this Luau feast, eating the roast pig and various strange foods with their fingers. At the high table, at which the Princess Kawananakoa was presiding, chairs were provided for the diners, as it was rumoured that Her Highness' bulk prevented her from rising if she ever sat completely down. Everyone present wore a lei round their neck, and behind H.R.H. stood two men with royal tapu poles. The Royal Chanter recited the life history of H.R.H. in the native tongue, while a row of Hawaiian women fanned the party with olapas, which are long fans made of little feathers, on bamboo sticks. Towards the end of dinner four Hula girls appeared between two palm trees and executed some marvellous native dances to the accompaniment of two men, who squatted on the ground beating gourds with their hands and singing weird and fascinating songs. The dancing was chiefly remarkable for the extraordinary hip and hand movement accompanying it. Between these dances one of the girls would come on and sing a native song. These songs were dreamy and restful, for after one or two harsh notes would follow a series of soft, melodious ones. It was not until long after one in the morning that H.R.H. left, to the accompaniment of a farewell 'Aloha' from all the natives present.

WEDNESDAY, 14 APRIL   We weighed anchor at 5.00 a.m. and shaped course for Fiji.

As some seas were breaking over the Quarter Deck, the proposed concert did not come off; this was made up for by H.R.H. and the Staff giving a small concert of their own round the electric piano before turning in.

FRIDAY, 16 APRIL   Shortly before 9.00 p.m., H.R.H. went on to the Flag Deck. Nearly all the officers and most of the ship's company were already crowded in the bows. Suddenly a voice was heard hailing from the bows, 'Ship ahoy!' The Captain[1] replied from the fore bridge, 'Aye, Aye.' The voice hailed again, 'What Ship is that?' The Captain answered, 'His Britannic Majesty's Battle Cruiser *Renown*.' The voice from the bows then said, 'I wish to come on board.' The Captain gave the order to stop both engines, and hailed the forecastle, saying, 'My engines are stopped. I am sending an officer to conduct Your Majesty to my bridge.' The visitor turned out to be His Aquatic Majesty King Neptune, who desired to pay his official call. A group of rockets shot into the air as His Majesty, gorgeously arrayed in his seaweed robes, crawled on board through the hawse-pipe, accompanied by his Sec-

[1] The Captain of H.M.S. *Renown* was Ernest Taylor, later Vice-Admiral Sir Ernest. Perhaps inspired by these tours around the Empire, he was elected for South Paddington in 1930 for the Empire Crusade Party, but only retained the seat until 1931.

retary (or imp), two members of his body-guard, and two bears, who crawled about on all fours.

A searchlight was switched on to the forecastle and fountains of water were played into the air from fire hoses.

An officer met His Majesty and his followers and conducted them to the triple-gun deck where the Captain and H.R.H. received them. After some speeches in verse, His Majesty and his followers partook of some liquid refreshment, and having been photographed returned to the sea for the night.

At 11.00 p.m., the ship crossed the line.

SATURDAY, 17 APRIL Shortly before 9.00 a.m., H.R.H. and Staff went to the after part of the Quarter Deck, where the remainder of the officers had already collected. All the men off watch were watching from the top of the turrets and corticene deck. At two bells in the forenoon watch, a fanfare of trumpets announced the arrival of His Majesty King Neptune. The Chief Herald came on to the Quarter Deck leading the procession followed by his four Heralds. Next came the Chief Bears, chief among whom was Captain North heavily disguised with target canvas thrumbed with spunyarn. After these followed the Judge, two of His Majesty's Body-guard, and His Aquatic Majesty King Neptune himself, accompanied by his Queen Amphitrite and his Secretary. The Doctor, the three Barbers, and four more of the Body-guard were following. On His Majesty's arrival on the Quarter Deck he was received by the Guard and Band, the latter playing 'A Life on the Ocean Wave'. The procession then proceeded right aft, followed by the rest of the Bears, the Deep Sea Police, the Barbers' Assistants, and the Doctor's Assistants. The Captain received His Majesty, and His Majesty made a short speech in reply.

A fanfare of trumpets was blown, and the Herald announced that His Majesty would now hold an investiture. H.R.H. The Prince of Wales was then invested with the Order of the Equatorial Bath, and he replied in four verses. Next the Admiral was made a Veteran of the Salt Water Division of the Most Excellent Order of the Old Sea Dog. The Admiral then replied, and in doing so introduced the Novices among the Staff, finally accusing Colonel Grigg of having attempted to stir up ecclesiastical strife, and the Flag Lieutenant of having aided and abetted him by not showing the Admiral the signals before they were sent out of the ship. At the end of the Admiral's speech, King Neptune thanked him for his loyalty in bringing to his notice the names of these two traitors. His Majesty ended up by saying, 'Arrest Mountbatten and the man named Grigg.' Whereupon the Deep Sea Police pounced upon their victims, handcuffed them and secured them with ropes. After this little interlude the investiture continued, Engineer-Lieutenant Platt receiving the Order of the Crusted Barnacle and Captain North the Order of the Ancient Cod. The Navigator and Captain were also invested with the Order of the Soused Herring and Ginned Sardine respectively.

Another fanfare of trumpets was blown and the Herald announced, 'His Majesty will now instruct the Novices.' The procession then moved forward along the port side and those in front mounted the platform which had been rigged just abaft 'A' Turret, where King Neptune made another speech.

At the end of this speech, H.R.H. sat down in the Barber's chair and the Doctor took his temperature, proclaiming it to be normal. His Majesty, however, objected to this, pointing to H.R.H.'s shaking knees. The Doctor took his temperature again and came to the conclusion that his thermometer had stuck on the first occasion, so he gave H.R.H. a No. 9 pill, which was about the size of a golf ball. The Chief Barber then lathered him thoroughly and shaved him with a razor whose blade was 3-ft long. Suddenly the chair was tilted backwards, and before he knew where he was, H.R.H. was in the grip of the Bears, who ducked him along the entire length of the bath.

Next the prisoners were brought forward and unhandcuffed, but the ropes were kept on them. The ship's company were ordered to 'off caps' while the Aquatic Articles of War were read. Then the warrant of Louis Francis Albert Victor Nicholas Mountbatten was read, which finished up 'and the prisoner not being allowed to call any witnesses on his behalf or to give any evidence in his defence, I consider the charge to be substantiated against him and do adjudge the aforesaid to be ducked four times four.' The Flag Lieutenant was then put in the Barber's chair (the rope which bound him being passed down to the Bears to pull him in by when the time came) and given a double spoonful of No. 5, after which he was lathered in black, purple and white, and tipped into the bath, where he got his full sixteen duckings. Next the warrant of Edward William Macleay Grigg was read, which, on the whole, was very similar in context to the previous one, but contained one unfortunate slip. Throughout the warrant, King Neptune was referred to as His Majesty, yet, later on, the man named Grigg was referred to as a Colonel in His Majesty's Grenadier Guards, thus, apparently attributing that Historic Regiment to King Neptune's Service. Even as he was being lathered the gallant Colonel found breath to say, 'What! What!' Hardly had this remark escaped him when he was shot backwards into the bath, getting his full nine duckings there, for his sentence had been 'to be ducked three times thrice'.

The rest of the ship's officers followed, and finally the men, who were done three at a time, the whole performance barely lasting two hours. Towards the end, many Conscientious Objectors were brought up, one of these being thrown in handcuffed and lashed up entirely.

TUESDAY, 20 APRIL   We passed many islands of the Fijian archipelago during the early part of the afternoon, and arrived in a heavy rain squall at Suva, anchoring about 4.00 p.m. Several war canoes sailed out to meet us and escorted the ship in.

The furniture which had been brought out from England in the ship for H.R.H. to sit on, on arrival at Government House, was quickly sent ashore so as to be ready for him on the morrow.

WEDNESDAY, 21 APRIL   The Governor[1] and all the important people of Fiji were awaiting H.R.H. on the pontoon, and those he had not met before were presented to him there. H.R.H. then inspected the Native Guard of Honour, who, with their great fuzzy hair, bare legs and feet, and kilt-like skirts, looked very fine indeed. Then the party drove through the town of Suva to a square, where the returned soldiers and sailors and the Fijian Labour Corps were assembled. H.R.H. shook hands with the returned men and inspected the Labour Corps.

H.R.H. held a small investiture for some officers and natives. A large party of natives dressed in coloured leaves were squatting on the grass square in front of the box. They first performed the Qaloqalovi and the Ai Sevusevu. After this, they made the yaqona drink, which they gave to H.R.H. and most of the Staff to drink, and which was decidedly unpleasant in taste. These ceremonies were accompanied by amazingly well-timed and rhythmical swaying of the body and clapping of hands. An address was then presented by the Fijians, after which the Fijian Chiefs themselves were presented. An immense number of native mats were then presented to H.R.H., as well as whales' teeth, models of a native canoe and a native hut, and also a native 'jazz box'.

The square was then cleared, and 400 picked natives advanced to

[1] Sir Cecil Rodwell.

The Prince of Wales and his entourage as portrayed by S. G. Wells of *Punch* in June 1920.

above: Sir Godfrey Thomas and
Mountbatten aboard H.M.S. *Renown*.

right: Admiral Halsey.

dance the Meke. Their faces were blackened, their dress consisted of bright coloured leaves, and each man carried a large club or battle-axe. The Meke then began, and it was indeed a weird and wonderful sight. The native orchestra accompanying the dancers consisted of some men banging poles on the ground and singing their native chant. The warriors then went through a mimic battle, splitting up into several parties, and moving together with great precision.

The party changed for dinner and dined quietly at Government House. After dinner, the party witnessed the firework display, given by the *Renown*, from the verandah, and then they drove to the Grand Pacific Hotel to attend a ball given in honour of the officers of H.M.S. *Renown*. One of H.R.H.'s first partners was the lady typist to the Chief Indian Agitator, much to the consternation of Government House.

THURSDAY, 22 APRIL   Weighed anchor at 6.00 a.m. and sailed for Auckland.

New Zealand

*New Zealand had the reputation of being the most
loyal of the Dominions, and it had lived up to it by
its behaviour during the war. Eleven per cent of the
population had volunteered for active service and 16,302
had been killed.*

*The wartime coalition between the Liberals and the
Reform Party had broken up in 1919 and the Reform
Party (the more conservative of the two) had remained
in power on its own. In the election of 1919 it had won
a large majority of the seats, though in fact it had less
than half the votes – the rest being split between the
Liberals and the Labour Party.*

*Fortunately for the visitors – in particular, if Mount-
batten's diary is to be believed, the Admiral's Secretary,
Arthur Janion – a proposal to introduce prohibition to
New Zealand had narrowly failed to gain an overall
majority in a referendum held shortly before the Prince's
party arrived.*

SATURDAY, 24 APRIL 1920 About 9.30 a.m. ship arrived in the
Auckland Harbour entrance and proceeded up harbour. Shortly after
this an immense flotilla of small craft met the ship and escorted her in.
There must have been several hundred of these craft all round the ship
gaily bedecked with flags and streamers. There was a Salvation Army
Band on board one of them, which played hymns. About 10 o'clock
H.R.H. came on to the bridge and then proceeded to his special
platform above the bridge. He was at once recognized by all the people
in the boats, who cheered heartily and called out 'Coo-ee' and 'Kia
Ora'.

34

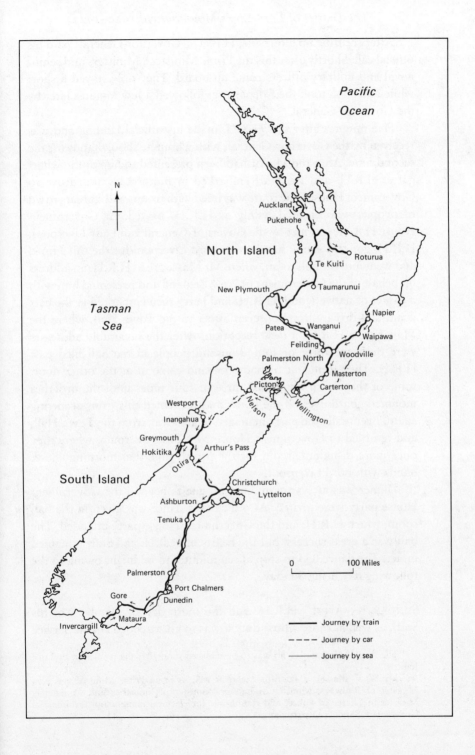

Pacific
Ocean

N

Auckland
Pukekohe

North Island

Roturua
Te Kuiti

New Plymouth   Taumarunui

Tasman
Sea

Napier

Patea   Wanganui
                            Waipawa
Feilding
Palmerston North   Woodville
Picton   Masterton
                        Carterton
Westport   Nelson
Inangahua   Wellington

Greymouth
Hokitika   Arthur's Pass
        Otira

South Island   Christchurch
                    Lyttelton
        Ashburton
    Tenuka

                0   100 Miles

Palmerston
        Port Chalmers
Gore   Dunedin
    Mataura
Invercargill   ——— Journey by train
                        ----- Journey by car
                        ——— Journey by sea

After securing up alongside, H.E. The Governor-General[1] paid his official call. Shortly after this the Prime Minister[2], Ministers and senior naval and military officers came on board. They only stayed a short while and soon took their departure, followed a few minutes later by the Governor-General.

Five minutes after this H.R.H. made his official landing and was received by the Governor-General, with whom he shook hands for the second time. After the Mayor had been presented to him at the wharf gates, H.R.H. and the Staff embarked in motor cars and drove to Government House. The route was lined with troops and a great crowd of people, who cheered wildly as H.R.H. passed. At Government House H.R.H. was met by the Governor-General and Lady Liverpool. H.R.H. got out, shook hands with Lord Liverpool for the third time, and went into the ball room, where Mr Massey read H.R.H. an address on behalf of the Government of New Zealand and presented him with a casket of native wood. H.R.H. and party then embarked in the cars again and drove through Queen Street to the Town Hall, where the Mayor gave H.R.H. a civic reception. After the invariable addresses were over, the three or four thousand people in the hall filed past H.R.H. They went out of one door and came in at the other door, some of them even filing past three or four times until the orderlies mounted guard over all the doors and prevented this from occurring again. Eventually the party managed to get away from the Town Hall, and returned to Government House by a different route, where they once more dismounted and for the fourth time that morning shook hands with Lord Liverpool.

Dinner was at 7.30 p.m., and no guests beyond the Government House party were invited. At 9 o'clock a dance was given in the ball room, which H.R.H. and the Government House party attended. The ball was a great success, but the hearts of H.R.H. and Staff remained intact. The dance had to stop at ten minutes to midnight owing to the following day being Sunday.

SUNDAY, 25 APRIL H.R.H. and the more devout members of his Staff, as well as those whose duty it was to go, attended Divine Service

---

[1] The Earl of Liverpool, who was to be replaced soon after the royal visit by Lord Jellicoe.

[2] Mr W. F. Massey, a Pooh-Bah who as well as being Prime Minister was also Minister of Railways, Minister of Labour, Minister of Industries and Commerce, Minister in Charge of Police, and responsible for electoral matters and the Imperial Government Supplies Department.

at the cathedral. The chief diversion during the service was caused by the entrance of a small dog who trotted up between the choir, sat down, and proceeded to scratch himself. Having relieved himself of his fleas, he smiled at H.R.H. and positively laughed at the choir. This was his doom, for a choirman rushed out and seized him, pushing him into the organ, where he proved of great assistance to the organist.

MONDAY, 26 APRIL   At 10.15 a.m., H.R.H. left for the Domain, where a children's demonstration on a large scale had been organized. The whole amphitheatre was black with people, and about 6000 children were drawn up forming the word 'Welcome' in enormous letters. The second item was a fine display of physical drill by several thousand boys, who took their time from one small boy perched up all alone on a high stand. No words of command were given. There was only one instructor (whose chest measurement we were told was 46 inches) blowing a whistle for each movement. The display ended very impressively by children who wore red, white and blue caps, forming an enormous Union Jack.

Shortly before the end of lunch H.E. left for the races, followed at 2 o'clock by H.R.H. H.R.H.'s party arrived at Ellerslie race course about 2.30 p.m., in time for the third race. The party proceeded to the royal box, and the odd 30,000 people present turned their eyes on H.R.H., and, even while the race was in progress, most of the ladies kept their glasses on the royal box. After this race, H.R.H. walked round to look at the horses and the totalisator, which takes the place of 'bookies' in New Zealand. Great crowds followed H.R.H. wherever he went, cheering at intervals. At the totalisator H.R.H. and most of the Staff 'invested' in betting tickets for various horses. The party then proceeded to the stewards' stand, whence they witnessed the fourth race, the Prince of Wales's Cup. The favourite won this race, H.R.H., the Admiral, and the Flag Lieutenant all winning 'dividends' on it. The fifth race, which was the steeplechase handicap, was witnessed from the grand stand, H.R.H. again winning on the favourite.

TUESDAY, 27 APRIL   At 10.00 a.m., H.R.H. left Government House and drove to Auckland railway station. The party were attired in plain clothes, and, owing to the leading car being a closed car with just the back portion let down, H.R.H. and the Admiral were repeatedly hit on the head by gifts, such as pipes and books, etc. The party entered the rear car of the train, which was luxuriously fitted out. As the train drew out of the station, H.R.H. waved a farewell from the observation platform. In fact H.R.H. and the Staff were kept busy waving in turns to groups of people all along the line.

The first stop was made at Pukekohe, the constituency of the Prime Minister. An enormous crowd of school children were drawn up on the platform, who waved small Union Jacks and sang the 'God Save' and the 'God Bless',[1] as usual. H.R.H. received an address here and in his reply made a few facetious remarks anent the Prime Minister, who was travelling in the royal train. H.R.H. then shook hands with about 60 returned soldiers, using his left hand as his right hand was nearly worn out.

The train was rather late and, therefore, increased speed which shook the coaches very much owing to the narrow gauge of the rails. At 4.35 p.m. Rotorua was reached safely. H.R.H. walked to the cars through the station yard, which was lined by some old Maori warriors and soldiers from the hospital. The party proceeded by a roundabout route to the Grand Hotel, excited Maoris running alongside the cars and shrieking with joy.

After the party had had tea, H.R.H. went for a walk to Whakarewarewa and saw the hot pools and Maori village, which looked very quaint and mysterious by night.

H.R.H.'s party and H.E.'s party dined privately at the hotel, and after dinner went to a small dance given by the ladies of Rotorua. There was just one really good dancer there, a Miss Nolan, who had come down from Auckland. H.R.H. and party returned about 1 o'clock, and just before retiring to bed a small scrap occurred, in which part of the contents of a fire bucket was upset over Captain North, Sir Godfrey lost his hat, and H.R.H. chased the Secretary all along the corridor back to his room. After this the party retired to bed.

WEDNESDAY, 28 APRIL   All the engine drivers came out on strike at midnight for higher wages, using the opportunity of H.R.H.'s visit to win their point with the Government. The Government, however, are remaining obdurate, and everybody is at present marooned at Rotorua except the official and naval parties, whom the railway men have consented to take back to Auckland.

---

[1] The 'God Save' was, of course, the national anthem; the 'God Bless' was 'God Bless The Prince of Wales', originally written in Welsh to music by Brinley Richards, translated into English by George Linley. The hope expressed that olive branches would twine around the sacred bulwarks of the Throne of England seems both unfair on Wales and militarily unwise.

Lord Claud states that he felt an earthquake during the night, which excited him considerably. Later, he came to the conclusion that, as he had heard it at 1.30 a.m., it must have been the 'young people' turning in.

H.R.H. and Staff left the hotel at 9.30 and motored to Ohinemutu. They were met at the approaches to the village by two half-naked Maoris, who ran backwards uttering fearful yells and putting their tongues out at intervals. (The effect was somewhat marred when we learnt that the wilder of these two savages was Captain Walker, late of the N.Z. Pioneer Battalion.) These challengers led the party to the village square, where the whole tribe was assembled. H.R.H. took his seat on the platform, and a 'haka' was then performed. An address was presented, to which he replied briefly in English, and it was translated into Maori by Dr Pomare.[1] The maidens of the village then gave a very effective canoe song, the tune of which rang in the heads of the Staff for several days. The party paid a visit to the Maori Church, walking past a line of the lady performers, all of whom took a turn at kissing H.R.H.'s hand in the most affectionate manner.

The next item was a visit to the village of Whakarewarewa. The party proceeded on foot in the pouring rain to the hot springs region, quite close to the village. They were shown the various blow-holes and boiling mud pools, but the large crowd which followed in their train made it very difficult for any but H.R.H. himself to see much. Pohutu geyser had, in the meantime, been soundly soaped, and on arriving there the cauldron was found to be bubbling furiously, and the experts were full of assurances that the geyser would spout in ten minutes' time. The cauldron continued to bubble furiously, but, perhaps owing to the torrential downfall, nothing further had happened at the end of half an hour, and the patience of all was becoming exhausted. At this juncture, some of the Maoris started singing to pass the time, starting off with Maori songs, suddenly switching off to 'Annie Laurie' and ending up with a ribald rhyme about the Kaiser (who was made to rhyme with 'geyser'). Even this did not induce Pohutu to spout, and as everybody by this time was wet to the skin, it was given up as a bad job.

There was another dance in the evening.

H.R.H. and the Flag Lieutenant put Lord Claud and the Secretary down for calls at 5.00 a.m. on the office slate.

[1] Dr M. Pomare was the Member of the Executive Council representing the Native Races and in charge of Maori Councils.

TUESDAY, 29 APRIL   Lord Claud and the Secretary complained that they had been called at 5 o'clock. The Secretary merely said 'Thank you', but Lord Claud, when he was called for the second time at 5.15, had quite a lot to say.

The Maori reception, which had been abandoned on the previous afternoon owing to the rain, was held at 9.30 a.m. and attended by very large crowds of spectators. H.R.H. motored at 9.25 a.m. to the Maori camp on the race course. When H.R.H. alighted he was met by H.E. and Lady Liverpool, the head of all the Maoris, and Dr Pomare, the latter's daughter fixing a kiwi feather mat round the shoulders of H.R.H. The party was then challenged by the Arawas and Matatua tribes, who performed the ceremony of 'taki' amid much noise and shouting. Most of the Maoris were stripped and painted up in their war paint for the occasion, but some of them retained incongruous garments such as highly coloured boots, top hats and checked trousers. H.R.H.'s party then proceeded down the lines of the massed tribes, the road being kept clear by lines of Maori girls, some of whom, be it said, were exceedingly lovely.

Sir William Herries, the native minister, accompanied by 64 chiefs and chieftainesses, presented an address of welcome, with its whariki (Maori mat). This was probably the best, certainly the most poetic, address yet received by H.R.H., and H.R.H. made an appropriate reply, translated, sentence by sentence, into Maori by Dr Pomare. Then followed the dances, of which there were 22 in all, each tribe taking it in turn to perform their dances. These, as a rule, constituted a war dance, a haka, and a poi dance, but variations of the haka, such as the taparahi and parowha were also presented, one tribe giving the powhiri (dance of welcome). Perhaps the most attractive of the poi dances which were given by the girls was the canoe dance. Some of these dances were purely wild, primitive outbursts, while others were somewhat marred by the use of modern pianos, fiddles, and mouth-organs. One notable feature of the morning was the appearance of the Hon. A. T. Ngata, a well-known member of parliament, who, in native costume and stripped to the waist, led his tribe, the Ngatiporou, in their dance. The performance lasted close on three hours, ending by a massed Ngeri given by the entire assembled tribes, who yelled out their farewell, 'Ka Mate! Ka Mate! Kia Ora! Kia Ora!' at the conclusion of the dances. H.R.H. and party advanced down the steps to receive the gifts, which included some fine Maori mats.

Nobody changed into evening clothes for dinner. Immediately after dinner Lord Claud returned to the Maori camp, where he attended their dance in the big marquee, 'getting off' with an elderly chieftainess, who wished to present him with a huia feather before his return but was not there when he left, so Lord Claud never got his feather. The remainder of the Staff practised the canoe poi dance, giving a farewell performance to H.E. and his party just as they left for the station, the Admiral acting as 'coxswain' of the party. After this, the Captain and Flag Lieutenant drove to the Maori camp and joined in the dance in the big marquee, where they succeeded in 'getting off' with a young Maori chieftainess and some fat old Maori ladies. The Flag Lieutenant was given a kiwi mat. When the time came for them to leave, several of the Maori girls and matrons accompanied them to the cars, failing in their endeavours to kiss the Captain, but succeeding with the Flag Lieutenant!

FRIDAY, 30 APRIL   The train arrived at Auckland at about 7.45 a.m. Several strike pickets showed their intense loyalty by cheering lustily as H.R.H. descended from the train.

On arrival on board breakfast was served, and at 9.15 a.m., H.R.H. motored out to Maungakiekie (One Tree Hill) Golf Course. The Admiral, Colonel Grigg and Captain Legh played a three-ball match together and drove off first followed by H.R.H., Sir Godfrey and the Flag Lieutenant. At the fifth green, Captain Rhodes[1] arrived with the information that the strike would probably be settled by 4 o'clock and that the party would leave in the royal train at that time to carry out the North Island Tour. Like Sir Francis Drake, H.R.H. continued his game, but the Admiral's party knocked off after the twelfth hole in order to get back to the post office, where several conferences were held, which consisted chiefly in listening to telephone conversations between the Governor-General and the Prime Minister, who was in Wellington.

H.R.H.'s game was considerably upset towards the end by a crowd of garrulous and excited women, who followed him closely for the last two holes. Everybody returned to the ship for lunch.

The Admiral and Colonel Grigg had to rush back to the post office before they had finished their lunch to attend further conferences, and, by the time the train was due to steam out, the entire party were

[1] Captain Tahu Rhodes, Military Secretary to the Governor-General.

waiting on board. About 4 o'clock the Admiral returned with the information that the strike was still on.

SATURDAY, 1 MAY   At 7.30 p.m. it was decided that, as the strike was still on, H.R.H. would travel to Wellington in the ship. Accordingly H.E.'s party came on board for dinner and spent the night on board, in readiness for an early departure next day. At 10.30 p.m. the strike was declared off, and orders to go by train were given. The party, however, spent the night on board.

SUNDAY, 2 MAY   The party breakfasted and lunched on board. They attended church, which, by the Captain's orders, was cut down to 25 minutes, left the ship and walked to Auckland station, accompanied by the usual enthusiastic crowds, who rushed on to the platform before the train's departure. The train left at 3.50 p.m.

A stop was made at Frankton Junction about 6 o'clock for a matter of 10 minutes. Although this was not an official stopping place, great crowds, mostly railwaymen, had collected. One of the men's leaders jumped on to the observation platform and made a small speech, assuring H.R.H. of their loyalty, and distress in having caused him inconvenience.

At 7.20 p.m. Te Kuiti was reached, and this being an official stopping place, H.R.H. was met by the Mayor and Councillors, who conducted him to a small platform jutting out into the station square. The 'God Save' and the 'God Bless' were sung, after which H.R.H. walked among the people, shaking hands with the returned soldiers. A quarter of an hour after arrival the party re-embarked and proceeded to Taumarunui, which was reached about 9.15 and where a very similar performance occurred.

Ohakune had telephoned through to Taumarunui that great crowds were collecting there, and H.R.H. ordered the train to be stopped there for 10 minutes at about 11.40. The crowd cheered lustily and gathered round the observation car, from whence H.R.H. waved his hat. Poker was played up to arrival at Ohakune. The Staff and Retinue were provided with better sleeping accommodation this time, but the Admiral and the Colonel preferred to stick to the saloon.

MONDAY, 3 MAY   At 10 o'clock New Plymouth was reached. H.R.H. and party disembarked and got into cars, which drove them through New Plymouth to Pukekura Park. A guard of honour of some very small schoolboys was drawn up in the centre of the park, which was an artificially levelled grass plot bordered on three sides by grass terraces. On the terrace opposite H.R.H.'s stand some girls in blue and white formed the letters 'H R H' and in the centre of the green several hundred school children formed a gigantic Prince of Wales's crest, holding stalks of tuitui to represent the feathers, and enormous ribbons with '*Ich Dien*' on them. H.R.H. shook hands with the returned soldiers and walked over the grounds down the lines of school children, crossing a trestle bridge erected by some boy scouts in 15 minutes. After this the party re-embarked, driving by the same route to the station, where the crowd was again permitted to rush the platform. The train departed at 11.15 a.m.

The train arrived about a quarter past two at Patea. It was on the shores of Patea that the first inhabitants of these islands are supposed to have landed. The reception here consisted of a simple platform ceremony, a very amateur band playing the 'God Save' on arrival and the 'God Bless' on leaving. The Mayor was considerably flustered, and forgot to read the address or to call for three cheers for H.R.H. until reminded to do so by 'Zoo' William Fraser.[1] H.R.H. shook hands with the returned men, walked up and down among the school children, and returned to the train, the train leaving shortly before half past two.

The train arrived punctually at a quarter to four at Wanganui. Outside the station a very smart guard of honour of senior cadets was drawn up, which H.R.H. inspected before motoring to Cook's Gardens. After the inspection H.R.H. held a small investiture. The returned soldiers then hitched drag ropes on to the royal car and dragged H.R.H., accompanied by the senior returned man and Lord Claud – whose day on it was – once round the arena, casting off the drag ropes at the saluting base. The royal car, followed by the rest of the procession, then left Cook's Gardens, having to make rushes like tanks at the steep part of the bend of the cycle track in order to get out of the saucer-like field.

The party then went into the hotel and had tea, after which, H.R.H. and some of his Staff motored out to Wanganui Collegiate School, which is a sort of Eton of New Zealand, built in a very modern bungalow style in red brick. The boys were all drawn up in the

[1] Sir William Fraser, a gallant old gentleman of eighty-two who was in charge of the arrangements for the Prince's tour of New Zealand. He had been Minister of Public Works till 1920.

Great Hall in their cadet uniforms, and the headmaster made a short welcoming speech to H.R.H. After H.R.H. had replied the boys cheered and yelled and clapped, the 190 of them making far more noise than an average crowd of twice the number. The party then went right through the dining hall, chapel and classrooms before returning.

Dinner was slightly late, owing to the fact that the boiler had just burst and flooded the kitchen. However, H.R.H. was able to leave by about 9.00, and motored to the Opera House, where a concert was being given by the returned soldiers' association, at which he remained for about half an hour. A move was then made to the citizens' concert at His Majesty's Theatre. The programme started on H.R.H. taking his seat beside the Mayoress in the dress circle. A number of singers had been imported from Christchurch, Wellington, etc., who gave extracts from various operas, and there was also a certain amount of local talent, including a violin solo, and a recitation by a gentleman who appeared to have dined rather well. The last item on the programme was a Tschaikowsky selection by the Wanganui garrison band, who had recently won the inter-band contest of New Zealand. They had only been playing for a short time when all the lights went out and the theatre was plunged into complete darkness. Except for a few muffled shrieks there was no panic whatever, and the band rose magnificently to the occasion by at once striking up a march, which they knew well enough to play in the dark, being the one they had practised for months and won the contest with. The lights were turned on again in a few minutes and the programme was completed without further incident.

TUESDAY, 4 MAY   As the train left a powerful, yellow car started off along the road which ran parallel to the line. The car was bedecked with many flags, and carried six occupants in all including three children, who all waved flags frantically. The car kept level with the rear of the train as far as Palmerston North, taking some corners on two wheels.

At Palmerston North, the train passed through a magnificent square which was almost a park in itself. Two elderly ladies returned the two missing colours of the 3rd Regiment of Foot Guards to H.R.H. They had been in the possession of the Dalrymple family since the year 1801, after the siege of Alexandria. An old man presented H.R.H. with a stock whip which he had cracked before the King and Queen at Melbourne. Immediately on leaving the yellow car was again observed racing along the road by the train. H.R.H. and the Staff yelled encouragement from the observation platform as the car almost skidded into the ditch in avoiding two other cars. The railway line now followed the course of the Manawatu River, and after passing through a tunnel the party, who were having lunch, were amazed to find the old car on the trail, shooting along the opposite bank of the river at 30 miles an hour faster than the speed limit allowed for that gorge. A little later the road came close to the railway line and the entire occupants of the train leaned out and waved. The train stopped for water at Woodville, and the car stopped also, H.R.H. and the Admiral descending and shaking hands with the occupants. Apparently they had not been a bit frightened, or worried by anything except sheep.

After a short stop the train proceeded and arrived at Napier at 4.30. Large crowds had collected at the station and were kept back by soldiers and fences. H.R.H. and party drove to Nelson Park. H.R.H.'s car had the name of the firm from which it had been hired painted in large letters on a placard which was stuck up in front of the bonnet. On each side a large royal coat of arms had been painted, and the owners of the garage calmly proposed to hire out this car as a taxi after H.R.H. had left, with the coat of arms still on. The matter, however, was satisfactorily settled before H.R.H. drove away from the park again.

WEDNESDAY, 5 MAY   The 'Zoo' sprang a surprise on the party by asking if the train might be stopped at Waipawa, which apparently was his constituency. He assured H.R.H. and the Staff that there were no returned men to shake hands with, no speeches, and no crowd. In fact, from Sir William's description it was hard to understand why H.R.H. should stop at Waipawa at all. Always ready to oblige, however, H.R.H. had the train stopped at Waipawa, where a dense crowd had collected. A special dais had been built out from the platform. Crowds of school children had collected. Many returned men were fallen in, and a local band, dressed in a sort of pantomime uniform, which was a mixture between naval white and household cavalry uniforms, played patriotic tunes lustily. The Mayor made a speech, chiefly notable for repetition, to which H.R.H. had to reply extemporaneously, but no addresses were exchanged.

H.R.H., Colonel Grigg and the Flag Lieutenant got into the cab of the locomotive for the next trip. H.R.H. thoroughly enjoyed himself, blowing the whistle when necessary and handing in the right-of-way tablet.

The crowds at Woodville were amazed to see H.R.H. descending from the engine, and when they realized whom it was they cheered and cheered with great enthusiasm.

Masterton was reached about five minutes past three, and H.R.H.'s party motored to the public park through the town itself, which is quite big and important. H.R.H. proceeded to the dais in the centre of the park, and the fat little Mayor, bristling with importance, read out in a clerical tone a rather original address on behalf of the boys and girls, commencing with 'Beloved Prince'. The party then fought their way through dense crowds to where a large hole had been dug in the ground. A red, white and blue tripod had been erected over the hole, and, by means of a small purchase, H.R.H. lowered a young oak tree into the hole. Two girls dressed in pseudo-nautical rig with fancy *Renown* cap ribbons handed H.R.H. a little spade about the size of a teaspoon, with which he shovelled three diminutive sprinklings of dried earth from a silver bowl into the hole. The royal oak having been planted, H.R.H. returned to the stand, said 'Good-bye', and then the party motored back to the station, leaving about a quarter to four.

Carterton, which was reached about four o'clock, provided the comic relief of the day. It is doubtful whether any of the inhabitants were completely sober, and to top it all, Colonel Grigg could not be found at the critical moment. No address was, therefore, presented, but H.R.H. said a few words. Colonel Grigg was found by Lord Claud, shortly after the train had left the station, in the ministerial car, whither he had retired after alighting on the platform as he did not think the address was going to be read out.

The train arrived at 5.25 at Cross Creek, where the kitchen car and another car were unhitched. Here the high-geared engine was uncoupled and three 'Fell' engines were put on, one in front, one in the middle, and one in the rear. These locomotives are provided with special horizontal wheels which grip the centre rail which runs from this station to the station at the summit of the Rimutaka range of mountains. There is no teeth-gearing in the centre rail of any sort, the grip being merely a friction grip. The train now began one of the steepest rail ascents in the world, up an average gradient of 1 in 15, at one turn of the line as steep as 1 in 13. Altogether, three short tunnels were passed through on the way and some amazing twists and turns were taken. There is a continual draught blowing down the gorge which on windy days is so strong that wind shields have to be provided to prevent the train being blown off the line. The maximum speed of the train was so slow that it was possible to get out and walk from one coach to another, which was actually done by some people. The summit station was reached at 6 o'clock, the three 'Fell' locomotives removed and an ordinary one coupled on, which took the train down a long gentle slope into Wellington.

Wellington was reached punctually at about 7.30 p.m. Mr Massey and the important people in the district received H.R.H. on the platform. An enormous crowd had gathered outside the station, which was successfully kept back by the police while H.R.H. and the Staff drove off in the cars. By the time the procession reached Lambton Quay the crowd broke loose and stormed the cars. The orderlies successfully prevented anyone from climbing on to H.R.H.'s own car – in which he was standing up to let the people see him – but all the other cars carried between twenty and thirty people all the way up to Government House. Owing to the stupendous crowd it was impossible to proceed at more than a fast walking pace, with the result that the entire crowd moved with the cars, and the streets being comparatively narrow, this produced a most tremendous compressing effect, and some people would insist upon trying to run between the cars. The fourth car, in which Captain Rhodes and his servant were, ran over a woman who was trying to run behind the car in front and had fallen down. The chauffeur put his gear in reverse in a desperate effort to save the woman, and the car leapt back on to the fifth car, crushing the leg of a boy who was sitting on the bonnet of the fifth car. The boy was removed, still cheering, but the fifth car was smashed up, and the Admiral's Personal Staff who were occupying it had to jump out. The crowd very obligingly threw them into Captain Rhodes's car, and the journey continued. H.R.H.'s car passed over the foot of a man holding a baby in one hand and waving his hat in the other, but he took no notice of this whatever.

THURSDAY, 6 MAY   At 4 o'clock H.R.H. drove to Newtown Park, where a military review on the same lines as that at Auckland took place, though livened up by all the benches of the spectators collapsing sideways one after the other like a row of dominoes. On return tea was served, and then H.R.H. held a privy council, to initiate H.E. Sir Godfrey, who had been specially sworn in as an assistant clerk, was the only member of the Staff permitted to attend this important function, and one of H.E.'s aide-de-camps guarded the entrance with drawn sword. A mysterious-looking black box, supposed to contain important documents but believed to contain fishing tackle, was carried into the room and the privy council refused to open it until everybody else had withdrawn. H.R.H. and the Staff were dined by the Wellington Club, and after dinner returned to Government House, coming in through the window to avoid detection by the hundreds of guests who were arriving for the great ball.

FRIDAY, 7 MAY   Shortly before noon H.R.H. drove to the Parliamentary Buildings, where the usual massed school children stunt was taking place on a large scale, the number present being about 10,000. Owing to the awkward shape of the grounds no fancy lettering or patterns could be made by the children, but they sang patriotic songs instead.

After lunch H.R.H., accompanied by the Admiral, drove to the Athletic Park where they watched the first quarter of an hour's play of the rugger match between the Army and the Wellington teams. It was a very good match to watch and the party were sorry to have to leave so soon. They drove to the *Renown* – which was lying at King's Wharf – and boarded a small tug from her. This steamer conveyed the party across Wellington Harbour to Petone, about 7 miles away. After having passed down between two lines of yachts, the tug anchored and the *Amokura* – the New Zealand training ship – sent three pulling boats to take H.R.H. and party ashore. A pageant had been arranged by the Early Settlers to represent the colonizing of New Zealand. In the first picture a Maori war canoe was seen to pull ashore, the natives leaping out – shivering in the cold owing to their semi-nude condition – proceeded up the narrow gap left for them by the crowd to H.R.H.'s platform and disappeared from sight in the crowd. A considerable delay now occurred. This was owing to Captain Cook, who was due to land next, having been so overjoyed at the prospect of landing for the second time, after so many years, that he had celebrated this landing at the local pub rather too well. A new Captain Cook was quickly found, who was almost overcome by this unexpected honour, and walked ashore rather uncertainly followed by a squad of four Marines whose bayonets were of four different sizes. The Maoris met Captain Cook and made friends with him, and a box which was being carried ashore plainly marked 'Old Scotch Whisky' was set down and violently kicked by the Marines. Suddenly a delightful little black pig jumped out and disappeared among the crowd. The Missionaries, and then the Early Settlers, followed, and after the pageant had been concluded H.R.H. went to the small Maori encampment near by, where some mats were hung round his neck, while the canoe's crew yelled out their 'Ka Mate! Ka Mate!'

The party then got into the cars – which had been brought out from Wellington – and drove to Petone Station. For the first part of the way the local band marched in front, playing vigorously, but they were persuaded to draw aside and let H.R.H.'s party pass. The Hutt Valley people were almost worse than the Wellingtonians in throwing confetti at H.R.H.; one girl even going so far as to throw an entire box, which burst and poured its contents down H.R.H.'s neck, to his intense annoyance. The party re-embarked at Petone Station in the royal train and proceeded out to Trentham to the Military Hospital, where H.R.H. shook hands with the patients and nurses, and afterwards walked round the wards. The party returned by the train to Lambton Station and drove straight back to Government House. After a quiet dinner at Government House H.R.H. drove to the Town Hall for the Citizens' Ball.

Immediately on arrival an official set of 'Lancers' was danced owing to the unfortunate fact that the local band possessed 'Lancer' music. It was a sight not to be missed. H.R.H., the Admiral and Captain were the only members of H.R.H.'s party to have to perform, and they, none of them, knew too much about it. H.R.H. tried to be graceful, in which he was greatly assisted by his partner, Mrs Massey. There was room for about 500 guests, and, of course, 1300 had been asked, with the result that, although the official party managed to get their supper all right, the supper queues for the rest lasted until 2 a.m.

MONDAY, 10 MAY H.R.H. and Staff settled down to a long cross-country motor drive to Nelson, and found, to their amazement, that the party filled 22 cars, this being exclusive of the servants and luggage, who were on their own. The long procession started off and flew through lovely country in clouds of dust, resembling the headquarters of an army in headlong flight. The next two hours of the drive were spent in negotiating mountains, the road being one long succession of hair-pin turns, flanked by a precipice on the left. Luckily, the drivers were first class, as H.R.H.'s car fairly set the pace, and the only car where anything approaching panic showed itself was No. 3, owing to the fact that the Admiral's Secretary, gorged with a heavy lunch, went sound asleep on the box-seat, and at all the really dangerous corners, lurched across and almost knocked the steering wheel out of the chauffeur's hands. However, Nelson was reached without mishap, and as soon as the party had removed the thick layer of dust with which they were covered from head to foot, H.R.H. mounted the church steps in front of which a very large crowd had collected and received and replied to the civic address. Nelson fully made up for the deficiencies of other halts as regards cheering. Once they had started nothing could stop them, and on the few occasions when one section of the crowd paused for breath, the Mayor shouted to the bandmaster, 'The King, Tom, The King', and the gap was filled up by the National Anthem, which must have been played 20 times during H.R.H.'s short visit.

As always happens, two hours had been allowed on the programme for the above item, which had only taken 40 minutes. There was no point in hanging about, so it was decided to carry straight on. Consequently, H.R.H. and Staff, through no fault of their own, arrived at this next engagement, not only punctually, but considerably before schedule time. As a special reception had been arranged to take place before the crowd were admitted, H.R.H.'s unexpected arrival, and the order to throw open the doors at once, caused wild confusion, and the greatest difficulty was experienced in sorting out 'Early Settlers' and 'Next of Kin', with special platform tickets, from the onrush of the general public. However, all went well; the doors were closed when people started coming round for the second time, and H.R.H. got away at 6.15 to the Commercial Hotel, where the party were staying.

The programme had shown that H.R.H. was to be escorted to the Civic Ball by a torch-light procession, but the party little knew what they were in for. On leaving the hotel, each leading car was surrounded by a number of firemen carrying Bengal flares on long poles. These emitted a suffocating smoke, but were otherwise harmless. The pièce de résistance, however, came when each fireman lighted a long Roman candle and brandished it in every direction, pouring showers of burning sparks on the heads of the occupants of the cars. The firemen, being provided with helmets, regarded it as a great joke, but as such it was not shared by those who had holes burnt in new hats or overcoats, of whom there were many. A bill for the damage is being sent in to the N.Z. Government with the request that, in future, fireworks at point blank range may, like confetti, be discouraged as a form of public welcome.

WEDNESDAY, 12 MAY   H.R.H. left soon after 9.00 a.m. and motored down the lower Buller Valley to Westport. The weather was very fine, though cold, and the scenery of this end of the gorge far more impressive than that of the upper part. On arrival at Westport, the usual functions took place, and H.R.H. was presented with a number of gifts, including a carved Maori stick and a locket made of Westland coal. Three quarters of an hour were spent at Westport, and the party returned to the motors through ranks of cheering school children, who put down a heavy barrage of chrysanthemums as they passed.

H.R.H. drove the leading Cadillac most of the way back along the Buller Gorge, and arrived safely at 2.00 p.m. at Inangahua Junction, where the train was waiting. Most of the party lost no time in sitting down to lunch, but H.R.H. and Colonel Grigg went for a walk, as the train was not due to start for some time. There was no sign of them at the time fixed for departure, but the whistle of the engine proved effective, and they emerged from the bush only a few minutes late and the train then started. At 7.15 Hokitika was reached. The party attended a dance in the Hokitika Drill Hall. Colonel Grigg, who paid 'a surprise visit to the cloakroom early in the evening, found a party of souvenir hunters going through the pockets of all the overcoats – later investigation luckily proved that the only articles looted were a few cigars.

THURSDAY, 13 MAY   It is not known how many of the Staff availed themselves of the prospect of seeing the sun rise on Mount Cook. Anyhow, people were astir early. Lunch was taken in the train after leaving Greymouth. A diversion was caused in the middle by the rear car nearly leaving the lines from the excessive speed at which the train had been running for some time. Most of the things on the table capsized, and H.R.H. himself rushed along the corridor to beg them to go slower.

At Otira Station, the party left the train and found a number of coaches awaiting them for the drive across Arthur's Pass. The scenery in the Gorge was as fine as the weather, and most people took advantage of the slow pace at which the coaches mounted the steep incline to walk to the summit of the pass, some 3000 feet above sea level. From the watershed, the procession of coaches dropped down quickly to Arthur's Pass Station, where the train in which H.R.H. travels during the rest of his time in N.Z., was waiting. During the half-hour prior to its departure, H.R.H. walked to the mouth of the

Otira Tunnel. This tunnel, 5 miles long, is nearly completion, and will form the connecting link between the south and west coasts. After being photographed with the engineer in charge, H.R.H. boarded the train, which at once left for Christchurch.

On arrival at Christchurch at 7.30 H.R.H. was met by the Mayor, Dr Thacker, Councillors and others and motored through dense and enthusiastic crowds to the Christchurch Club. The party dined in day clothes, as the luggage could not get up in time owing to the congestion in the streets. They changed after dinner, when H.R.H. went to Captain Tahu Rhodes's private dance.

FRIDAY, 14 MAY The morning was wet and drizzly, and nobody ventured out, but H.R.H. and Sir Godfrey played squash in a dripping wet, open court, later on.

In accordance with the Mayor's plan, a large rally of boy scouts took place in the square outside the Club just before lunch. H.R.H., however, did not go out to inspect them, as it was not on the official programme and no previous warning had been given. Not to disappoint these scouts by not being inspected at all, the Admiral, accompanied by some of the Staff, inspected them, and was very heartily cheered, but as Captain North and Colonel Grigg, who were accompanying the Admiral, appeared on the ground, a lady was heard to remark, 'What a disappointment.'

After this, the Admiral accompanied the Mayor in a car to see about the various local arrangements. Dr Thacker stopped the car in the Cathedral Square, and standing up as suddenly as it was possible for him to do so, addressed the traffic as follows: 'Citizens. This is Sir Lionel Halsey. Once he was your Captain; now he is your Admiral. Give him three cheers!' This, to the Admiral's extreme embarrassment, was repeated no less than seven times at various parts of the town. The surprised pedestrians responded enthusiastically on each occasion.

SATURDAY, 15 MAY The party left shortly before lunch, and drove to Riccarton Racecourse, where after witnessing the second race – the first one being over – they retired to lunch with the Stewards. Immediately after lunch H.R.H. and the Admiral mounted fiery steeds and cantered off to the starting point for the next race. This race had two false starts, which caused some people in the grand stand to wonder whether H.R.H. was not starting the race himself. On his return from the starting post H.R.H., feeling skittish, lightly leapt a hurdle, and, elated at his first success, put his gallant steed at the second hurdle. The animal, however, felt sulky, and refused, sending its royal rider over its head so that he landed on a tender portion of his person. Luckily no serious damage was sustained, and the party returned to the grand stand amidst thunderous applause.

After tea, H.R.H.'s party walked back through the Botanical Gardens, where they met the Curator, who showed them the tree which they wanted H.R.H. to plant some time. Coming to the conclusion that there was no time like the present, H.R.H. planted it then and there in the dark, in the presence of three witnesses. From H.R.H.'s point of view, this was the most satisfactory tree-planting yet done.

SUNDAY, 16 MAY   H.R.H. attended Divine Service at the Cathedral, accompanied for the first time in this trip by every single member of his Staff. The service was quite pleasant, and when the choir sang in tune they sang very well indeed. A very long service had been arranged, but by the Admiral's intercession of the night before, it had been cut down to within reasonable limits. As the party was leaving the Cathedral one of the vergers hit Captain North hard on the head with the butt end of a billiard cue which he was carrying.

The party then drove to Christ's College – which is another one of the three great schools of New Zealand. Those boys who had not been sent home owing to influenza were crowded on the lawn, and cheered heartily as H.R.H. arrived. Most of them had mothers and sisters present. H.R.H. first inspected the plans of the new building, and then walked round the present building, finally entering the hall, where he made a short speech to the assembled boys.

About 2.15 p.m., H.R.H. drove to Chalmers Military Hospital, where the usual hospital stunt was gone through. H.R.H. then inspected a party of boy scouts on his way out to the Military Sanatorium at Cashmere where the men of the *Renown* were being looked after. On the way he received a great ovation from the Christchurch Maternity Home. Sir Godfrey Thomas and the Admiral's Secretary, who were out for a walk, edged their way up to the front of the crowd as H.R.H.'s car passed and waved their hats, shouting, 'Isn't he lovely!' but received no recognition.

MONDAY, 17 MAY   The party departed from Christchurch at 10.00 a.m. They travelled by a special train, which was very nicely fitted up inside, though the coaches were some 16 inches narrower than those in the North Island. There seemed to be more officials accompanying H.R.H. on his tour through the South Island. Although the servants travelled in the pilot train with the luggage, no less than 73 people were travelling by the royal train.

The first stop was made at Ashburton at 11.25 a.m., and the party motored to the Domain in 16 motors – quite a record for such a small place. The usual stunt was gone through, a notable feature being the organized waving of small Union Jacks which the school children carried, and the number of cadets who fainted in the guard of honour. Ashburton Domain is very pretty, and not unlike parts of the Old Country, in fact, the whole of Canterbury looks very English, and very picturesque. The line from Christchurch is practically one straight level line, and the best stretch throughout the Dominion, the train touching a speed of 60 miles an hour at one time.

Temuka, which was reached at a quarter to one, was a platform show, and well arranged. A feature of the show was the accompaniment of the cheering first by drums and later by cornets. The Mayor had, unfortunately, lost his best set of teeth, and his second best somewhat impeded his articulation.

The 'Zoo' did the dirty on H.R.H. by suddenly announcing that he was having the train stopped for a few minutes at Palmerston, thereby breaking up everybody's after-tea rest. On arrival at Palmerston no crowd was observable, but presently half a dozen people appeared. On looking closer these turned out to be occupants of the train. However, the 'Zoo' appeared and conducted H.R.H. and the more energetic members of his Staff to the Station Square, where a few returned soldiers and some school children were gathered together. After the usual stunt H.R.H. and party re-embarked, and the train left.

Not content with this, the 'Zoo' arranged a slowing up seven miles further on, but, having got the wind up again, he neglected to have H.R.H. informed so that H.R.H. arrived too late to wave from the platform.

The train made up a full half hour on the trip to Dunedin and arrived almost up to time. At the Dunedin Club, where H.R.H.'s party is staying, the Dunedin Pipe Band was drawn up, playing the 'Athol Highlanders' March'. They were remarkably good, and while H.R.H. paused to listen on the steps, four of the senior members of the Staff danced a wild and excited Highland Schottische in the hall. The servants, who had arrived by pilot train, had the gear ready this time, and dinner was at half past eight. Shortly after the fish course everyone had to stand up, as the Dunedin Male Choir had arrived unexpectedly and fired off by singing the 'God Save'. After this they sang some excellent songs, which were thoroughly enjoyed by all, H.R.H. going out and talking to them when they had finished. H.R.H. then drove by more or less the same route he had arrived by, to the Art Gallery, where the first Citizens' Ball was being given. There were only some 300 people present, which was a pleasant relief after Christchurch, but as the hall was only designed to hold 200, the relative crush was nearly as great. Perhaps it is because the Staff have become spoiled by the perfect dancing of the Christchurch maidens, but everyone was agreed that it was not such an easy matter to dance with the Dunedin girls. An unofficial set of Lancers was danced, in which H.R.H. and most of his Staff participated, and which they appeared to enjoy hugely. Shortly after supper the party returned to the Club, where H.R.H. and the Admiral retired upstairs, while the remainder of the Staff remained below and danced a 'haka', with Captain North as the leader.

TUESDAY, 18 MAY   The party drove to the Dunedin General Hospital, being received a short way from the gates by a number of the students carrying bones, dummy figures and skeletons, which they waved frantically as they ran alongside the cars. H.R.H. entered the main hall, where the nurses were assembled and some half-dozen children in cots. From here a move was made to the end of a corridor, where H.R.H. shook hands with wounded soldiers, and then walked along to a big lift, into which he and half of his Staff got. The gates were closed and everyone waited, but nothing happened. After about a minute or two the lift suddenly went up, stopping as suddenly half way between two floors. H.R.H. pressed a button in the lift and it descended, overshooting the mark and going half way down into the basement. More buttons were pushed and the lift once more ascended, but stopped again a few feet above the original floor. Eventually, after another short wait, the lift successfully did the trip to the top landing, where the occupants disembarked and visited the wards.

On return, the crowd as well as the nurses broke through, making it very difficult to get to the cars. The 'Zoo', shouting 'I must get forward', and, belabouring those who had the temerity to stand in the way, with his umbrella saved the situation by making a gangway to the rear cars. The party then drove along a very dusty route for some 15 miles. Shortly before 4.00 p.m. Port Chalmers was reached, this being the port of Dunedin. Here the usual small place stunt was gone through. The party then re-embarked and drove along the Lower Road back to Dunedin, stopping at one of the outlying suburbs – West Harbor.

Here the Mayor stood up and made a speech, in which he explained that he was not going to make a speech. Then, having called for three cheers for the King, Queen Mary and Admiral Halsey, he presented three small girls, who gave H.R.H. some bouquets. The party then drove on.

A telephone message arrived during dinner saying that a crowd of ten thousand were waiting in the Drill Hall impatiently for H.R.H., and could he come as quickly as possible. The party accordingly, without further delay, got up from dinner and drove to the Drill Hall where H.R.H. received one of the most enthusiastic welcomes he has ever received anywhere. Although, perhaps, ten thousand is an exaggeration, the crowd could not possibly have numbered less than between six and seven thousand, and nearly all were seated. H.R.H. and the Staff sat and listened to two or three items of the concert which were being given, and which were very good. The first item seemed a mixture of grand opera and bugle calls of the British Navy. Then came the singers of the night before – The Dunedin Male Choir – followed by a mixed orchestra with the Nell Gwyn dances. H.R.H. then made a short and good speech, which was cheered to the echo, and the party left and drove to the Art Gallery for the Otago Women's Club Ball, which was even more crowded than that of the night before, so that they did not stay long.

WEDNESDAY, 19 MAY   H.R.H. and Staff drove to Forbury Park for the military review. This was practically the same as previous big reviews, but contained all the improvements, thought out as the result of the other three, and was, therefore, the most perfect one to date. To the great grief of the 'Brigade of Guards', the odd-numbered ranks were turned about, which served to re-start the old argument as to whether this is right or not. The review was considerably enlivened by the arrival of two hares, which, dazed by the immense number of people present, raced up and down between the lines, being 'shoo-ed' back whenever they tried to get off the field, until, in despair, one of them galloped up to the Royal dais and slid under the platform, while the other one sought refuge in the refreshment tent. A great number of returned soldiers were shaken hands with, and then the party drove off to Carisbrook Grounds to witness part of a rugger match.

Before dinner, Captain North had called up Mr Fenwick and asked him to come to the Club 'to be knighted'. Mr Fenwick apparently understood this last remark as 'tonight', for when he arrived after dinner he knew nothing about what they expected of him. H.R.H. turned shy and refused to have any of the Staff present except the Admiral while he was giving the accolade, but his little scheme was spoiled by the 'Zoo', who slipped in unnoticed by anyone after Mr Fenwick had gone in. Owing to Mr Fenwick's apparent astonishment at being sent for, the Staff began to have grave doubts as to whether they had sent the right man in, and were contemplating what to do if it were the wrong man. After what seemed endless time to those waiting outside, the party re-appeared, and Captain North rushed up to Sir William, saying, 'Has he knighted the right man?' The 'Zoo' nodded his head, and all drew a sigh of relief.[1]

After this H.R.H. and all the Staff drove to the Kensington Drill Hall. A very good choir of some hundreds of women, waving red, white and blue ribbons to the time of the music, sang the 'God Bless' on the arrival of H.R.H. After a selection by the band and a song by the returned soldiers' choir, the girls sang the Hallelujah Chorus exceedingly well. The 'God Save' and 'For He's a Jolly Good Fellow' were then sung, and the party moved on to the Art Gallery, where the crowd was done in by the cars drawing up at a new entrance. The party went round the Early Settlers' Association's museum here, H.R.H. and some of his Staff playing the old hand organ of 70 years ago which is still in working order. H.R.H. then walked round to the south entrance, followed by a cheering crowd, to attend a dance given by the Overseas Club. After shaking hands with those few who had not been presented before, H.R.H. was presented with a green-stone watch for Princess Mary.[2] H.R.H. stayed considerably longer than usual, and finally was made a life member of the Overseas Club by the President of the Otago Branch, who appeared to be ignorant of the fact that H.R.H. was already their Patron.

THURSDAY, 20 MAY   About 1.25 p.m. the train stopped at Gore. The party embarked in motor cars and drove 100 yards up the main street. They then got out of the cars and walked another 100 yards up the

---

[1] Sir George Fenwick was unduly modest. As owner and former editor of the Otago *Daily Times* and active in many fields of New Zealand life he was a prime target for a knighthood.

[2] The Princess Royal, who was to marry Viscount Lascelles in February 1922.

main street to a dais which had been erected at the end. Here the usual stunt was gone through – school children and returned soldiers. This time the Mayor again presented councillors' wives to H.R.H. It is uncertain whether the councillors of Gore are Mormons or whether there are an unusually great number of councillors. Whichever the reason, there were between twenty and thirty wives to be presented.

Just as the party were settling down to lunch after the train had left Gore, the 'Zoo' arrived, and from his guilty look the party guessed what he was going to tell them. Of course he wished the train stopped at an unofficial place, though he firmly denied that it was a Government stronghold where the Government were trying to cull favour. Perhaps he was right, for when the train stopped at this place, Mataura, the local Mayor and his wife disembarked from the royal train, having travelled back from Gore, which was only seven miles off, in it. Perhaps the Staff were right, for it was the constituency of another M.P. who was travelling in the train, the Honourable Anderson. Certain it is that H.R.H. and the Admiral had their lunch disturbed, and had to go out in the snow to wave to a small crowd, which included neither returned soldiers nor school children, all of whom had gone by train to Gore.

Invercargill was reached at 3.00 p.m., and H.R.H. was received by a guard furnished by the 8th Southland Regiment. It should here be noted that it had been raining and snowing all day at every place until the moment of H.R.H.'s arrival. According to the people he brought with him 'Prince's weather', for wherever he arrived the sun shone and the clouds disappeared.

The 'Zoo' was perfectly splendid here, for when the local Mayor attempted to follow the party on to the parade ground, the 'Zoo' pulled him back by the collar of his coat, saying, 'No civilians are ever allowed on the parade ground.'

After dinner everyone went to the Garrison Hall and listened to two or three items of the usual type of concert. Only one row of seats was provided, so that nearly all the four or five thousand people present had to stand. As it was apparent that they had come to see H.R.H. and not to hear the music, a popular reception was arranged. Captain North made the arrangements with the Commissioner of Police to get the crowd away outside while H.R.H. announced what he was going to do and the Admiral explained how the crowd were to do their part. The Staff then leapt off the dais and cleared the front row of chairs out of the way and took up their stations as policemen, to pilot the crowd past H.R.H. H.R.H. did not shake hands with everybody, but stood at the bottom of the dais's steps and smiled on everyone as they passed. This meant that instead of doing 40 a minute he could do 120 a minute, and in just over half an hour the hall was cleared.

The party finally drove to the train and, as there are no sleeping cars in the South Island, had to camp out. The Admiral and Colonel Grigg as usual took the day saloon. Captain Legh, Lord Claud and Captain North took the Staff saloon, and were all very comfortable with the exception of Captain North, whose hot water bottle leaked over him. H.R.H. occupied his tiny sleeping cabin, while the Flag Lieutenant lay on the floor half under his bed, and the remainder of the Staff slept in the ministerial portion of the train. The servants were practically crowded out altogether, and on the whole it was a very weird night journey.

FRIDAY, 21 MAY   At 8.45 a.m. the train was stopped for a few minutes to enable the whole of the train staff and officials on board to get out and shake hands with H.R.H., who made a short farewell speech to them and was photographed with them. The train then proceeded, arriving at Christchurch at 9.00 a.m. From here, H.R.H. and Captain Rhodes departed for 'Te Koraha' to change into hunting clothes. The meet of the Christchurch Hounds was at Charing Cross, some 25 miles out of the town. H.R.H. had rather a queer mount and took two tosses over two wire fences in the first short run, later settling down to a very good day. They killed once in the very beginning, but after that they had much difficulty in finding any more hares. H.R.H. then went down to the ship.

An official dinner was given on board to the Governor-General, the Prime Minister, and all the most important people of the Dominion. No speeches were made, to H.R.H.'s intense satisfaction and H.E.'s intense disappointment. Whether it was because the Staff, including the New Zealand officials travelling on the train, had just come from the 'dry' district of Invercargill, or whether the wine was unusually potent, is not known, but the dinner certainly went with an additional 'zip' and some of the diners seemed to enjoy themselves hugely. After dinner, H.R.H. dealt out a few Victorian Orders, knighting Major-General Sir Edward Chaytor and Sir William Fraser.[1] The dear old 'Zoo' was completely overcome by what apparently had been an entirely unexpected honour, and babbled and prattled about it for

[1] Sir William was of course a knight already, but now added the KCVO to his previous honours.

hours in the most delightful way, trying to get the star pinned on to his coat, although he had no special fittings for it. The Staff had been growing quite fond of their old 'Zoo' and will all miss him very much in the coming trip.

SATURDAY, 22 MAY   The ship cast off from the jetty at 6.30 a.m. and proceeded out of harbour, steaming up the west coast of the island and passing through Cook's Strait in the afternoon, and then shaping course for Australia. H.R.H. appeared, looking very 'fat-headed', on the bridge when the ship moved off.

TUESDAY, 25 MAY   The wind and swell had completely disappeared by lunch time, and later on the sun came out, so that the day finished up perfectly.

During dinner a message was received from a Mr Soul, congratulating H.R.H. on his safe arrival. Everyone remarked, 'We haven't arrived yet', and thought the congratulations rather premature.

After dinner another 'haka' rehearsal was gone through, H.R.H. and the Admiral joining in for the first time. About 9.00 p.m., H.R.H., accompanied by some of the Staff, went down to the Gun Room, where they spent a very good evening, making much noise. Colonel Grigg played some 'Poi' music whilst all the 'Snotties' got on the table and did a canoe dance.[1]

---

[1] It was after an evening of this kind that the future Admiral Willis noted gloomily: 'Not a bad form of rag when in the mood for it but . . . I fear H.R.H. and Staff were rather bored.' Some Staff may have been, but H.R.H. seems usually to have relished this entertainment. 'Snotties' were midshipmen.

Australia

Australia was in some disarray in 1920. W. M. 'Billy' Hughes had formed a national government during the war and was held to be a traitor by many of his former supporters. His Nationalist Party had won a convincing victory in the general election of December 1919 but there had already been serious economic problems and the Prime Minister had made himself unpopular by pushing through substantial pay increases for ministers and members of the legislature. To add to his problems there was much labour unrest, particularly in the public service.

Australia had been proclaimed a Commonwealth in January 1901, when the six former colonies, now designated Original States (New South Wales, Victoria, Queensland, Western Australia, South Australia and Tasmania) joined in a Federation. The apportionment of powers between State and Federal authorities caused much initial trouble and was a live issue during the Prince's visit. The seat of the Federal Parliament was at first Melbourne, but a new Federal Capital was already in the process of construction at Canberra.

Republicanism was a potent force on the left wing of Australian politics and the Prince's entourage looked forward apprehensively to a certain amount of hostility from elements of the labour movement. In fact very little of the sort was encountered, a tribute both to the good manners of the Australians and the tact and skilful public relations of the Prince.

WEDNESDAY, 26 MAY 1920   At 6.15 a.m. the weather was clear, the sea was calm, and the outlook for entering up to time was favourable.

Three quarters of an hour later the ship ran into a thick fog bank and reduced speed. When some four or five miles off the Heads the fog thickened, so the engines were stopped. The ship had to be through the Heads by 8.30 a.m., at the latest, otherwise the tide would be too strong, and, owing to her great length, she would become uncontrollable while passing through the narrow channel. When the fog, therefore, lifted slightly, the Admiral made haste to push the ship on, but she ran into another and denser bank. She turned 16 points and hove to, anxiously waiting for the fog to lift, most of the Staff remembering Mr Soul's fatal greetings. Just before 8.30 it was realized that it would be too late to catch the morning slack water and a message was despatched to the Governor-General[1] to say that the *Renown* herself, anyhow, could not enter during the forenoon slack water. A reply came to say that hundreds of thousands of people were waiting in the streets already for H.R.H., and the Admiral, therefore, decided to go by destroyer. Half the escorting flotilla, which was waiting inside the Heads, were summoned by wireless, but in the fog no definite rendezvous could be given, and the destroyers missed the ship. Guns were then fired every fifteen seconds, which soon brought the three destroyers into sight. Everything was in readiness on board, and immediately the destroyer was alongside, the detectives, clerks, servants, orderlies, Press correspondents, photographers and signalmen got on board. H.R.H. embarked, and within three minutes of her first coming alongside, the *Anzac* was under way steaming for Port Phillip at 25 knots. As the land was neared the fog thinned, and inside it was merely slightly misty. The destroyers went straight over a very shallow patch, causing a mountainous wake to follow. The *Anzac* then reduced speed, and passed between two of the lines of the Australian Fleet, the ships being manned, and cheering H.R.H. as he passed.

The *Anzac* berthed alongside New Pier at Port Melbourne. After inspecting the guard, H.R.H. crossed over to the other side of the pier and embarked in the *Hygeia*. The *Hygeia* is an old paddle-steamer, and was used owing to the historic interest attached to her, as she had been used for the King when he was out in Australia. After she had shoved off, an old, old Merchant Service Captain was brought up and presented to H.R.H. He turned out to have been in command when the King had made the trip on board 19 years ago. The *Hygeia* berthed at St Kilda Pier at 3.15 p.m. which was only three quarters of an hour

[1] Sir R. Munro-Ferguson, later Lord Novar, a level-headed Scot who was to be replaced after the royal visit by Lord Forster.

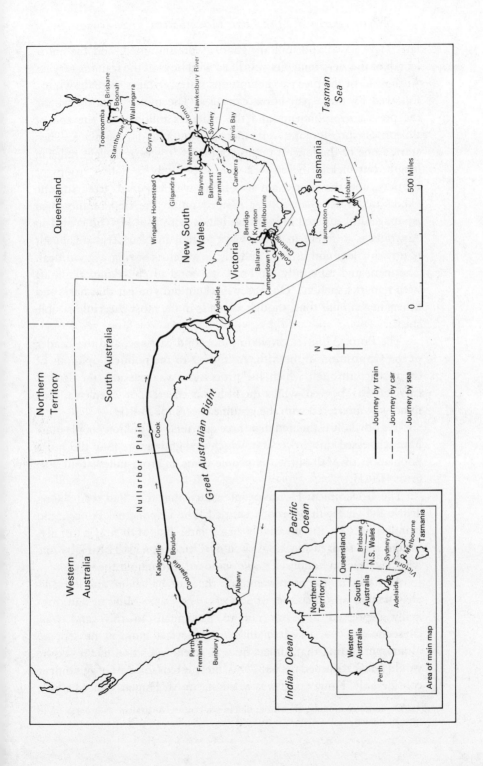

late. Here naval and military guards were mounted, and the entire length of this very long pier was lined with boys of the training service. At the end of the pier two sumptuous state carriages were drawn up, followed by three pair-horse carriages. The motor cars containing the press correspondents and the orderlies followed at the end of the procession, looking very incongruous and out of place. Then started one of the longest drives yet made. It was over eight miles in length, but luckily the crowds were kept back by police, troops or barriers, and the procession was in no way impeded. Even so, one exhilarated Australian soldier jumped on to the step of the royal equipage and insisted on shaking hands with H.R.H. The crowd in Australia is different in many ways to that in New Zealand, but it is no whit less enthusiastic and loyal, which is saying a good deal. The men, and especially the boys, are fond of chy-aking[1] the Staff with remarks such as, 'Oh, Percy – where did you get that hat?' and others in a similar tone, though all made in the most cheerful possible spirit.

The Prime Minister drove in the second carriage, and the Leader of the Opposition in the fifth. According to the political opinions of the district through which the procession was passing, the second carriage was 'boo-ed' whilst the fifth was cheered, or vice versa. This in no way interfered with the genuine cheers for H.R.H.

It is officially estimated that three quarters of a million people must have witnessed this procession, which is slightly more than the entire population of Melbourne, as people came in from miles around to greet H.R.H.

The Government House people stated that they had read a long article by Mr Keith Murdoch entitled 'The Unpunctual Prince', and blaming H.R.H. for invariably being late. The Staff are, naturally, furious that such insinuations should be made against H.R.H. by one who has been an honoured guest on board throughout the trip.

At 9.30 p.m. the party went into the state ballroom, and immediately danced an official set of Lancers. The Prime Minister had originally expressed a desire not to participate in this, and was, consequently, not asked to do so. At the last moment he sent an ultimatum stating that, unless he was given a position in the set, he would refuse to attend the ball. This interrupted Colonel Grigg's dinner considerably. However, it was worth it, for Mr Hughes danced a little

[1] Or, more commonly, chiacking; nineteenth-century Australian slang meaning to tease or banter.

above: Renown navigating a landslide in the Panama canal (30 March 1920).

below: H.R.H. and Mountbatten bathing in *Renown*'s so-called pool.

above: A 'Soap Frill' is administered before H.R.H. is initiated on Crossing the Line (17 April 1920).

below: The arrival at Auckland, escorted by an armada of motor boats (24 April 1920).

above: Government House, Wellington.

below: H.R.H. gingerly uses his left hand to greet returned servicemen at Ashburton, one of seven towns visited the same day (17 May 1920).

The centre of Canberra. H.R.H. and his staff walk to the point where he is to lay the centre stone of the new city (21 June 1920).

set of Lancers all by himself, and really, the remainder of the dancers hardly worried him. Then H.R.H. shook hands with everyone, and the ball commenced. Of course, it was crowded at first, but very soon the crowd thinned, and dancing became possible. The bands of the *Renown* and *Australia* officiated, much to the disgust of the Musicians' Trade Union, who have entered a protest against the use of ships' bands ashore. The ball closed about 1 a.m. and all retired to bed.

THURSDAY, 27 MAY   At 9.50 a.m. a military guard of honour marched up to the front of the house, and H.R.H. went out and inspected it. Hardly had he returned inside when a naval guard of honour arrived, and so H.R.H. again went out and inspected that. He then entered the ballroom for the levée and investiture. First, those with the right of private entrée, made their bows. This did not take long and was quickly followed by the investiture. For the first time this trip there was a V.C. to bestow. After the investiture the public levée was held, to which about a thousand people had come, nearly all of whom appeared in top hats. This did not take longer than some forty minutes, and was well organized. After this, thirty-four addresses were presented, of various shapes and sizes, each by three representatives of the body concerned. Of course, some of the address-givers arrived late and had to make the presentation in the passage outside.

At 6.45 p.m., H.R.H. drove to the Commonwealth House of Parliament through a most enthusiastic mob. Here H.R.H. was received by Mr Hughes, who first conducted him to the Senate, where he introduced him to the President,[1] who escorted him to the dais. After an exchange of addresses with the Senate, H.R.H. was taken to what the Prime Minister affectionately termed the 'House of Reps'. The same stunt was gone through here, H.R.H. as before shaking hands with the members afterwards.

The party then proceeded to the Queen's Hall, where the official dinner, at which over 300 were present, was given. Mr Hughes made a most impressive speech at the end of dinner, followed by H.R.H., who was in great form and made quite one of his best speeches, which was liked enormously by all. After this a returned soldier got up and sang the 'Men of Harlech' in an exceedingly fine voice. The decorations were original, consisting of illuminated flowers, maps and constellations. In the meanwhile, H.R.H. had given instructions that the

[1] Senator Thomas Givens.

mounted police were not to accompany him owing to the danger to the crowd. This was not strictly carried out, but even so, great crowds pressed round him and several men jumped on to the car trying to shake hands, but were speedily knocked off by the orderlies. At Government House H.R.H. sent for the Chief of Police and arranged with him to have the mounted police withdrawn altogether.

FRIDAY, 28 MAY   H.R.H. boarded H.M.A.S. *Franklin* which was doing duty as Royal Yacht. On arrival among the Australian fleet, a salute of 21 guns was fired by all saluting ships. The royal yacht then steamed down between 'A' Line and the Supernumerary Line, turning 16 points at the end and proceeding up in front of 'B' Line, turning again at the end, and doing the same thing for 'C' and then for 'D' Line. As she passed each ship cheered. The most effective cheering was that of the submarines of the J Class, the ships' companies in clean white sweaters looking particularly effective. It was a misty morning, and it was not possible to see quite to the end of the lines, which was really rather lucky, as it made the small Australian fleet of some 35 ships in all, look considerably larger. After the Review the *Franklin* anchored near the *Australia* and the party proceeded on board for luncheon with the Commodore commanding H.M.A. Fleet.

Back on shore, the cars drove to the Victoria State House of Parliament, through great crowds. The Melbourne crowds are falling into bad habits – confetti is appearing in great and unpleasant quantities, and the 'touching' mania has started, only, owing to the hearty disposition of the Australians, the touches are more like blows, and H.R.H. and the Admiral arrived half-blinded and black and blue.

The State Exhibition Building is an enormous one made in the form of a stunted 'T'. The three wings were packed tight, each containing some 6000 people. At one end the choir bravely struggled with a few original tunes, such as the 'God Save' and the 'God Bless', 'Rule Britannia' and the 'Hallelujah Chorus'. H.R.H. mounted a dais which had been erected for him, and the gate of the first penn was opened, allowing a thin stream of people to file past. They were not shaking hands with H.R.H., of course, and everyone was disappointed when an average of only 90 a minute could be raised. However, the gate was opened to its full extent and the people were let through five abreast so that an average of over 170 a minute was eventually attained. The pressure became so extreme in one part of the building, owing to the people in the rear crowding up to see H.R.H., that over 100 fainting cases occurred and three hospital cases. After an hour and a quarter, the room was nearly empty, when suddenly the doors of the middle chamber opened and a fresh avalanche burst in. Messengers were hurried up to close these doors and prevent the people from entering, but by the time that they arrived on the scene all the people were in, but luckily these did not exceed a thousand. In all, at least 20,000 people filed past H.R.H., who stood the test gallantly, and they were got past in just under two hours, which says a lot for the organization, especially when it is taken into consideration that this was the first event of its kind to take place in Australia.

The evening papers contained a cabled account from London, stating that in a leader, which had appeared in *The Times*, an attack had been made on H.R.H.'s Staff for 'curbing his boyish and generous outbursts, and generally imperilling the success of the trip'. This time it was H.R.H.'s turn to express indignation against this attack on his Staff.[1]

SATURDAY, 29 MAY   Just before lunch the boomerang expert arrived and some of the Government House party came out and stood near him while he threw them. Of course, this was the worst place they could stand, for the boomerangs always came back, and they had to throw themselves on to the ground and try to cover their heads as though for an air raid, which amused those watching from the house considerably. The spectators then started to try to throw, the only successful one being Colonel Grigg.

Immediately after lunch H.R.H. motored to Essendon where a short 'exchange of address' stunt was done. The cars then pushed on to the Royal Agricultural Society's Show Grounds at Flemington. As soon as he had been received H.R.H. went down from the royal stand to the track to watch the parade of specially selected horses and cattle. Next, he witnessed a wood-chopping competition, in which some half dozen men each had to chop in two a standing block of 45-inch girth. The winner did it in under a minute. Next, a sheaf-tossing display was given, in which the highest sheaf was tossed 54 feet. The party then walked over to the south side of the grounds and entered a shed

---

[1] The leading article, of 27 May 1920, announced that the Australians considered the Prince 'Simple and generous-minded and without side', but were disposed to think that his Staff was 'inclined to check these impulses'. Whether these impressions were justified or not, concluded *The Times* – leaving no doubt that it thought they were – 'We have no doubt that the Staff will realize that their first duty is to remove it.'

which contained prize rams, wethers, pigs and poultry, which H.R.H. inspected thoroughly. Cadets were lining the route in the show grounds, but though they looked well disciplined from a distance, no sooner did the leading car come level with them than some of them attempted to touch H.R.H., and others made facetious remarks to the Staff. The cars stopped at a large shed where there were examples of all Australian products, quite artistically arranged. When he had seen this show, H.R.H. returned to the trotting track and watched a high-jump display, in which the winning horse succeeded in jumping a seven-foot high gate.

The party had exactly half an hour to dress for dinner and start off on the next stunt, which was the dinner by the Naval and Military Boards given at Menzie's Hotel. There were only about 40 present, and the table was made in the shape of a boomerang. The dinner arranged was a twelve-course one, but after the meat course 'The King' was drunk and smoking started, and the last three or four courses cut out so as to enable H.R.H. to drive on to the Grand Hotel to fulfil another illegitimate function, but rather an important one, as it was a 'press' dinner. The Chairman made a very pleasant speech, to which H.R.H. replied, but, for the first time, words failed him about half way through, though in a most effective manner, so that he sat down amidst thunderous applause.

SUNDAY, 30 MAY From the programme, with the exception of church, this day appeared free. In actual fact, this was far from being the case, for after church official photographs were first of all taken, a perfect battery of over thirty cameras taking three pictures each, so that at least a hundred plates were secured of the group. Then H.R.H. planted a tree in the Botanical Gardens quite near by, and visited the Royal Stables. The Prime Minister and Mrs Hughes came to lunch, the former being in riding rig. It was noticed that he was only wearing one spur, and this was pointed out to him by H.R.H., but it turned out that he always dressed like this.

Immediately after lunch, H.R.H. and the Prime Minister set out for a twenty-mile drive to Sassafras, the Prime Minister's country home.

Not far from the eventual destination the Prime Minister's car stopped, and the party alighted to find two girls sitting on horseback, one of them holding a small soft animal with a small pointed nose peeping out from under one of her arms. She was very excited, and

wanted to know whether H.R.H. would accept 'Joey', who turned out
to be baby wallaby not two months' old yet. He was accepted with
great joy and turned over to Inspector Burt,[1] who pointed out that
confusion might arise between the wallaby and Captain Legh unless
the name was changed. H.R.H., therefore, called him 'Digger'. The
calvacade then proceeded and rode at a tremendous pace for about
two hours through the most delightful country, along muddy and
twisting roads. The Prime Minister was most amusing, and every now
and then, for no apparent reason, he would disappear in a cloud of
dust or a shower of mud, according to the nature of the road. At first,
some apprehension was felt concerning him, but one of the girls who
had joined the party pointed out that it was merely his horse running
away with him, which it apparently did at frequent intervals.

After what really proved a most delightful ride to everybody, the
party returned, to find an immense crowd around the cars, who cheered
and yelled, but luckily did not frighten the horses. The party drove off
followed by an enormous procession of cars, producing a tremendous
dust cloud. H.R.H., turning round, saw two or three cars trying to
pass, and thinking they were in a hurry, let them get on ahead. At least
forty cars followed, and H.R.H.'s car was swamped in dust, so he
turned up a side road which appeared to be too bumpy, and had to
turn back, and only by dint of keeping in the middle of the road and
keeping the rear of the traffic back could he avoid being smothered by
dust again in the main road. At the Prime Minister's house an enormous
crowd had collected, and here again the police got more in the way
than the crowd. One of the mounted men's horses kicked H.R.H.'s
car very hard, and one of the foot police tried to stop even H.R.H.
himself from getting past. On arrival H.R.H. made a terrible faux pas.
Seeing two men standing at the far end of the hall, to whom the Prime
Minister waved his hand, saying, 'This is my son,' H.R.H. went up to
the one in evening dress and shook hands. He turned out to be the
waiter. While waiting for dinner 'Digger' was brought into the room
and made to jump small logs of wood, which he did very successfully.
He is a most loveable and delightful animal, full of quaint little tricks
and not much bigger in body than a very tiny rabbit. The party now
drove back to Government House, where they changed into evening
clothes and found a lot of pretty girls gathered in the hall.

As it was Sunday night only ludo could be played, according to

[1] Alfred Burt, the Prince of Wales's private detective.

His Ex., who is a Presbyterian, but it was played in the ballroom to the accompaniment of a gramophone and pianola, and was hardly distinguished from ordinary dancing. After midnight, as it was no longer Sunday, one good dance was indulged in before the party finally broke up.

MONDAY, 31 MAY   This day being the anniversary of the Battle of Jutland, a naval march past took place by a thousand men, from the *Renown* and all units of the Australian Fleet. All the men marched remarkably well considering that they had never been drilled for it. H.R.H. took the salute at the last bend in the drive.

Everyone changed into plain clothes again before lunch, and at 1.45 p.m. the cars were reported ready. After driving for a good half hour through endless and crowded streets, the Melbourne Cricket Ground was reached and the party at once proceeded to the Royal Stand. The first thing noticed was Government House, which could be plainly seen from the stand, in spite of the half-hour's drive. In the great open expanse of the cricket ground 6000 school children were seated, making a gigantic map of Australia with the words 'Our Prince' in the middle of it. A whistle blew and, to the inevitable tune of 'Johnny's in Town', which seems to have sprung into favour in Australia again, all the children forming the map rose and marched off the field, following the contour line of the map on their way to the gate. This left the children forming the letters on the ground, and as another whistle blew they ran off as hard as they could, to the intense amusement of all the spectators. Next the band struck up the Rifle Brigade March, and some 3000 junior pupils, whose average age can't have been more than seven, marched in, coming up the centre of the ground in eight lines, each boy holding his partner by the hand. All were dressed in the Welsh national costume made up of black and a very pretty shade of green. The school teachers left their little charges, and at another whistle alternate sections of their lines marched into the intervening gaps. The whole parade now danced an old Welsh folk dance with the most amazing grace. No mistake was made by anyone, and it was one of the prettiest and most successful shows yet witnessed.

TUESDAY, 1 JUNE   At 9.40 a.m., H.R.H. left Federal Government House and drove to Spencer Street Station, where he boarded the royal train and departed. This train, unlike the New Zealand train, is enormously wide, the gauge being 5 ft 3-ins. Although only the State

Governor's car was used by H.R.H., it was magnificently appointed and very comfortable, containing, among other things, two bathrooms with long baths, and several separate compartments.

The train arrived at Geelong at 11.15 a.m. A military guard of honour and a guard of the R.A.N. Reserve were mounted outside the station, and after the Mayor had received H.R.H. he went out and inspected them. The naval guard was really rather pathetic. It was commanded by an R.A.N. Lieutenant-Commander, who seemed dazed. The second in command was an old Surgeon, who found some difficulty in drawing his sword. Some of the men had their caps on the back of their heads, looking even more untidy than a liberty-man can do ashore. Most of them were chewing 'gum', and altogether it was not too amusing a spectacle. Very different to these were the bluejackets who lined the route to the Town Hall.

After a trying tour round the grounds, the party fought their way out to the cars and drove to an exhibition of the local products. This was very interesting, and showed what a surprising variety of things can be produced in one small town. Perhaps the most interesting was the shearing of a sheep with electrical shears. Everyone was feeling sorry for the sheep, when suddenly the fuse blew and the shears refused to operate. Perhaps it was as well, as the sheep would have had to have been wrapped up in blankets if it had been sheared completely, owing to the cold weather.

Luncheon was served in a magnificent dining room in the train, and at 12.30 p.m. Colac was reached, H.R.H. being received by the President of the Shire. Motor cars were provided, which drove everyone to the Town Hall. It had just been raining, but on H.R.H.'s arrival 'Prince's weather' set in again. Addresses were exchanged with the President outside the Shire Hall, and then returned soldiers were shaken hands with. The police being somewhat inadequate, the Staff joined hands with all the police there were, and kept the crowd back on their own. Everyone then drove back to the station, and to the inevitable tune of 'Johnny's in Town' the train drew out of the station.

The terminus of the day, Camperdown, was reached at 3.00 p.m., and here the first ludicrous incident of the day occurred, for on arrival there were only two Ford cars present and these were intended for the servants – who have been officially called 'attendants' to avoid the eternal misunderstanding which occurred in New Zealand. On arrival the guard and band marched off and H.R.H. and the Staff followed, some difficulty being experienced in avoiding keeping time with the band, which would have looked rather ridiculous. The Crossley cars which had been sent up from Melbourne by train were awaiting the party, and drove them to the house of Mr Black – 'Glenormiston'. This is a charming house, quite like an English country house, both as regards the interior and the views from the windows of the surrounding country. After tea H.R.H. went for a short walk, and, as far as possible, everyone rested.

There has been a great scheme since the party left, to give H.R.H. a free week in Melbourne before sailing for Sydney. He is becoming terribly overworked, and cannot possibly continue at this rate. After dinner, which was quite informal, the Admiral called up Colonel Grigg and made the final arrangements about this week, but was an hour late in coming on to the dance as a result.

Mr Black rushed round the place with sheafs of written instructions on the subject of H.R.H.'s movements, asking continually for the detectives and orderlies, etc., and it was a fearful blow to him when neither detectives nor orderlies accompanied the party to the dance, which took place at Mount Noorat, some three or four miles away. An excellent jazz band provided the music, having specially come down from the 'Palais de Danse' in Melbourne, and H.R.H. and the Flag Lieutenant played the drums occasionally during the evening. A Miss Browne, who was staying at 'Glenormiston', and was among the party, behaved in a most astounding manner. She would start by asking her partner, 'What is your favourite topic of conversation?', shouting at him 'Don't spit' the moment he attempted to answer, and then offering to tell him a scandalous story in French. As the evening got on she became worse, and the Staff wondered what was at the back of it and whether she always behaved like that. The dance finished at about half past one, and everyone drove back and retired to bed.

WEDNESDAY, 2 JUNE   After the train had left luncheon was served, and at 2.00 p.m. Ballarat – or as it should be officially spelt, Ballaarat – was reached. The city, which boasts some 40,000 inhabitants, is apparently divided into two for legislative purposes: Ballarat, and Ballarat East; with a result that two Mayors, who are very alike and rather resembled Tweedle-dum and Tweedle-dee were awaiting H.R.H. on the platform and introduced two sets of Councillors. Outside, a collection of gaily coloured cars was drawn up, which it was at first imagined belonged to a tourist party, but later turned out to be those intended for the royal party's use. They were covered in cheap red, white and blue ribbons, Union Jacks, French flags, imitation standards and Prince of Wales's feathers, etc. In front of each bonnet a wooden triumphal arch had been erected, with the word 'Welcome' on it, and to cap it all an enormous stuffed wallaby was strapped to the running board of H.R.H.'s car so that the orderlies could hardly jump on the car, when they were required. Having made the party look ridiculous by providing these absurd cars, the local council thought that they would give it that tone of dignity so necessary for H.R.H.'s movements, and arranged an escort of light horse to trot before and after H.R.H.'s car. The two Mayors, like Mutt and Jeff, followed in the next car, and the rest of the Staff had fat councillors distributed in their cars; the last staff car having, as well, a lady, aged six, who wept copiously most of the time. After driving for a long while in circles, which turned out to have been done to give Ballarat East a fair turn, the City Hall was reached, and, owing to the jealousy between Mutt and Jeff, an impartial Colonel read the address. H.R.H. on starting his reply, began: 'Mister Mayors . . .' No sooner had he started than a cornet player struck up the 'God Bless', and, at last, in desperation H.R.H. stopped reading the address, saying that he really could not compete with the band. It now came on to rain, but, owing to the elaborate decorations, it was impossible to put the hoods up without spending some ten minutes in cutting down flags and streamers, which there was not time to do at this place. The party now drove a good long distance to the Arch of Victory, where H.R.H. dismounted and went on to a platform. This opportunity was seized to cut the decorations adrift and get the hoods up, but the colours ran out of the decorations, giving the cars a camouflaged appearance.

This account seems to have been ridiculing Ballarat so far, but it must be admitted that nowhere has a crowd been put to such a test of loyalty, and answered it so well, as in Ballarat, for it rained solidly during the next two hours and not one person in the whole crowd was seen to move off, even along the dull parts of the route. This Arch of Victory had been built by the efforts of 500 girls working for the firm of Lucas. They had also planted some 4000 trees, each tree representing a local soldier, along a 14-mile avenue, which they call the Avenue of Honour. The arch was not quite completed, but was considered ready for opening, and after a hot air speech by somebody, a dear old lady came up and made a long speech, in which her 'Hs' got terribly mixed up, finally presenting H.R.H. with a pair of gold scissors with which he cut a string holding the garlands across the arch. As he cut it a tremendous explosion was heard and the garlands swung clear. The arch was now apparently opened, and much clapping took place. The next thing that happened was that H.R.H. had to lay a coping stone. It seemed an odd thing to lay the coping stone last of all, but perhaps it was better than not laying it at all. A lady representing the Lucas girls then stepped on to the platform and presented H.R.H. with a pair of laboriously worked satin pyjamas. At the end of this little ceremony she turned to the 500 girls and said in a loud voice, 'Are they to wear on his honeymoon?' Back came 500 unanimous replies, to the intense amusement of all and the discomfiture of H.R.H.

Tea was next served, at the end of which one of the Mayors got up and took five minutes to say that he was only allowed a minute to make his speech in. He then called upon one of the Town Clerks to make a speech in half a minute. After the Town Clerk had complained for some three or four minutes about only being allowed half a minute to make his speech, he was stopped by everyone rising and going off, much to his distress.

The party then drove back to the station and departed. Melbourne was reached shortly after half past six and everyone drove to Federal Government House. After an official dinner, a departure was made for the State Governor's House, where a small ball was being given. This was the first official ball at which there was room to dance. Miss Browne was there, and quite different and well behaved, which has led the Staff to believe that the causes of her behaviour of the night before were only temporary.

Mr Keith Murdoch has written to the Colonel explaining that the attack on the Staff was not due to him, and that some local correspondent must be blamed; he is, therefore, exonerated from any suspicion that may have rested on him.

THURSDAY, 3 JUNE Most of the Staff accompanied H.R.H. to the Grand Hotel for the luncheon with the Executive of the Returned Sailors and Soldiers' Imperial League of Australia. On the way it was noticeable that the cheering and crowding of the people had abated considerably. This was due to a leader in the morning's paper pointing out how tiring this was for him. It was a dark and stuffy room rendered more so by great flags being hung over all the windows. The tables were well decorated but the seats were very close together.

At 3.00 p.m. Melbourne University was reached, where H.R.H. was received by the Chancellor. H.R.H. was taken to a small dressing room, where he donned the gorgeous red gown of a Doctor of Laws. A procession was then formed, with the most important people leading, and everyone walking in two by two. The route to the hall was lined by undergraduates in uniform. Inside there was a large congregation of 'undergraduates' in petticoats and gowns. After all were seated the Chancellor made a welcoming speech, everyone standing up at the end of it, while H.R.H. was presented for the Degree, which was then conferred upon him by the Chancellor. An address was presented to H.R.H., which was read to him in Latin, H.R.H. excusing himself for not being able to read his reply in Latin, read it in English. The Premier of Victoria[1] now did an amazing thing. Although he is not a member of the University and really in no way connected with it, being present as an honoured guest and occupying a spectator's seat, he thought fit at this point of the proceedings to jump up and call for three cheers, which, however, was enthusiastically responded to.

FRIDAY, 4 JUNE   Kyneton was reached at 10.05 and was a platform stunt. The 'God Save' was played by a comic band in Hussar uniform with Panama hats, but the 'God Bless', which was also sung by the school children, was played by a harmonium and fiddle. When H.R.H. began to read his reply to the address, two of the orderlies held up boards with the words 'Silence' painted on them. This had an extraordinarily good effect on the people, who preserved absolute silence while H.R.H. was speaking, for about the first time on record.

Shortly after noon the train drew up at Bendigo station. The Prime Minister and the Premier of Victoria were accompanying H.R.H. and apparently a wrangle had ensued as to who should have the honour of presenting the Mayor to H.R.H. This honour apparently fell to Mr Hughes, or anyway, he walked quicker than Mr Lawson, for it was he who did the presenting. Bendigo is Mr Hughes's constituency, and although in one part of the town he is quite popular, a certain section, and a very noisy section at that, dislike him. The Mayor got rather frightened at the idea of driving with Mr Hughes, as he had just bought a new set of robes and did not think rotten eggs would improve them. He therefore got four soldiers, some of them wounded, to stand on his car to protect himself and Mr Hughes. Although no attack was made there were lots of loud shouts of 'Hyoooes', and he was likened to stinking fish and such other pleasant things. Again it must be stated

[1] Mr. H. S. W. Lawson.

that no boo-ing in any way interfered with H.R.H.'s cheers, and as 'Billy' Hughes is exceedingly deaf he probably thought that he was being cheered as well.

After lunch the party drove to the Unity Gold Mine. At first, the project of going down the mine was abandoned; but when it turned out that it was a holiday and that those miners who were down were volunteers to demonstrate the working to H.R.H., he consented to go down, and accordingly changed into brown overalls and a miner's blue cap. All the Staff followed suit, and even 'Billy' Hughes put on brown overalls, though as he neglected to tuck the tails of his morning coat into his overall trousers, they hung out between the brown coat and the brown nether garment, looking somewhat comic and later exceedingly dirty. The party went down in three loads in the cage which travelled at 500 feet a minute. The face which the party went to was 1255 feet below the surface. Except in a very few places it was possible for the tallest of the party to walk upright, and the mine was well lit by candles all along the route, so that the candles which had been supplied to the party to carry, and which, incidentally, kept on blowing out as they walked along, were, luckily, unnecessary. At the face drilling operations were witnessed, and some of the party, finding little nuggets of gold in the quartz, got permission to knock them out with a pick. A flash-light photo was taken at another face which was visited later, and then the party returned four at a time, Mr Hughes standing at the bottom of the shaft telling 'funny' stories about what happened when the rope broke. However, everyone reached the surface safely and, having dressed once more, went to the cars.

About half past seven Spencer Street station, Melbourne, was reached and everyone drove back to Federal Government House.

SATURDAY, 5 JUNE H.R.H. drove to the Anzac Hostel at Brighton where he was received by the Mayor and prominent citizens, and then went in to see the wounded and invalid soldiers. There were only some twenty of these, and they were nearly all doomed men, yet you could not have found a more cheerful crowd anywhere. One man, who had only a fortnight to live, was more cheerful than anyone. H.R.H. talked a long while to each man and gave him his autograph.

At a quarter to eight everyone drove off, mostly in closed cars, to Her Majesty's Theatre. At the entrance a great crowd had collected. Two attendants, in gold livery with powdered wigs, blew a fanfare on coach horns. Quite a good little bull-fight now occurred, which warmed the Staff up before going in to a very cold auditorium. The ante-room had forest scenery placed in it, and the theatre inside was beautifully decorated with flowers, crowns and festoons. Each seat in the stalls had balloons, filled with gas, tied to them, but this was a slip, for as soon as the curtain went up so did the balloons, until the attendants went round and begged people not to let any more go as it was upsetting the actors. The gala performance consisted of *The Bing Boys on Broadway*, interspersed with such items as 'Selections from *Renown*'s Band', grand opera songs and pageants. These prolonged the show, and Government House was not reached until nearly midnight, but the show had been good and on the whole much appreciated.

SUNDAY, 6 JUNE   At Government House two or three girls were invited to dine and later on the Fairbairn party joined up, so that another small Sunday dance could be held in the ballroom to the accompaniment of the pianola. The cook's pram, which was wheeled in at half time, suffered considerably, for the Captain insisted upon wheeling H.R.H. down the length of the ballroom at breakneck speed, turning round so sharply at the end that he spilled him out and damaged the pram considerably. Unfortunately the cushions fell out as well and next minute a rugger scrum had been formed and a good game was soon in full swing which lasted until the insides of the cushions were sent flying in all directions, giving the room a very debauched appearance. Everyone retired to bed before midnight.

FRIDAY, 11 JUNE   H.R.H. went out to Moonee Valley Racecourse at Essendon, where he did some bigger jumps than he had ever done before. When he had finished his ride he motored to a hospital. He had meant to go to the Austin Consumptive Hospital, but, by some mistake, he was taken to the Macleod Hospital, which contained some 130 wounded soldiers. Unintentionally, this became a surprise visit, and H.R.H. saw the hospital in its true unvarnished state. It was not exactly clean, nor was there any appearance of smartness about any of the inmates, and on the whole H.R.H. was very disappointed with it; but then, as he was later informed, this hospital has never been very brilliant. It is to be hoped that his visit has done something to smarten it up.

H.R.H. now motored to the hospital he had originally set out to see, and, by some mistake, they had not been warned of his coming, so that a second surprise visit was paid; but, as he only wished to see the ward containing the twenty odd wounded soldiers, this did not matter so much, and he found the place in very good order.

In the evening Mrs Fairbairn gave a small dance, which H.R.H. attended accompanied only by his equerries and the Admiral's Staff. While sitting out in the gentlemen's cloak room, H.R.H. discovered a wardrobe full of marvellous clothing, in which he immediately dressed himself up, having an opera hat many sizes too large for him over his head, a coat equally as big, and a pair of white boots about size 15. The Flag Lieutenant, who was with him at the time, followed suit; and both their partners dressed up in red and pink boot bags, which looked very becoming. H.R.H.'s appearance caused much laughter, but it is doubtful whether he could dance very well with two pairs of boots on. H.R.H. was virtuous and stuck to his Cinderella record, though the party only got back at three minutes to twelve.

SATURDAY, 12 JUNE   H.R.H. and party left about 4.15 p.m. and drove to Parliament Buildings. From there they drove to the ship officially. The crowd fully made up for their week's restraint and gave H.R.H. a grand send off. Only a very few officials were allowed to see him off and hardly had they seen him officially on board than he quietly slipped ashore again and visited the Missions to Seamen in Flinders Street, where he talked with a stoker who had been in the old *Renown*.

At 7.45 an official farewell dinner party was given on board to the Governor-General and various other important people. The Lord Mayor, who was present, emulated the Bishop of Barbados, and became thoroughly merry. Just before dinner it came on to rain heavily so that the awnings got soaked, and although it had stopped raining after dinner, the water dripped from the saturated canvas through the ceremonial awnings on to the deck. Luckily, the reception deck had been prepared as well, so that by the time the dance guests arrived after dinner everything was ready for dancing up there. The dance was an entire success, although Mr Armytage went round with a revolver searching for his wife who had been locked into the Gun Room for six dances. Many heartbreaking good-byes were said at the end of it, the young Marine having to be fetched back to the ship by force just at the moment he was trying to conceal himself in a certain car.

A record in ship visitors was created in Melbourne, for well over 100,000 people visited her here, alone, which is only slightly less than the total number in New Zealand.

SUNDAY, 13 JUNE   H.R.H. kept up his record by appearing on the bridge at 6.30 a.m. Just as the ship was shoving off, from the far end of the pier came 'coo-ees' and cheers, although it was still·dark, and as the ship swung past the next pier the crowd which had collected at the end also cheered raucously. Even after the ship had got under way a white boat full of maniacs followed the ship singing 'Abe my Boy', the 'God Bless' and the 'God Save', and then shouted out: 'We want the Prince.' H.R.H. leaned over the bridge and waved his cap many times, but they took no notice of this as they did not seem to imagine that he could really be up at this hour of the morning.

MONDAY, 14 JUNE   The ship reached Jervis Bay about 1.30 p.m. and anchored quite close to the College steps.[1]

The College is in a very isolated position on the edge of Jervis Bay, surrounded by thick bush, and the nearest railway station is more than 20 miles distant. After the drive round, H.R.H. inspected a number of dormitories, classrooms, etc., and eventually went out on to a special platform that had been built to watch the rugby football match between the Ship and the College. However, as the *Renown* XV had not yet put in an appearance, H.R.H. climbed down and walked across the ground to a spot where a number of returned and wounded soldiers were among the spectators. These were called out and formed into a line, and he shook hands with each of the 50-odd men present. By the time this was over the missing team had turned up and the match started.

The *Renown* players were not in the best possible training after their fortnight at Melbourne, and their only advantage was their superior weight in the scrum, of which they took full advantage, and kept the ball down in the College 25 for some time at the beginning of the game; but the youth and agility of the Cadets, and the experience of some of the Officers who were playing for them, eventually told, the final result being a victory of 19 points to 9 for the College.

A quick visit was paid to the hospital, where there were a few Cadets with 'flu and one with measles, who peered pathetically at H.R.H. from the window of a detached isolation hut. The party then walked down to the jetty through the workshops and returned to the ship by 5.50.

A large dinner party assembled at 7.45, at the end of which the

---

[1] The Royal Australian Naval College.

four or five ladies present danced for a short time, but the gentlemen of the party drifted off one by one to the Ward Room to find old shipmates, and the celebrations necessitated by the renewal of so many old-time friendships resulted in what is said to be the most hectic night the Ward Room has ever seen. It started very quietly with a duet at the piano, which, followed by a poi dance, quickly developed into scenes that baffle description. Through the haze of tobacco smoke visions remain of 'Boss', the bulldog, peering with a puzzled expression at two Admirals whirling round the room locked in each other's arms; the Second Naval Member clearing the floor with his full weight of 16 stone, and later lifting the *Morning Post* correspondent and chair bodily on to the table; and, lastly, an enormous pool of arterial blood spreading over the deck from the nose of a member of the Ward Room, who was carried away and never re-appeared. The guests from the College and the *Brisbane*, battered, bruised and dishevelled, but thoroughly happy, left the ship soon after eleven.

WEDNESDAY, 16 JUNE   About 8.00 a.m. *Anzac* and five destroyers fell in with *Renown* and escorted her in to Sydney. Once inside a number of small craft escorted the ship for a few yards, but as the ship was going rather fast the majority could not keep up with her. There were, anyhow, not so many as at Auckland actually following the ship. A royal salute was fired by all ships in harbour. The ship anchored in Neutral Bay just under the lee of Admiralty House. The official calls were got over very quickly and quietly, and at 10.45 H.R.H. made his official landing.

Sir Godfrey and Colonel Grigg had a great moan with the Prime Minister who had insisted upon taking a hat box in the carriage with him so that there was no room for anybody's legs in the middle. The purpose of this hat box was revealed as soon as the procession was started, for 'Billy' opened it and took out a squash hat which he donned in place of the silken head-gear, presumably not to lose the labour votes in the city.[1] Just before entering Government House he changed back again, presumably not to lose the 'best people's' votes at Government House. The Lord Mayor, who drove in the last carriage and who, apparently, had been at a dinner to Cardinal Mannix before his departure, at which seditious speeches are alleged to have been made and the King's toast was omitted, was soundly 'boo-ed' from one end

---

[1] 'You can't be too careful,' Mr Hughes explained. 'That top hat might cost thousands of votes.'

of the route to the other almost as enthusiastically as H.R.H. was cheered.[1]

The old Crossleys from Melbourne were there and conveyed the party to the Commonwealth Bank for the Governor-General's dinner. The first traffic block on record this trip occurred just after leaving the landing stage, as a sight-seeing char-à-banc got stuck right across the route. The police in Sydney are at present rather useless, as they are capable neither of holding a crowd back nor of stopping people from running alongside the cars. One man who held on to the second car and refused to let go had to be turned off by the orderlies. No sooner had he been pushed off than he ran up with the intention of striking one of the orderlies on the back of the head. As luck would have it, the orderly saw him, and turning round in time, pushed him in the face, so that he went head over heels backwards. In the big streets they had kept the barriers up, so that progress was easy and everyone was able to see H.R.H. as he stood up in the leading car.

The dinner took place on the third floor of the bank, and two or three hundred guests must have been present. Mr Hughes rushed through his speech after dinner. It could not be heard at the ends of the room and was very indistinctly delivered. However, as Colonel Grigg pointed out, it will sound very good in the papers. H.R.H. got up and spoke very clearly and distinctly, though his speech did not appear to be so good as the one he made at Melbourne.

THURSDAY, 17 JUNE   H.R.H. appeared for the first time in military uniform on board and left shortly before ten in the barge, landing at Man-o'-War Steps and walking up to Government House.

A levée on similar lines to that of Melbourne was held here, but it was considerably enlivened by the presence of the Governor, Sir Walter Davidson. There were three gentlemen to be knighted, and one lady to receive the D.B.E., and as H.R.H. gave the accolade, or pinned on the decoration, His Ex. would drone forth, in a heavy, sentimental voice, particulars of the gallant deed that had won the recipient his decoration. Sir Charles Wade, one of those who were knighted, had apparently founded the Commonwealth Bank, which caused the Governor to go into perfect ecstasies over a description of the bank.

[1] The Most Reverend Daniel Mannix was Roman Catholic Archbishop of Melbourne – not a Cardinal. He was an Irishman, born in Cork, and had spent most of his life at Patrick's College, Maynooth. His anti-British sentiments were notorious and he continued to air them until his death at the age of ninety-nine.

The presentation of the lady, Mrs Chisholme, went off so quickly that His Ex. was unable to say all he wanted to, and was still droning about a canteen she had made at Al Kantara, after she had left the room. After the people with the right of private entrée had been through, about 700 others came past and then a short 'stand easy' was held before the presentation of addresses started. Sydney must contain very modest and unassuming societies, for only seventy-two of them presented addresses to H.R.H. and, wonderful to relate, nobody giving addresses had more than twenty-five accompanying him, with each of whom H.R.H. had to shake hands although most of them had already been round once at the levée. H.R.H. must have shaken hands with more address-givers than people at the levée, and it was very strenuous work listening to the small prepared speeches which the spokesman of each party had to get off his chest although they had been requested to hand in their addresses in silence.

Two ordinary-sized rooms had been cleared for dancing, which, at the most, would hold about 250 couples. Twelve hundred guests had been invited, so there was not room to stand, much less dance. A few people attempted to dance, but could not keep it up long. Most people retired to bed fairly soon. Among others present was Lieutenant Flora Sandes, of the Serbian Army. She is the sister of the *Daily Telegraph* correspondent on board,[1] and appeared in uniform, booted and spurred, her breast covered with decorations. H.R.H. chatted with her for some while, but couldn't bring himself to dance with her.

FRIDAY, 18 JUNE   Shortly after ten H.R.H. drove to the Town Hall. A popular reception on the same lines as that of Melbourne now started, but not more than an average of 120 could be raised as the doors were very narrow and the people had to climb up steps to get to the hall. A queue of many thousands was waiting in the streets between barriers, and, after about an hour, a halt was called and H.R.H., having partaken of some light refreshment, shifted up to the top of the stairs, where the people now passed by him. As, however, they had to go up and down the steps, only another thirty a minute were done, and as a report came back at twelve o'clock that another 11,000 were still waiting and people could walk through on the same level the whole way, and the average sprang up to 250 a minute, so that by ten minutes past one practically everybody had been done,

---

[1] Mr John Sandes was the *Daily Telegraph* correspondent.

certainly all those who had been originally in the queue and promised a view of H.R.H.

At about 7.20 p.m. H.R.H. and the entire Staff drove once more to the Town Hall for the State Government's dinner, at which over 700 were present, not including large numbers of ladies in the gallery who watched the men eating with great interest.

At the end of dinner the Hon. John Storey, the Premier,[1] made a fairly good speech, which had the merit of being short. H.R.H., who had only thought of preparing a speech at lunch-time that day, rose to great heights and, for a short speech, made one of his best.

SATURDAY, 19 JUNE Dinner was at Government House, and some four or five girls came to it.

After dinner, the guests for the dance began to arrive, and everyone went up on the verandah to watch the fleet illuminations, searchlight display and fireworks. The band were discouraged from bringing a drum, as it was 'noisy and rather beneath the dignity of Government House'. H.R.H. played the castanets given him by the Melbourne Jazz Band, and tried to induce the bandmaster to send for his drums. About an hour later H.R.H. went up to the band again, and found a boy in brass buttons, who claimed to be the bandmaster's son, and, incidentally, the drummer, but he had not brought the drums. He was, therefore, despatched again, and returned about the last dance with the drums. The leader of the band, who had looked upon the wine when it was crimson, now sought out H.R.H. and tried to induce him to play a tune on the drums which he had had specially brought, in fact he chased H.R.H., the Governor and the Admiral for the next half hour trying to induce them to play the drums. He quite upset the Secretary's evening whisky and soda, which was of unusual dimensions, even for him. Eventually, however, the Governor dealt with him, and everyone retired to bed.

SUNDAY, 20 JUNE In the evening some half dozen girls were invited. After dinner – wonder of wonders – His Ex. suggested to the Dame that the gramophone should be moved into the ballroom to enable those who wanted to dance. As it was Sunday night Dame Margaret was duly horrified, and playfully slapped her erring spouse on the hand while she exclaimed: 'You naughty man! You naughty man!' However,

[1] of New South Wales.

she very tactfully retired and the gramophone was pushed in and a very good little impromptu dance came off. At 10.10 H.R.H. and the Staff took their departure.

They arrived at the station about half past ten to find enormous crowds awaiting them, who cheered lustily. This train beats all the others, including those used on the Canadian tour, for its sumptuousness and magnificence. H.R.H., the Admiral and Colonel Grigg each have one enormous state room with a large four poster bed and private bathroom attached.[1] Both the sitting room and dining room are much the cosiest and most tastefully decorated that have yet been used by H.R.H.

MONDAY, 21 JUNE The party drove to the Federal Capital site, Canberra. Some apprehension was felt that the Federal Capital might be missed altogether and H.R.H. never arrive as a result. This fear was groundless, for the champagne corks could be heard popping from miles off in the Government tent. On a hill, which a notice board kindly explained was Capitol Hill, was gathered a vast concourse of motor cars in which were all the old friends from Melbourne and Sydney. Immediately on H.R.H.'s arrival he was taken to a large marquee in which some three or four hundred officials and their wives were waiting. These officials had been brought up in special trains from Melbourne and Sydney. Luncheon – which was very well done – was also brought up an immense distance. This meal and getting the people for the meal must have cost the Government something in treble figures. H.R.H. was down, on the official programme which was supplied to the guests, to make a response to the toast of his health, which he got out of very cleverly by simply getting up and saying: 'Thank you.'

After lunch a move was made to the centre of the site of the Capitol. H.R.H. shook hands with returned soldiers, before walking up to the stone he was to lay. This stone had an inscription on it, in the middle of which 'Prince of Wales' appeared, and in the centre of the 'O' was a small gold dot, which was to be the centre of the entire city, all

---

[1] Mountbatten told his mother: 'When they heard out here that I was coming out with David, they constructed all the specially built railway coaches with two adjoining compartments of the same size, the other one being intended for me. This has given the Admiral some very comfortable billets, as he has taken those intended for me. I don't believe he even realizes this, but the general in charge of our transport told me it privately as a good joke.'

avenues and roads radiating from it.[1] At present, of course, there is no sign of the city, although £1,000,000 has been spent on it already. There is in existence, however, a very good water supply and drainage system for the houses when they are eventually built. There are, also, a great number of foundation stones, as H.R.H. remarked in his speech; but beyond that there are only two or three tin shanties and a power station to show where this magnificent capital is going to stand.

The space which had been reserved for the officials had been completely swamped by the crowd of Canberrans, who had been waiting many hours to see this function. The stone, which turned out not to be a foundation stone at all, but a paving stone, was lowered very smoothly and quickly by the master mason; all that was required of H.R.H. being that he should hit the stone twice with a wooden mallet and declare it 'well and truly laid'. He had some hesitation in doing this as the spirit level seemed to indicate that the stone was not quite true, but it was explained to him that this was the identical level that had been used by his father 19 years ago, and apparently was no longer quite true.

With much trouble the children got through from the back to pass in front of H.R.H. Nowhere in Australia in the small places do they seem to take their children into account very much, or give any facilities for them to see H.R.H., and, unless an effort was made by the Staff, no children would see him at all. After this a bull-fight would have occurred, but for the two lines of returned soldiers, who put their hands on each others shoulders and formed a body-guard round H.R.H. and the Staff, and walked with them as far as the cars. The soldiers very nearly lifted H.R.H. on to their shoulders at this point, but, luckily, there were some sensible ones among them who strongly discouraged this idea.

From here the party embarked in the train without further ceremony and arrived back in Sydney at a quarter past ten.

TUESDAY, 22 JUNE Shortly after 1.00 p.m. H.R.H., accompanied by most of the Staff, drove to the Town Hall. There were almost unprecedented crowds out owing to the fact that this was the end of the dinner hour, and H.R.H. received a great ovation from them.

A luncheon at the Town Hall was given by the New South Wales

---

[1] On subsequent visits to Canberra Mountbatten used always to visit this stone, causing a fearful furore in 1976 when he found that it had been removed.

Branch of the R.S.S.I.L.A.,[1] of which H.R.H. is now Patron-in-Chief. The tables were placed in the ante-room as there were not more than two or three hundred present. The food was rather indifferent, even for an official luncheon, but the hosts made up for this in their efforts to please. The menus, unfortunately, had special places reserved, headed 'Autographs', with the result that H.R.H. – who at first refused, but later consented for the blind soldiers – and all the Staff, had to sign their names many, many times for the various returned men. At the end of luncheon, H.R.H. shook hands with everyone, and a departure was made by motor for the Centennial Park, where the first big parade in Australia was held. The only men on parade were returned men and veterans. There was no sign of discipline while H.R.H. was inspecting them, the men lounging about, talking as they felt inclined. Finally, at the end of the inspection the men marched past. Just before this was due to start the crowd broke through all along the line. A body of several hundred ex-soldier policemen were marched up, and at a given signal they scattered and pushed the crowd back. At first the troops marched past in fours, but, as the detachment from the 1st Division was not quite completed after half-an-hour's marching, something had to be done, and the men were therefore made to march past in eights. Now, it must here be mentioned, that the march past was magnificent, the men marching really splendidly, which was very unexpected after their original slovenliness. About 10,000 men marched past.

WEDNESDAY, 23 JUNE A children's display, somewhat on the same lines as previous big ones, was witnessed. The first item was a flag display by 8000 children, the flags producing the same dazzling effect as the white sleeves had done on the last occasion.

This was followed by a gigantic tableau consisting of the three feathers in the centre surrounded by symbolic groups of the various colonies, with the words 'Many Happy Returns' on either side and below the crest; it being H.R.H.'s 26th birthday. At a given signal all the children closed round and sang the usual songs. Before leaving H.R.H. went down to the ground, and as there were no facilities for him to walk among the children he climbed on to the conductor's stand so that they could all see him. He then took his departure for Sydney University.

[1] Returned Sailors and Soldiers' Imperial League of Australia.

Much the same occurred here as in Melbourne, H.R.H. receiving the LL.D. Degree, with a gown of such dazzling colours as to cause him to ask the Chancellor whether this had not been specially invented for him. Several addresses were exchanged during the show as the authorities and undergraduates could not agree to one address.

THURSDAY, 24 JUNE   The entire Labour Government of the State went in the royal train on this occasion. After half an hour's train journey Parramatta was reached. This was the first spot settled in all Australia, and not far from the platform the original Government House could be seen. The official stunt was done in the open from the end of the platform. Very large crowds had collected all round, and after H.R.H. had shaken hands with the returned soldiers and chatted with the oldest serving man in the force, who was a native of the place, the crowd were allowed to come on the platform, which considerably upset the Mayor and local dignitaries, but enabled them to catch at least one good view of H.R.H. as the train left.

A stop was made at the 'town' of Wilberforce, which was considerably smaller than an average English village. This was quite the shortest official stunt ever done by H.R.H., for he never even got out of the car, but shook hands with the five returned soldiers from the back seat of the car. The Mayor made a really short hot air speech, and without giving anybody time to sing more than the 'God Save' the party drove on to Sackville Reach.

A river launch called the *Premier* was secured to the landing-stage, which everyone now boarded. She then shoved off and proceeded down stream at about ten knots. This was another one of the typical parliamentary jaunts at the country's expense. A sumptuous luncheon, consisting chiefly of oysters and champagne, was laid in the after part of the launch, and after she had been under way about an hour everyone sat down. The Minister for Works tucked his napkin into his neck, which turned out to be rather lucky for his coat. The Treasurer, who sat opposite, objected to the N.O.s among the party as they had never been on the 'lower deck'.[1] He also made himself popular with H.R.H. by telling him that the returned soldier's badge that he wore was worthless; by trying to stop him waving his hat to the Home for Inebriates, the occupants of which were waving wildly at the launch as she passed; and finally by refusing to listen to his arguments when

[1] The Secretary for Public Works was Mr John Estell, the Colonial Treasurer Mr John T. Lang.

he tried to explain that he could not subscribe to a particular pet drought loan of this Minister's. Mr Storey, the Premier, was the one man of the party who almost made this day on the Hawkesbury River bearable; but even he could not resist the temptation of breaking his promise to H.R.H. and making a speech at the picnic lunch, but it must be admitted that it was a most charming little speech. The speech was followed by what one of the Ministers described as the 'light 'orse 'ooray'. This consisted in all present having to tap the table ten times with their forefingers, then ten times with the flat of their hands, finally banging the table ten times with their fists while they stamped on the deck with their feet. By the time this had been done once all the glasses on the table had gone over and most of them were smashed, as the tables were of flimsy construction and shook violently, but this did not deter some of the gallant ministers from 'drawing their swords', as they put it, which consisted in drawing a table knife from an imaginary scabbard which these military enthusiasts seemed to imagine was worn on the right side. Not content with having smashed up all the glasses, they then had a second 'light 'orse 'ooray', and finally succeeded in smashing up most of the plates.

By this time, the Minister for Education[1] was so worked up that he insisted upon singing a song, in which his colleagues joined. A sickly smile which spread over H.R.H.'s features was mistaken by the glee party as a smile of approval, so that they burst forth into another half a dozen songs, yelling at the unfortunate Staff to join in. This, however, was a merciful change from the cross-examination which H.R.H.'s party had to undergo at the hands of their hosts if they sat down for a minute. A very expensive gramophone which had been provided, presumably at the public expense, was now turned on, and the Commonwealth cinematographer took pictures of this 'day of rest'!

It must here be mentioned that the Hawkesbury River is one of the most charming in all Australia. The day was perfect and the scenery was really beautiful and thoroughly enjoyable, and, had it been possible for H.R.H.'s party to go by themselves, there is no doubt the day would have been a pleasant one. Actually, this was the most difficult day of the whole trip, up to date, though individually, no doubt, each of the Ministers is a most charming fellow.

Shortly after sunset the *Premier* steamed under the seven span

---

[1] Presumably Mountbatten meant the Minister of Public Instruction, Mr Thomas Mutch.

railway bridge and turning up to starboard arrived at the landing stage at Brooklyn.

The English mail, which had arrived at noon, was brought up by train, and everyone spent this trip reading their letters. H.R.H. was the only one who apparently did not find his mail very cheering.[1]

A couple of hours' run brought the party to Toronto, which was reached shortly after seven. The party walked straight down to the pier jutting out into Lake Macquarie where a motor launch was waiting. The foreshore was lined with Chinese lanterns, which looked very pretty indeed. The lake, which had a coastline of about 350 miles, is connected with the sea, but the trip which H.R.H. took only lasted ten minutes going at slow speed. At the final landing stage everyone disembarked and walked up to the two houses which were being lent for the use of the party for the night.

FRIDAY, 25 JUNE The launch *Helen* was lying alongside flying the Standard of the Duchess of Argyll which was subsequently changed by the Signalman attached to the retinue for the Prince of Wales's Standard, after all had embarked.

About a quarter past ten Walsh Island was reached, where the party disembarked, H.R.H. shaking hands with some of the returned soldiers among the dockyard hands at the pier before walking through the yard to the slips, where H.R.H. was to launch a ship. It was remarkable and satisfactory to note the genuine enthusiasm of the dockyard labourers, and their pleased expression at seeing H.R.H. among them. A small platform had been built round the bows of the ship, with a table on which was a wooden map of Australia. Through the centre of this ran a boomerang placed vertically, the end of which was cased in steel, with one edge sharpened like a knife. When the moment came for the launch all H.R.H. had to do was to pull down the boomerang, which cut the string holding the bottle of wine back so that the bottle was automatically broken over the bows, while H.R.H. christened the ship *Enoggera*, though owing to the noise the crowd was making no one heard what he said. The next movement of the boomerang cut through a small hemp rope, which actually did the final releasing of the ship and did not merely give the signal, as in most other launches, to the men, to let her go. The *Enoggera* moved gracefully down into the water, and then the Minister of Works made

[1] 'It is very difficult to keep David cheerful,' Mountbatten told his mother, 'at times he gets so depressed and says he'd give anything to change places with me.'

a little speech introducing H.R.H. to the workers, ending up by saying: 'We have now launched four ships.' He was immediately howled down by cries of 'Five', for he had forgotten the one launched that very minute.

The launch reached the Steel Works of the Broken Hill Proprietary Company slightly before half past eleven. These works are run on very novel lines by the Manager, whose salary is rumoured to be £15,000 a year. Every man is paid for piece work, and can earn more here than anywhere else. They are in no way connected with outside unions and up to the present have never had a sympathy strike, though the Manager's propaganda agents feel that they will be dragged into the strike which is due to come off throughout the Commonwealth in October.

A move was then made towards the light train, which was to convey the party through the works. Everyone mounted on what at first sight appeared to be a gaily decorated station platform, but suddenly a 'toot' was given and the entire platform moved off, revealing itself to be the actual train, so highly decorated and camouflaged as to be almost unrecognizable. A shield in the centre of the car bore the inscription E A C G A P D, which was at first imagined to be a Welsh word but on enquiry proved to be H.R.H.'s initials. The first stop was made opposite the open hearth furnaces, where the party witnessed the casting of some white-hot molten metal, which dazzled and fascinated everyone. The party disembarked from the train and walked over to an adjacent shed, where they watched a short thick bar of red-hot steel being lifted out by a crane and placed on a bed of rollers which started rolling, thus moving the enormous block to a set of specially shaped rollers. Just before it reached this set the travelling rollers stopped and two rams came out and placed the bar in the exact correct position. The rollers were then started once more and the block was pressed between the upper and lower shaped rollers, flattening out and lengthening it considerably. The rollers were now reversed and, having been brought closer together, pressed the bar still further. The rams came out again and turned the bar the other way up so that when it went through the rollers it was again elongated and made more nearly square in cross section. This performance was repeated several times. The long bar, which was still red-hot, now travelled to a new set of shaped rollers. After still further elongation here it was put through the final stages of this set, which rolled the bar out into the shape of a rail. It was then moved further down to a circular saw which cut this long rail into three normal lengthed rails, which had a slight bend in them. They were next travelled down to the end of the shop on rollers and pushed across on to a metal bed to cool. As they cooled they straightened themselves, but the final straightening was put in when they were cold. Finally magnetic cranes lifted a dozen at a time and piled them in special heaps. The entire process was most fascinating to watch.

After this the Mayor entertained H.R.H. at luncheon. He made a short hot-air speech in proposing H.R.H.'s health, for which the latter thanked him briefly. This luncheon was very much a 'C 3' one, in fact, as Captain North told the Mayor on the way back, 'H.R.H. had never had such a luncheon before.' The Mayor took this to be a compliment, thanking him and saying very proudly, 'We do not do things by halves in Newcastle.'

Sydney was reached at 6.20 p.m. At Government House H.R.H. busied himself giving away presents and photographs to all those who had been assisting him during his stay in New South Wales. At 7.15 p.m. the party moved down to Man-o'-War Steps, where the Governor-General and officials said good-bye. Although it was now dark, large crowds lined the shore and cheered and cheered as the motor launch containing H.R.H. shoved off.

SATURDAY, 26 JUNE The Wallaby, 'Digger', appears to enjoy being at sea. He is full of life and rushes round the after cabin in great leaps and bounds, usually ending up by jumping on a chair.

SUNDAY, 27 JUNE The rough sea produced by the westerly gale proved too much for H.R.H. at lunchtime. He moved into the Flag Lieutenant's cabin, as that was nearer amidships than his own and the motion was less noticeable there. Another reason may be that this cabin is done up in a quiet shade of blue, while the colour scheme of H.R.H.'s is worked out in a pretty, but on a 'sea-sick day' startlingly bright yellow colour. The motion became gradually worse, so the H.R.H. finally decided, not only to have his meals in this cabin, but also to sleep there, so that the usual occupant slept in H.R.H.'s cabin. There are no casualties to report among the rest of the Staff, but then the ship, considering the state of the sea, was behaving magnificently.

MONDAY, 28 JUNE The gale, which had eased up slightly during the night, gradually gathered renewed vigour. The seas became so terrific as to make it imperative to ease the speed of the ship to eleven knots to prevent the flare of the long forecastle from being completely pushed in. Even so, the ship took the seas in very badly forward. At times the sea would come in green as far as 'A' turret and break into a shower of spray upon the breakwater, shooting up right over 'B' turret, while cascades of water found their way through the hawse pipes and 'A' barbette to the lower deck. In the sick bay four men were kept baling day and night to keep the water under, and the bad cases had to be moved to a lower deck. Hands were kept baling the whole time forward of the main watertight bulkhead.

Most of the Staff, including H.R.H., who felt better in the fresh air, went on to the bridge to watch this exceedingly spectacular sight. Sir Godfrey saw one terrific sea lift the forecastle wash-deck locker off its seatings and deposit it the other side of the breakwater. Although the sea was very confused, some of the seas were estimated to be at least 30 feet in height, and are quite the worst yet encountered on either trip.

WEDNESDAY, 30 JUNE The ship anchored just outside the inner harbour of Albany at 2.00 p.m. From the ship Albany resembled nothing so much as Scapa.

At 3.40 p.m. H.R.H. embarked in the barge. The barge conveyed him to H.M.A.S. *Swordsman*, who at once proceeded, at about twenty knots, into the inner harbour and alongside the town jetty. Although a special request had been sent to the Governor and officials receiving H.R.H. to be in travelling clothes, they were all in pot hats. But then, perhaps they always travel in these clothes.

It was intended that H.R.H. should motor round the Marine Drive, but a note in the programme said 'W.P', and the 'W' did not 'P', for it came on to rain as the Marine Drive was about to be started, so the cars turned in to the railway station, where the royal train was already drawn up. The State Organizer had handed round neat little pocket books containing an abridged programme and some half a dozen tickets and passes. This is the first state where 'red tape' has been met with, though a little more of it might have kept some of the un-official hangers-on in check. Everyone required a pass to get on to the railway station and a ticket to board the train, and when once inside the ticket had to be again produced by all unless they wanted to be turned out. The Transport Officer stated that this train was the most homogenous train yet used for H.R.H. This may be so, but it certainly was not so comfortable as previous trains, although this was largely accounted for by the fact that this State has the narrow gauge, as in New Zealand. H.R.H. had a specially constructed car right aft, which was perfect in every respect save that no doors were fitted anywhere, curtains only dividing the sleeping compartments and the corridors.

The Governor[1] is also travelling by this train, and has his coach hooked on next to H.R.H.'s. The 'Golden West' is usually so hot that the train throughout was fitted with fans. On this occasion it was actually freezing, but no form of heating apparatus existed anywhere, and the hot water for washing was brought to most people in tea cups.

As Captain North was about to turn in, a train attendant who said he hailed from Pontypool looked in and asked if he would like a 'night-cap', and receiving a reply in the negative, said, 'Why not? The Government's paying for it, and when the Government says "'Ave a good time," I says "'Ave a blinking good time."'

THURSDAY, 1 JULY   At 5.30 a.m. the attendant of Number 2 sleeping car, overcome, as he afterwards explained, by the presence of royalty, went round to some of the occupants and woke them to ask them if they were warm enough.

At 10.00 a.m., the train drew in at Perth railway station. The Governor descended first in order to be on the platform to greet H.R.H. This gave the Staff an opportunity to assemble in the rear car, for the Naval Members found it very difficult to walk down the narrow corridors in epaulettes and cocked hats while the train was in motion.

The usual crowd of bigwigs greeted H.R.H., and the party then trooped out to a large and apparently solid platform which had been erected in the station square. H.R.H.'s appearance was the signal for tumultuous cheering from a large crowd which had collected. He first inspected the guards of honour, and immediately after this exchanged addresses with the Mayor. In the meanwhile, the crowds pushed the police bodily forward and forced their way up a long line of cars. The Staff, who were to occupy these cars, viewed this encroachment with great apprehension, as a bull-fight in one's best rig is rather an expensive game. However, the officer in charge of the guard saved the situation by giving the order, 'One pace step back, march!' In obedience to this order, the two ranks of the guard moved backwards, taking the crowds with them!

[1] Sir Francis Newdigate-Newdegate, who had previously been Governor of Tasmania.

Meanwhile those on the platform were not without their troubles, for when the Premier[1] stepped on to it there was a loud creak and one of the boards gave way. Luckily, everybody managed to move on to another set of boards, and the carpet laid over them prevented anybody from falling through.

The procession arrived shortly before 11.00 a.m. at Government House, where Lady Newdigate-Newdegate, Miss Newdigate-Newdegate and the Newdigate-Newdegate parrot, which has an unfortunate habit of biting people, met them. H.R.H. and the five senior members of the Staff, who are staying at Government House, were shown to their rooms.

Immediately after luncheon swords and epaulettes were put on for the levée, which took place in the ball-room. The levée was conducted on the same lines as previous ones, the most noticeable feature being the ball-room itself; it was certainly the most attractive one yet come across in Australia. Only some twenty addresses were presented, of which at least 20 per cent were presented by the Acting Primate of Australia, who seemed to spend his time going round the room in a large circle joining up with various address-giving bodies. H.R.H. in his time has had addresses given him by some very queer-named bodies; the prize, however, must certainly go to Western Australia for their address-givers' 'The Ugly Men's Instructional School Committee', who incidentally perpetrated the joke of the trip on H.R.H. by making him a Life Member.

The general levée which followed was, for the first time, really general, resulting in a weird mixture of people, including bare-footed school children, pattering past the dais.

FRIDAY, 2 JULY   At 9.50 a.m. H.R.H. proceeded to the Barrack Street Jetty where a queer old tub, the *Zephyr*, was lying alongside. This launch was boarded and as soon as everyone was on board she shoved off. The steering arrangements were by means of a steam valve connected direct with the engine and placed horizontally. Perhaps this preyed on the helmsman's mind, for when the Admiral gave orders for the halyards of the Standard to be secured to the cleat on the mast itself, he objected on the grounds that it would interfere with his view for steering. He could not explain, however, how he was going to see with the mast itself there.

---

[1] James Mitchell, Premier of Western Australia.

The Swan River, down which the *Zephyr* was proceeding, provided very different scenery from the Hawkesbury River, though this is probably to some extent accountable for owing to the fact that this was very near the mouth of the river, whereas in the former case the party never got within twenty-five miles of the mouth.

An hour's run brought Fremantle into sight, and suddenly a creaking was heard and all fittings on deck, including the mast, funnel (which was of the telescopic type) and stanchions with awnings spread, etc., were lowered down to within three feet of the deck. This was necessary in order to pass under the two bridges, which are very low.

Shortly after this the launch berthed alongside Cliff Street Wharf. As Captain Legh stepped ashore an excited old man rushed up to him and said in a very respectful voice: 'Excuse me, sir,' and pointing to the officer in charge of the guard whose only decoration was the Military Cross, 'Can you tell me: is that General with the V.C. Sir William Birdwood?' To which Captain Legh replied without a smile: 'I think you are making a mistake: it is Marshal Foch!'

The weather held fine until H.R.H. reached the Town Hall, and he had literally not been ten minutes inside the building when a regular downpour started. Within a civic luncheon had been arranged on teetotal lines, the only drinks that were offered being tea or ginger ale. Nevertheless, those of the Staff who were insistent enough were given whisky. The waitresses were all volunteers, and in most cases the daughters of the ladies and gentlemen sitting at luncheon. Immediately after the King's health had been drunk, H.R.H., not unnaturally, lit up a cigarette, which quite scandalized some of the dear old ladies present, who had never heard of a 'gentleman' smoking at his luncheon, and were nearly prostrated with horror when informed that in England ladies not infrequently join the gentlemen with a cigarette. The Mayor made rather a poor speech at the conclusion, which was saved by being astoundingly brief. As H.R.H. rose from his seat the rain miraculously stopped, and by the time he had re-embarked and driven off the sun was shining once more.

The cars now took the Perth–Fremantle road, two or three hold-ups occurring on the way, in one case a rope being stretched across the road. Government House was reached about 4.30. The weather, having behaved itself perfectly up to then, broke about 4 o'clock and it set in to rain for the rest of the day. H.R.H. was billed to attend a trotting meeting at 9.00 p.m., but a message came through to say that as it was so wet H.R.H.'s coming had better be off. This message arrived in the form that as it was so wet the meeting was off; and nobody worried any further about it, until desperate calls came through on the telephone about dinner time saying that the meeting was not off and that an enormous crowd was expecting H.R.H. H.R.H. left Government House at 9.30 to drive to the trotting grounds. The fact of H.R.H. having to go worried some people rather, as these meetings are alleged to be somewhat crooked at times, but the spectacle of the one race H.R.H. witnessed was so unusual as to cause everyone to forget their qualms. It was raining hard and the hoods of the motors were put up on starting; but as H.R.H. wished to drive round the course for all to see him, the cars were stopped and the order 'Down hoods' was given. The first two cars got them down very much quicker than the other cars, with the result that when the third car arrived in the arena the leading cars were three quarters of the way round so that this car had a small race on its own round the course, skidding at the muddy corners in a most dangerous manner, and cheered on by the crowd.

H.R.H. descended at a specially erected covered-in pavilion, where he was presented with a heavy gold-mounted riding whip. He was asked if he would start the race for the Prince of Wales's Cup and, accordingly, proceeded to the middle of the ground. This was no easy matter, as the ground was soaking, and the party were attired in silk socks and evening pumps. The spectacle of the Admiral's Secretary with a pair of gold-laced trousers pulled up to his knees, walking on the heels of his half-wellington boots, as the soles were leaky, through the quagmire, is one not easily to be forgotten. Arrived in the centre, H.R.H. fired a pistol, which started the trotting race, a further downpour of rain, and a race on the part of the Staff to seek the shelter of the motor cars. From here they witnessed one of the most extraordinary races anybody had ever seen. The whole course was illuminated by enormous electric lights, and some sixteen horses were competing, of which three or four were ridden and the remainder driven. They simply skimmed round the course, the race consisting of three or four laps; and the weird artificial light thrown over the scene produced a spectacle which beggars description. After this one race, H.R.H. had to depart, but before finally leaving the course he had to place a wreath on the winner. This necessitated a further wade through the swamp, which finally finished off the dancing pumps of the party.

SATURDAY, 3 JULY At the march past, which was billed to take place that afternoon, it had originally been arranged for H.R.H. to ride, but

left: H.R.H. with his beloved pet wallaby, Digger.

below: Derailment in Western Australia. Mountbatten, in the furthermost coach, is clambering out of H.R.H.'s window (5 July 1920).

above: H.R.H. somewhat unconvincingly lends a hand sawing down a giant karri tree. He was feeling ill at the time, hence his rather lacklustre performance (5 July 1920).

below: Landing at Hobart, Tasmania (19 July 1920).

owing to the wet and slippery condition of the asphalt streets this project was abandoned, and H.R.H. motored down the lines. While H.R.H. was at the extreme end of one line, a tall and stately gentleman in a grey lounge suit walked up the lines, carefully inspecting the Naval Detachment, no one daring to stop him or even ask his name. This gentleman turned out to be Mr Everard Cotes, the Reuter correspondent, attached to the party.[1]

H.R.H. now arrived at the saluting base and the march past started; a naval detachment coming first, then a military detachment. In the middle of the military march past a staff car proceeded slowly down the line between the saluting base and the column on the march. No one dared to stop this car either, and it stopped of its own accord just beyond the saluting base, where Mr Everard Cotes got out!

In the evening a State Banquet took place in the Government House Ball-room. The top table was on the dais and was of normal height, but the caterers seemed to imagine that the other tables should be of the same height as the top table, which could only be arranged by having the table-legs about eight inches higher than usual, with the result that the food was on a level with the diners' mouth, which is not so convenient as it sounds.

SUNDAY, 4 JULY At 6.30 p.m. H.R.H. left Government House for the station. At a quarter to seven the train drew out, the crowd having been allowed on to the platform just before it left, as usual.

To make a comfortable night trip the royal car had been placed in the middle of the train, as on these narrow gauges the rear of the train swings about very considerably.

The official programme showed no stops until the following morning, but, of course, the usual thing happened – some of the ministers travelling on the train had constituencies along the line. At the first stop, Mundijong, the Honourable George, Minister for Works, in whose constituency this stop was made, climbed off the train at the front end of the ministerial car and tried to lose himself in the crowd, a difficult matter, owing to his great height and unmistakable face, though his clothes were very similar to those worn by most of the country people, and started speaking to H.R.H. from the crowd, saying, 'I am afraid it is rather damp here, but you see it has not

---

[1] Mr Cotes wrote *Down Under With the Prince*; the best thing which can be said about it is that it is slightly less dreadful than Sir Herbert Russell's book on the royal tour of India.

damped our spirits.' H.R.H. retorted very quickly, 'But then, it would not damp you in any case, as you are travelling on the train.'

MONDAY, 5 JULY The train drew in at Pemberton at 7.00 a.m., and the cars behind the royal car were uncoupled and drawn to the other side of the main street, as when a long train is standing in Pemberton Station it completely blocks up this street. It rained like fury most of the night, and was still pelting spasmodically up to ten o'clock, when H.R.H. disembarked officially. H.R.H. went into a wooden hut where a walking stick made of the local jarrah wood and three black 'possums were presented to him. A sort of popular reception stunt was done after this, but, as everyone had macintoshes on and it was raining when H.R.H. came out again, at least 90 per cent of the people passed by H.R.H. without realizing that he was there, and those who did were far too shy to take any notice of him, although as a body they had cheered very lustily indoors. The saw-mills were inspected after this, where enormous logs, mainly of karri and jarrah, were cut up by circular saws for transportation. It was interesting to note the bright red colour of the sawdust. Everyone now embarked in a light railway, the only properly covered-in coach of which was the leading one, in which H.R.H. got. The train went about seven miles into the bush, where everyone disembarked to witness 'snigging' by cattle and horses. The first log was 'snigged' by 28 head of oxen yoked together two at a time and four abreast. The logs were some 20 to 30 feet long and all quite 15 feet in circumference. A metal shoe about two feet long was placed under the leading end, and when the drivers cracked their stock whips all the oxen gave a great tug together and started the log off. At the word of command the leading oxen would wheel to the right or left, although the driver giving the command was right in the rear. Light railway lines are usually constructed in the valleys so that logs can be 'snigged' down hill, as up hill work can only be done with steam engines, which method is not used out here. Another log was now 'snigged' by two dozen horses harnessed three abreast. They did not appear to be so good at the job as the oxen, although they also were rather wonderful.

Moving a little further away from the railway line the party came upon a small gang of men busy felling karri trees. They had already made a large wedge-shaped cut with their axes on one side of the trunk in order to make the tree fall in that direction when the time came. Two men were busy on a great two-handed saw, sawing through the trunk at the height of about three or four feet from the ground, stopping every now and then to drive in wedges to prevent the weight of the tree jamming the saw-blade. Presently the party were warned to stand clear, and the wedges which had kept the tree from toppling over at the cut side were removed. The top of the tree began to move slightly forward, an ominous cracking sound making itself heard at the cut. Gradually the tree gathered momentum and crashed down, carrying small trees and branches from bigger ones with it, making a noise similar to a preliminary roll of thunder before the final thud, which came as the great tree hit the ground. The tree measured 135 feet to the first branch and was some 12 feet in circumference.

The party now witnessed two more of these karri trees being felled; H.R.H. being photographed holding one end of the saw at the third karri tree. He was not feeling very strong, however, and did not attempt to do any sawing.

The party next proceeded to an enclosure near the saw mills in which six blocks of wood 15 ins in diameter and three feet long were placed horizontally, prevented from rolling by battens. A wood-chopping contest was now witnessed, in which six competitors were handicapped, the champion of all Australia starting fifteen seconds behind the winner, and only taking one minute to chop the first log in two. The wood choppers had to stand on the log they were working at, and the winner suggested that H.R.H. should have a try with his axe. This he consented to do, but after having a couple of chops at a block the two halves opened out and he slipped off, and came down exceedingly heavily on a corner of one of the supporting battens, hurting the very place he had hurt in Christchurch at the races. The winner demonstrated the sharpness of his axe, even after having chopped the block in two, by shaving part of his arm with the blade. Finally a departure was made for the train.

Manjimup was reached round about half past two, and, although the train stopped, no one got out, H.R.H. waving to the few people about from the observation platform, whence he had an uninterrupted view owing to the royal car being at the end.

The car next ahead was the ministerial car, which was also a gorgeously fitted-up concern. Just in front of this ran No. 1 sleeping car, which accommodated the Staff and servants. Then came a dining car and four more coaches, the whole being drawn by two very heavy and powerful locomotives. A short distance ahead of this train ran the pilot train, and at frequent intervals along the line 'line-watchers' were stationed to report if anything went wrong.

Nevertheless, at 2.45 p.m. a 'jolt-jolt-jolt' was felt by the occupants of the last three cars. Lord Claud stepped towards the corridor to find out what was the matter. H.R.H., who was sitting on the fixed bunk in the last compartment, and the Admiral, who was writing letters there, also noticed the 'jolt-jolt', and remarked to one another that their coach must be off the line. This was actually the case, as the Flag Lieutenant discovered on running back from No. 1 car, where he had been when he first noticed the jolting, to the ministerial car. He at once looked round for the communication cord, but found none, as they are not fitted in the Australian trains as yet. He then ran forward to get the engine stopped just as the last two coaches overturned with a great crash, dragging No. 1 car off the rails and listing it over to the left. Luckily, owing to a cow (which, as H.R.H. later declared, deserved the M.V.O.) having been in the way just previously, the train had not yet gathered up normal speed.

Luckily the specially fitted strong couplings held, and the dead-weight of the rear cars brought the train to a stand-still in a very short time. The Flag Lieutenant jumped out of No. 1 car and raced aft to the royal car, which was lying on its side on a slightly sloping embankment with the wheels considerably higher than the roof. From the roof water was pouring from the tanks, and no sign of life could be observed until in answer to a hail a few choice but unrecordable words from H.R.H. set everyone's mind at rest. As the cars overturned H.R.H. had rolled himself up into a little ball as he described it, putting his feet against the end of the bunk; so that eventually he found himself with his weight on his feet. The Admiral, who had been sitting on the arm chair, was tipped over on to his shoulders, bruising himself. Through the left-hand windows, which were underneath, the occupants could see the ground passing below as the coaches were dragged along. H.R.H.'s own four-poster bed smashed over on to its side, and all the loose fittings came down with a crash.

In the rear saloon, Lord Claud was thrown the entire breadth of the coach, which shook him up rather severely. The P.M.O.'s right leg went through one of the bottom windows, giving him a nasty gash. Captain North ended up in a kind of cocktail, consisting of benedictine, cherry brandy and port, which had been on the table and shot over him as the table upset. A heavy sofa also joined in the mixture and pinned his legs down. In the meanwhile faint cries of 'Help!' came from the drain pipe of the rear compartment of the ministerial car, where the Honourable George had been caught at a most inconvenient moment! The Premier, Mr Mitchell, owing, perhaps, to his natural rotundity, did not suffer much hurt.

Meanwhile, people began to arrive on the scene from the front of the train. Luckily, although it was not raining at the time, only one fire broke out from the overturned cars; and this, which took place in the ministerial car, was promptly put out by one of the train attendants. Everyone now started shifting gear out of the three derailed coaches into the front coaches, one of the first things H.R.H. passed up being the precious cocktail shaker. The officials responsible for H.R.H.'s safety were still looking very white when H.R.H. himself appeared through one of the corridor windows and cheerfully remarked: 'Well, anyway, at last we have done something which was not on the official programme.' This was greeted with much laughter, and three very heart-felt cheers.[1]

He now proceeded to examine the line, which was torn up and twisted for a distance of 80 yards behind the rear coach as though it had been shelled. For another 230 yards behind this again, the marks on the sleepers indicated that the coaches had been off the rails for all this distance. The cause of the accident was easily traceable: the rails were only 48 lb to the yard ones instead of the usual 80 lb ones. The line in this unfrequented part of the country is unballasted, and the combined loosening effect of the continual rain and the unusually heavy weight of the pilot and royal trains, had finally bent out the left-hand rail at a curve in the line, and the left-hand wheels of the rear cars came off their rails at this point. As there were no marks on the right side of the sleepers, it is presumed that the right wheels must have remained on their rails; which would partly be accounted for by the fact of the train swinging out to the right as it went round the left-hand curve. There is no doubt that everyone had a miraculous escape. Had the train been travelling faster, or had the embankment been steeper, the accident would almost certainly have proved fatal. As things turned out, it was taken as 'the' joke of the trip, and everyone laughed heartily over their experiences, especially those of the Honourable George.

Picton Junction was reached in the neighbourhood of 10.00 p.m., and here the breakdown train arrived almost simultaneously, having

[1] 'This remark was really rather clever,' Mountbatten told his father, 'as we have made it a rule never to do anything which isn't on the programme.'

made a record trip from Midland Junction. H.R.H. went over and inspected the enormous crane and went for a short trip in the train as it was shunted out, eventually returning to one of the ordinary sleeping coaches in his own train, which he was sharing with the Admiral for the night.

TUESDAY, 6 JULY At Bunbury an enthusiastic cleric had arranged a Thanksgiving Service for H.R.H.'s safe deliverance, which he greatly hoped would be attended by the latter in person. In this, owing to the early hour of the morning, he was disappointed.

Perth was reached over an hour later at about 2.15 p.m. H.R.H. was met at the station by the Governor, and everyone drove back to Government House. As a result of the accident, H.R.H. received a most tremendous ovation from the crowds, which lined the route almost as thickly as on the first day. The Archbishop had arranged a Thanksgiving Service at St George's Cathedral to which he hoped H.R.H. would come in person, but in this he was disappointed owing to the lateness of the hour, 5.00 p.m. However, the Admiral went.

WEDNESDAY, 7 JULY H.R.H. was again photographed by himself, as the last one had made him look as though he was about to be sick.

Immediately after this everyone drove in motor cars along the main street of Perth to Parliament House, where the State Luncheon was being given by the Governor of Western Australia, this being the second State meal within five days. It went off very successfully, and although H.R.H. was feeling far from his best when speech-making time came round, the short speech he made was very well received.

Captain Barker, the Cinematograph Operator, returned about dinner time, having travelled cross-country for two days, as he had been left behind to take pictures of the tree-felling at Pemberton. He reported that the very train H.R.H. and party had used to get to the tree-felling met with an accident later in the day, about five hours after the other train accident, three trucks becoming derailed in this case, owing to a log having fallen across the line!

THURSDAY, 8 JULY Great crowds once more lined the route as H.R.H. departed, and cheered and shouted 'Come back again' at the station. The same officials as had met him saw him off, and were very nearly 'seen off' themselves by the crowd, which was let through unexpectedly early and fairly rushed the platform. The train left amidst a perfect uproar, and then the rain came down in torrents.

After the train had departed a large poker party was formed, everyone retiring to bed fairly early in spite of this.

FRIDAY, 9 JULY   Punctually at 10.00 a.m. the train drew in at Coolgardie, and H.R.H. and the Staff disembarked and walked across to the usual type of platform erected in the station square, where the returned-soldier stunt was gone through. At the outbreak of war, Coolgardie made a list of their eligible men, and three months later a list of the men who had enlisted; and these lists are said to have exactly tallied. Another pleasing feature about the reception was the substitution of a casket containing specimens of gold for the usual address.

After ten minutes the train departed for Kalgoorlie, which was reached after an hour's run. Mr Adams, one of the correspondents, in his telegrams to the West sent from two or three stations along the line, finished each one up with 'Royal train still on rails', which he said would go down well in the West, though he doubts if he will ever be able to show his face in the East again. H.R.H. held a small investiture in the hall. As he came out a man in the crowd refused to take his hat off, even when told to do so by a returned soldier standing near, he was promptly knocked down but as soon as he stood up again, quickly removed the offending head-gear, although by this time the procession had moved off for the Oval, via Hannan Street – which is the main street, possibly owing to the fact that it has twenty-six pubs in it. At the Oval some 4000 school children were grouped to form the word 'Welcome', after which they marched past H.R.H. It may here be mentioned that there is a certain 'red-rag' element in these mining centres which is most noticeable in a body called the A.W.U. (Australian Workers' Union). Prior to the visit this union passed a resolution forbidding their children to attend this show, which they called a display of capitalism. Hardly had they passed this resolution than they asked the Chamber of Mines for two days' holiday on full pay to celebrate the occasion. Needless to say, in the face of their previous resolutions this was not granted. The final burlesque, however, happened at the Oval, where not one child was missing at the roll call. In fact one notorious member was present himself, wearing a red tie. When asked why he had come, he replied, 'I've got two children in the procession, and the missus made me come to look after them.'

Everyone went by car to the city of Boulder, which is merely a smaller edition of Kalgoorlie and connected to it by tram as it is only about three miles distant.

One of the more important of the half dozen great gold mines was visited, the one chosen being the Great Boulder Mine. Here the party witnessed the whole production of the metal from the ore. The process is worthy of a short description. The ore is lifted by cages from the face – which is anything up to three thousand feet below the surface – and is travelled on broad belts to the ball mills, where it is automatically shaken into a trough which leads to the centre of these mills. The latter are revolving at a great speed with two tons of loose iron balls inside them which crush the ore into a fine powder. The next process is known as 'roasting', the powdered ore being stirred round over red-hot bricks till all the sulphur is burned out of it. From here it is travelled through the open air till it is well cooled. After this the amalgam process takes place, which consists in putting a large quantity of mercury into a trough with the ore. This collects about 30 per cent of the gold, amalgamating with it and sinking to the bottom of the shaker. This is a very simple method, but it does not get the full value out of the ore, so that while the gold amalgam is taken off to be smelted the rest of the ore is travelled on to the cyanide tanks. The smelting of the amalgam vaporizes the mercury, leaving the pure gold metal. At the cyanide tanks a solution of water and cyanide is stirred round by large paddles, and in this the powdered ore drops. Having been well mixed up it is then passed on to the filtering tanks. A great arm holding about a dozen filter bags is lowered into this tank. To the centre of each of these bags an air-pipe leads, and, when suction is put on, this pipe sucks the strained solution through the pipes and away. The arm holding these bags is then raised out of the tank and the suction dries the slimy ore which is clinging to it. As soon as this is dried the arm is turned right over and the bags are lowered into a rinsing tank where the waste slime is washed away by pure water, the final clearance being given by applying compressed air where the vacuum had been. The solution of cyanide had by chemical action extracted the rest of the gold from the ore, and this valuable solution is now pumped into the zinc tanks which contain cell after cell filled with fine zinc shavings. This zinc has the peculiar property of parting the gold from the cyanide and precipitating it to the bottom of the tank where the slime which had escaped the strainer mixes with it again. The gold-slime, which contains a very high percentage of gold, is then removed and put into smelting pots, the molten metal sinking to the bottom while the slime is skimmed off the top. It is then cast into bricks; one of which, worth £1500, H.R.H. handled.

The Great Boulder Mine is capable of handling some 550 tons of ore per day, though one ton rarely contains more than 16 penny-weights of gold, as compared with 60 ounces in Bendigo.

It was intended that H.R.H. should go to a Diggers' Concert after this, but the Mayor announced that the concert was off. The concert had been wisely postponed by the President of the Returned Soldiers' Association, a remarkably good fellow. It appears that the 'red-rag' element had turned out to prevent people from attending this perform-ance, as they said the prices were too high, so the prices were lowered, but still no one was allowed to go. Finally the seats were given away free, but still the 'Red-Raggers' remained outside preventing people from coming in. It was then that the President took the bold course of calling the concert off, for had there been any chance of H.R.H. turning up, there is little doubt but that the diggers, who had been 'celebrating' H.R.H.'s visit, would have gone out and engaged these 'Bolshies' in battle, an occurrence in which it would hardly have been suitable for H.R.H. to be involved.

SATURDAY, 10 JULY Between 2.00 and 3.00 a.m. the train entered the great Nullarbor Plain. This is a desert, entirely treeless, the only shrub that grows being the salt bush, which derives its moisture from the dew, as rain is very rare in these parts, and is practically never more than a foot or two in height. It was in these surroundings that the party found themselves when they woke up in the morning. There is a weird fascination about this great plain, which, to look at, reminds one of the sea, the horizon being distinct and unbroken all round. The sky was blue and almost cloudless. Looking ahead one could see the shimmering rails running straight on till they appeared to join and melt away in the distance, a second set of rails being occasionally visible in the air when a mirage occurred. From the observation car the same view was met behind. Beyond a few dingoes and an occasional wild turkey there was no sign of animal life. The line here runs perfectly straight and practically level for over 300 miles, which is the world's record for a straight run. The distance from Kalgoorlie to Port Augusta the eastern terminus, is practically the same as from London to Algiers (1050 miles).

A stop was made at about half past three, three miles on the western side of Cook. Nearly everyone disembarked and walked to a platform built of sleepers. H.R.H. talked to eleven returned men and then mounted the platform. Some fifty aboriginals, about an equal number of both sexes, were gathered here for the occasion and did a 'corroboree'. These natives belonged mainly to a tribe whose usual camping ground is on the edge of the Nullarbor Plain about 80 miles to the eastward, but some of them had come from Fowler's Bay, a distance of about 150 miles, and a few from the Musgrave Ranges, about 300 miles to the north. The last-named represented a tribe of aboriginals which had not, until a few weeks before, come in contact with white men. Most of these natives had trekked on foot, though some had been conveyed by train. They represented the very best specimens of aborigines in Australia. They were thin and lank, some of the men having long and matted beards, and nearly in every case long hair bound up with rabbit fur and hawks' feathers mixed with gum. But the part about them which H.R.H. admired the most was their legs, which, as he enviously exclaimed, were even thinner than his, so that they could have worn a better shaped riding boot, had they wanted to! These natives were living in about a dozen small huts called 'mia-mias', constructed of salt bush and sacking, and not more than three feet high. In front of each 'mia-mia' was a small fire. The fires had been started by the rubbing of fire sticks, a display of which H.R.H. later witnessed. The men were stripped naked save for a loin cloth, and their copper-coloured skins were grotesquely painted in red and white ochres, resembling nothing so much as camouflaged merchant ships, and it was noticeable that no two patterns were quite similar. At the commencement of the 'corroboree', which, it may be added, has been witnessed by remarkably few white men, and never known to have been performed in daylight before, the womenfolk, who are called 'gins' or 'lubras', and two or three very old men, squatted down in an open space in front of the platform. About eight fires had been lit in a large oval, the women folk squatting at the extreme and nearest end. In the meanwhile the men (or 'bucks') were all hidden behind a brush screen. The scene started by the women folk moaning a queer tune, the old men accompanying them by beating together boomerangs, while the women kept time also by slapping their thighs and beating their cupped hands together. The men made their appearance in single file shortly after the 'band' had started, stamping heavily with their bare feet upon the solid earth and producing a sound resembling a locomotive under way. They marched once round the oval and returned to their shelter, their steps having been barely eight inches apart. The rear of the procession was taken up by the medicine man, who, unlike the other bucks, carried no spear, but two 'waddies', which consisted of two sticks of heavy timber decorated with feathers, as also was the whole of his face, his entire body being painted in red and white stripes.

As the procession came opposite H.R.H. they gave him a shout of welcome and rattled their spears according to native custom. This formed the first figure of a series of religious performances. There followed five more figures, much on the same lines as this, the predominating feature in each case being the stamping of their bare feet, and the chief difference in the steps the fact that some were done without spears, one of their steps resembling the goose step. The party visited one of the 'mia-mias' which was set at a distance from the others and in which two youths were squatting. These had been kept apart from the general tribe, and especially the women folk, for two years, and had passed through six degrees of initiation into manhood, some of them grotesquely barbarous, the scars of which were later shown to H.R.H. by an old man. The seventh and final degree consisted in their re-union with the tribe, which occurred in the last religious figure.

After the religious dances were over a demonstration of spear-throwing was given, two or three good hits being registered on the targets, which consisted of stuffed sacks arranged as figures. The spears consisted of very thin long staves, sharpened at one end. When they are about to throw they place the butt end of the spear into a tooth-like notch at the end of what is termed a 'woomerah', an implement shaped somewhat like a scoop, being about two feet long and six inches across with a handle at one end by which it is held. To throw they hold the spear up with one hand and jerk the 'woomerah' forward, which gives the necessary impulse to the spear.

After this an exhibition of boomerang-throwing was given, at which sometimes as many as six were in the air at once, putting the wind up the spectators, who never knew whether they were going to be hit or not. H.R.H. had a try at throwing one himself, but was not very successful.

The natives presented him with a great quantity of presents, including some evil-smelling armlets filled with fat.

The Flag Lieutenant was given two weird-looking lizards, a mountain devil, which is reputed to change colour like a chameleon, and a barking lizard, which is supposed to bark like a dog when annoyed, though the veracity of this statement is doubted by Sir Godfrey Thomas, who has offered to pay 5/– every time it barks. They have been named Hector and Cuthbert respectively.

MONDAY, 12 JULY About a quarter past seven Lord Claud was dragged out of bed to deputise for H.R.H. at the inspection of a prize stud ram, which had just been sold to South Africa for four thousand guineas, and which had been brought several miles for H.R.H. to see.

At Smithfield, which was reached at 10.30 a.m., the Governor of South Australia[1] boarded the train. The train then departed for Adelaide, which was reached at 11.00 a.m.

The three old open Crossleys and the closed Crossley were here once more, and H.R.H. with the Governor and the Admiral embarked in the leading car. Adelaide is several times as big as Perth, and the drive was, therefore, considerably longer, though again, the town is only a third of the size of Melbourne or Sydney, so that it was not so long as at either of the two latter places, but a sort of happy medium. There were barriers almost the entire length of the route, the only pity being that the barriers were placed near the pavements on either side instead of having one of them in the middle of the street so that the people could get a closer view.

At Government House a dinner party was given, after which an official reception took place, which went off very well, Captain North and Captain Legh arousing much favourable comment by standing stiffly to 'attention' for three quarters of an hour opposite H.R.H. The reception lasted till about 10.30 p.m., after which about two dozen people remained behind and a little dance was given, which was great fun and at which everyone went mad, especially H.R.H. and the Governor. The former played with the six-year-old daughter of the house's toys, using them as a jazz set, while the latter conducted the band with a pencil. The dance lasted till 2.00 a.m.

TUESDAY, 13 JULY Shortly after 10.00 a.m. H.R.H. drove to the Jubilee Oval, where a boy scouts' demonstration was held, H.R.H. addressing a few words to them after his inspection. Finally they all

[1] Sir Archibald Weigall.

rushed forward, which, apparently is what they call a 'rally'. After the band had played the British National Anthem, the 'God Save', they played what is now being called the Australian National Anthem, 'Abe, my Boy', followed by 'Johnny's in Town'.

At 12.10 a.m. H.R.H. drove to Austral Gardens to meet the returned sailors and soldiers and nurses, etc. This was probably the best arranged stunt of its kind yet done, for all the men and nurses were seated in an open-air auditorium in front of a regular theatrical stage, on which H.R.H. and the Staff mounted. The President, an Officer with the V.C., made a short welcoming speech and received a very good reply. After this H.R.H. shook hands with the maimed soldiers in the front row. The sisters and nurses then filed past, and he shook hands with these also. A 'Digger' photographer put a large camera on a tripod within two feet of him and took numerous photographs: finally H.R.H. turned on him and said: 'That thing is as bad as a machine gun'; to which the digger smilingly replied: 'Sorry, Your Royal 'Ighness, but it's got to be did.' The party re-assembled and drove off shortly before two to the Victoria Park Racecourse where, after witnessing the first race, everyone went in to lunch with the members of Tattersall's. It was a very magnificent spread and there was an endless supply of champagne.

The cars had been escorted in by mounted police with drawn swords, but as these again were a great danger both to the cars and public, they were dispensed with for the return trip. As far as the betting was concerned it was quite a successful afternoon, but as far as rest and enjoyment for H.R.H. were concerned it was a rotten one, as, although the Adelaide crowd has a reputation for being quiet and unemotional, they cheered and yelled and stared at H.R.H. more than any other racing crowd during the whole trip so far.

THURSDAY, 15 JULY   H.R.H. started at 10.00 for the Military Hospital at Keswick. There were about 200 soldier patients there, and very fine workshops where the disabled men are trained in various ways.

The party was back at Government House by 11.30, and ten minutes later started again for the Exhibition Building, where H.R.H. was to attend a demonstration of women war workers. The demonstration had been well organized by an old Scots Guardsman, who had been in Australia many years teaching cadets, school girls, and even nuns to do physical jerks, and who had inculcated an absolutely Prussian discipline. Whatever the method, the results were excellent.

The room chosen for the demonstration was a very long one, and contained a small dais at the end. H.R.H. walked up the hall between two single ranks of nurses, and as soon as he was on the dais a march past began. The women war workers were all in white wearing the badges of their particular good work on their chests, each party carrying a standard in front giving its name. They marched right up the hall through the two ranks of nurses, and turned to the right or left as they reached the dais, taking up their position in very close order on either side, until the hall was absolutely full.

Some parties described themselves as 'Heavy Artillery', 'Light Horse', and so on, presumably to indicate the kind of soldiers they tended during the war. They were of all ages and sizes, marched very well, and looked very nice in the mass, though it was difficult to detect any striking instances of individual charm.

When the hall was full, Lady Hackett[1] read the women war workers' address in a frightened whisper. H.R.H. then read his reply, and added a few words of a less formal kind, ending up by saying that he always asked the diggers to regard him as a comrade and that he hoped the women war workers would do the same. This brought the house down, and the whole hall sang 'God Bless the Prince of Wales' with great fervour.

The only weak point in the demonstration was the women's band, which consisted entirely of women players, conducted by a wizened little man with a face like a sucked orange.

FRIDAY, 16 JULY   The party drove to Adelaide University. On arrival H.R.H. went inside to put on the scarlet hood and gown of a Doctor of Laws. The procession now formed up and wended its way to the great hall. The ceremony inside was typical of any degree-giving stunt, except for the fact that much singing of the 'God Save' and the 'God Bless' was indulged in, and H.R.H., instead of reading his address, made a very good little extempore speech.

After this show, H.R.H. shook hands with the returned soldier undergraduates, while other undergraduates sang 'Archie, my Boy' – 'Archie' being the Governor's nickname here – to the tune of 'Abe, my Boy'. This had the pleasing effect of doing honour both to H.R.H. by the tune, and the Governor, who was present, by the words.

The departure of the train from Port Adelaide was unique owing

[1] Lady Hackett-Moulden was the Lady Mayoress of Adelaide.

to the fact that the railway track passed down the centre of the main street, so that he passed once more through all the crowds that he had just left, almost actually touching the dais where the addresses had been read. The send off was a most enthusiastic one, and it is a pity that arrangements could not be made in all towns for the train to pass down the main street.

The journey to the Outer Harbour took a few minutes, and on arrival there H.R.H., after inspecting the guard of honour from St Peter's College, and passing through a line of women workers who had been most kind in looking after the needs of the ship's company of the *Renown* during the ship's period here, proceeded on board the ship.

MONDAY, 19 JULY At 7.45 a.m. *Renown* was met by two Australian destroyers, who escorted her in to the large and magnificent Hobart harbour, which, in appearance, is held by some people to beat that of Sydney. *Australia* was already anchored, and as the *Renown* passed, the former manned and cheered ship and fired a 21-gun salute. At 9.00 a.m. *Renown* anchored off Ocean Pier.

The official landing took place at 10.30. Before entering the cars H.R.H. went into a shed in which the returned soldiers were. There were too many to shake hands with, so H.R.H. just walked up and down the lines. At the entrance to the shed there stood a dear old lady carrying a Union Jack which she waved violently when the men cheered. She had, apparently, marched in front of every regiment in Hobart, thereby, no doubt, impeding their progress. She had also marched in front of Sir Francis Newdigate-Newdegate when he left Tasmania, and she, no doubt, wished to march in front of H.R.H., but he spoke a few kind words to her so that she had compassion on him and remained on the wharf.

THURSDAY, 20 JULY Departure was made by motor for the Town Hall. A note in the programme saying that the Town Clerk was going to unfurl a standard on H.R.H.'s arrival prompted one of the orderlies to take a standard with him. This was lucky, for on arrival a fat little man was seen to be 'unfurling' the Duke of Connaught's Standard. Luckily, he was stopped just in time and one of H.R.H.'s substituted; but the little man was deeply offended for he had personally written to Melbourne for this standard, having been told it was different from the Royal Standard, which it certainly was.

A State Luncheon was given inside the hall by the Governor of Tasmania.[1] The conversation on the part of the hosts at luncheon varied hardly at all, the subject they spoke about being the hydro-electrical possibilities of Tasmania. Not even the Premier[2] in his speech could avoid touching on it; in fact he spent several minutes quoting minute figures in connection with the hydro-electrical supply, which, he stated among other things, would produce 200,000 horse power, an amount which to him appeared to be staggeringly enormous, but made several of the ship's officers itch to point out that the *Renown* by herself could generate well over half of this stupendous power. H.R.H.'s throat being worse, he did not make a speech, merely standing up at the end of luncheon and in a hoarse voice apologizing for not being able to speak. A good band was in attendance, the bandmaster of which wore a very palpable wig.

The train for Launceston was due to leave at 12.00 p.m. The party arrived very shortly after twelve, but a quarter of an hour's delay was incurred in having to wait for the Mayor, who was changing out of his mayoral robes into his military uniform.

The gauge in Tasmania is the narrow gauge; and the train itself, although clean and obviously specially done up, might almost have been Stephenson's first effort. There was no corridor connecting the coaches, and the coaches were small and entirely without proper sleeping accommodation. The royal coach had very good billets. In the next car there was a compartment for four of the servants, the sleeping arrangements of which, although temporary, left plenty of room. Adjoining this there was a compartment, slightly smaller than any one of the three in the royal coach, which contained eight bunks, so close together and so small that the Staff had to pack into them like sardines when the time came, two or three ministers being also included in this compartment.

Although the engine driver had been warned to go slowly, he felt it incumbent upon him to make up time, and proceeded at a great rate. In the last narrow gauge, a speed indicator had been fitted in the royal car, and H.R.H., observing an indicator here which registered 11, thought the train could not possibly be only travelling eleven miles an hour, and pulled down the little handle alongside to see if that would have any effect. It certainly did; in fact it stopped the train, as it happened to be a connection with the Westinghouse vacuum brake.

[1] Sir William Allardyce.
[2] Sir Walter Lee.

This opportunity was seized to tell the engine driver that he was not to make up time, and the train proceeded at a more leisurely speed.

WEDNESDAY, 21 JULY   Launceston was reached at 10.50. About half past eleven the Brisbane Hotel was reached, where everyone was being put under the one roof, including, for the first time, all the pressmen and Ministers. This hotel was one of the most comfortable yet used on this trip.

After half-an-hour's wait H.R.H. and some of the Staff drove to the Anzac Hostel. H.R.H. inspected the inside of the hostel, which was indeed delightful. In the meanwhile the crowd pressed round, leaving only a small gangway, in which one of the diggers drew a circle with chalk, in the centre of which he placed a match-box on which were two pennies. When H.R.H. came out he was confronted with this. However, he appeared to know what to do, for he took up the box and tossed the pennies into the air, which is apparently a method of playing 'two up', which he is reputed to have played with the diggers in France. The enthusiasm of the diggers knew no bounds after this, and it was only with the greatest difficulty that the party forced their way through to the cars and drove off, arriving at the entrance to the Cataract Gorge. Having driven over the bridge, they were permitted to enter the asphalt footpath without paying the penny fee. This cataract gorge is really a magnificent sight, the South Esk having cut its way through solid rock to join the main river, the Tamar. The party walked along this path, H.R.H. in the van setting a brisk pace which the Mayor and Corporation, not to mention the Ministers, found some difficulty in trying to keep up with. After walking a mile the party came upon a picturesque little suspension bridge. There were quite 40 or 50 official pedestrians, and although they certainly did not keep step along the asphalt path, they appeared to do so when it mattered, on the suspension bridge; for it started swinging and bobbing in a most startling manner. To cap it all, H.R.H. stopped to view the scene presented, until the entire party were huddled together in the centre of the bridge, which now swayed worse than ever. Eventually, however, the bridge was crossed.

It had been arranged that H.R.H. and Staff should dine privately in their sitting room, but for practically the first time H.R.H. not only volunteered to go down into the general dining room for dinner, but insisted upon it. Shrewd guesses were made by the Staff as to which of the ministers' wives', or possibly waitresses', attraction was at the bottom of it; though to be quite candid there were no signs that they had guessed right during dinner. Dinner was chiefly enlivened by silver holders being provided to eat the asparagus with, which were used by the dinner party as castanets to accompany the band with, incidentally causing one of the waitresses to have a fit of the giggles.

THURSDAY, 22 JULY   A rather important event occurred about 10.15 a.m., for the Roman Catholic Archbishop called on H.R.H. to pay his respects and swear allegiance. He seemed a thoroughly good man, apparently in no way connected with Dr Mannix's intrigues.

After having given away presents, etc., H.R.H. departed for the railway station, arriving there rather late owing to the huge crowds.

Hobart was reached shortly after 6.00 p.m., the party driving through fairly large crowds direct to Ocean Pier. Everyone then departed by the barge for the ship.

SUNDAY, 25 JULY   Shortly after 10.00 a.m. *Australia* dropped astern and the destroyers followed *Renown* in to Sydney Harbour. She managed to get round the 8-point turn without difficulty, and let go her second anchor half a minute before programme time, which was 10.40. The first part of the route to the station was very thickly lined by enthusiastic crowds.

At 12.30 p.m. the train drew out of the station. It was the same train as H.R.H. had used before in New South Wales. It was a great blessing to be back on a broad gauge railway after the shaky narrow gauge ones, and it was certainly easier to sleep.

MONDAY, 26 JULY   Wallangarra was reached at 9.30 a.m. This is a small town on the border between Queensland and New South Wales. A carpet was laid from the standard gauge platform at which the New South Wales train was standing, to the narrow gauge platform at which the Queensland train was standing. Across this H.R.H. walked. A small crowd of interested spectators had gathered, but they were unusually silent. Transfer was quickly made, and within less than half an hour the new train had left.[1] At 6.00 p.m. the train ran into Wyreema and stopped at the platform, which was built on a curve, the super-elevation of the left rails giving the car a list of about 10

---

[1] The *Brisbane Courier* reported that the reception had been 'like a cold douche. Everybody was so much engrossed in the formalities of receiving the Prince that not a single cheer was raised.'

degrees to starboard. Luckily the train did not stop many minutes there, but moved farther up on to a siding for the first part of the night.

After dinner the State Organizer came aft with a telegram asking if a boy scout might present H.R.H. with a native bear before lunch on the next day. A vote was taken in the after saloon as to whether this gift should be accepted or refused. No one voted for it to be taken right home to England, but everyone except the Admiral voted that it should be accepted for a time, even if only for a day or two, to see what it was like. The Admiral made a very stirring speech denouncing the acceptance of the gift on the grounds that the beast would perish owing to the change of climate, and that the *Renown* did not want it on board. He was, however, counted out and the bear accepted *pro tem.*

TUESDAY, 27 JULY   At 7.00 a.m. the train proceeded to Brisbane, which was reached at noon.

Great crowds were passed as Brisbane was neared, and H.R.H. appeared clad only in breeches, boots and spurs, and his shirt, with a pair of 'brigade braces'. In this dignified rig he waved to the cheering multitudes. The Naval members again experienced great difficulty in going along the corridor in No. 3s, as the epaulettes would catch at all corners.

On the platform the Lieutenant-Governor[1] received H.R.H. The party embarked in the cars for the official drive. This drive was a howling success, which was not altogether expected, as the place was supposed to contain several disloyalists. Presently the procession passed Parliament House, where the party are being billeted. This is an imposing building, a mixture, on a small scale, of Buckingham Palace and Selfridge's. The old Government House was next passed, it is now being used as a part of the University. An undergraduate here, wearing a mortar board, enquired of one of the Naval Officers where he had obtained his cocked hat, and was told that it originated from the same place as his own head-gear.

A scout, and a girl – presumably his sister – arrived with a large hamper containing a native bear to be given to H.R.H. They were shown into the sitting room, and most of the members of the Staff collected to watch the presentation. Presently H.R.H. came in, and the basket was opened, revealing the most extraordinary animal imagin-

---

[1] of Queensland, the Hon. W. Lennon.

able. In general appearance it certainly bore a striking resemblance to an ordinary toy teddy bear; standing about one foot high on all fours, and being about eighteen inches long. Its fur was soft, and grey in colour, and its paws had sharp claws for tree climbing. The face, however, was most ridiculous; it reminded one vaguely of a Jew's face with a hooked nose, and had the stupidest possible expression, with a pair of tiny eyes set rather close together. It climbed up and all over the girl, who had had it for five years; and after H.R.H. had inspected it and left, she broke down and sobbed, while the bear cried like a baby. The bear spent the day in the Flag Lieutenant's room, crawling about and leaving an odour of gum leaves everywhere, these being its staple food. In the evening compassion was taken on the little girl who had given up her pet, and the native bear (or 'koala' as it is more properly called) was sent back by an orderly with a letter explaining why.

The sentries on guard at Parliament House seemed to be somewhat over-zealous, for they not only stopped Sir Godfrey and Captain North when they tried to get in – not knowing the password – but when one of the official cars was coming in, which they knew to be an official car from the number, one of them stopped the driver for not knowing the password, and when the driver tried to go on he jabbed his bayonet twice through the radiator, thereby costing the Queensland Government £10 for a new one. When H.R.H. returned, with the pilot car and the police car leading, they first stopped the pilot car, and being told that this was the Royal Procession coming back, still demanded the password. Eventually they let the pilot car through, but next stopped the police car, though not for long. By a stroke of luck they did not stop H.R.H.'s car.

Eventually Mr Cohen, the Minister for Works,[1] arrived back, having had a very cheery evening at the dance. The sentry on duty had known him all his life, and when the Minister said he wanted to get in, the sentry said, 'Good evening, Mr Cohen; do you know the countersign?' Mr Cohen said he did not know the countersign, whereupon the sentry said, 'Sorry, but you cannot get in.' So the unfortunate man had to return to the dance and ask someone for the countersign before he could get into his own Parliament House!

---

[1] The Minister of Public Works in the Queensland Government was Mr James Larcome. Possibly Mountbatten was registering a near miss on Mr J. H. Coyne, the Minister of Public Lands.

WEDNESDAY, 28 JULY   Shortly after eleven everyone drove to the Agricultural Exhibition. The naval brigade guard and band was drawn up, and had the appearance of being smarter than previous ones until the officer in charge of the guard gave the order 'Unfix' and the second officer shouted out 'No', whereupon the first officer said, 'All right; stand at ease.'

H.R.H. stayed till a quarter to four. The first event was a grand parade of fat cattle, horses and dogs, and after that a number of young ladies on horseback were let loose in the ring for a short while. Next came some trotting ponies, one pony putting up a great effort to break the trotting speed record. A galloping horse was pacing this animal, and had his work cut out to keep up with it. After this a stock whip cracker gave a rather wonderful performance, finally presenting H.R.H. with a whip, while the President presented one to the Admiral. He cut pieces of paper, held in the hand, in two; and he could crack the whip and let the lash coil round a man's neck without hurting him. A hunters' test for ladies was then held; the horse which was supposed to be the best unaccountably refused one of the jumps three times, and was disqualified. All the others were good, the last lady taking a fall, but not a very bad one.

THURSDAY, 29 JULY   The party proceeded to the site of the new Town Hall of the City of Brisbane to the no'th'ard of the river, passing, on the way, Wirth's Circus Tent, outside which four elephants were paraded, while a dancing horse was dancing about on a tub in the middle. The laying of the foundation stone of the new Town Hall was one of the most genuine yet done, owing to the fact that the stone was really laid, and not merely dropped a thirty-second of an inch into position. Several buckets of mortar had to be poured over the lower stone and smoothed over with an ordinary trowel. H.R.H. was then handed a magnificent gold and bejewelled trowel, and to the horror of the goldsmiths who had made it he lightly touched the wet cement with it, so that it had to be rubbed for several minutes before it could be got clean again. After this the heavy granite foundation stone, suitably inscribed with H.R.H.'s names, titles and distinctions, as well as all the names, titles and distinctions of his father, not to mention all the names of the Mayor, the Aldermen and the Town Clerk, was swung forward and lowered into place. The legs supporting this stone were very rough and chipped ones, and had been hastily painted white, while the heads had received a gorgeous coat of gold leaf. After the stone had been declared 'well and truly laid', the party moved off in the cars and returned to Parliament House for luncheon.

At 7.30 the party departed for Finney's Departmental Stores, where they were taken up to the top landing, which was a sort of restaurant, in two lifts, and found it had been converted into a banqueting hall to seat some four or five hundred people.

The meal was endless, lasting over three hours, and the speeches did not come on for a very long while. No less than four toasts were proposed and seven speeches made, which is really the record this trip. The Hon. J. A. Fihelly, the Acting Premier, made quite a good speech in proposing H.R.H.'s health, evoking a very good laugh by saying that even he would hesitate to take upon himself the responsibilities that were coming to H.R.H.! One point that seemed to strike one was how pleased he was the Premier was not there, so that he had had the honour of going about with H.R.H. H.R.H.'s reply was distinctly good, and very well received.

Throughout the evening many speakers sailed rather close to the wind; but when the party finally got up, shortly before eleven, one could not help feeling that under the circumstances the evening had been a success.

H.R.H. now descended by one lift, while all the rest of the Staff, and many others besides, descended in the other one. The attendant in charge of the last-named lift said there were too many people on board and the rope would probably break. Luckily his worst forebodings did not come true, but when the ground floor was reached the lift overshot the mark. With great presence of mind the attendant moved the lift down to the basement, but here again the lift overshot the mark, and it was only after a struggle that the door was burst open and the occupants were able to get out. The attendant led a sort of 'follow my leader' over the cabbages, crates and wholesale goods and up a narrow staircase into the ladies' millinery department, whence, after another struggle, everyone managed to fight their way out and into the crowd.

FRIDAY, 30 JULY At about 2.25 everyone set out on foot for the Botanical Gardens. They started off in the wrong direction, but were automatically stopped by the enormous crowd which had collected round the gates and through which no opening could be found. Luckily the police had placed barriers at the other gate. Five minutes' walk had brought the party to the usual type of raised platform at the edge of one of the paths, which had been barricaded off for the people to walk past. It was quite a well-run show, and a fairly good average was maintained. The whole affair did not last one hour.

After this H.R.H. shook hands with some returned soldiers who were lining the route in the park. Everyone then returned to Parliament House, while H.R.H. set off hospital stunting. H.R.H. first motored to the Red Cross Convalescent Home at Grangehill, where he visited the patients – about twenty-five in number – afterwards shaking hands with all the hospital staff. From there he motored to Rosemount Military Hospital, where also he shook hands and conversed with all the patients. After that he visited the Enoggera Military Hospital, inspecting most of the buildings and having tea with the matron in charge. Not sufficient time had been allowed in the programme to visit this hospital, consequently H.R.H. was an hour late in leaving.

SATURDAY, 31 JULY The party left Parliament House at quarter to eleven, and drove, through fairly crowded streets, to the Central Station. This is the station at which the party had originally arrived; it is a very large one with a domed glass roof, reminiscent of some continental stations.

About half past four Boonah was reached in a perfect downpour of rain. The two Majors Bell were there on the platform to meet H.R.H., and the party waded their way through mud and torrents of water to a very bedraggled-looking platform, which H.R.H. mounted. He made a short speech thanking the soldiers for turning out in such a downpour to see him, and then shook hands with the returned soldiers and war workers.

It turned out that the Bells had thought it too wet to send the horses, and the party, therefore, had to go by car. Eight cars had been sent up for this purpose from Brisbane. They had been used to convey the party to the station at Brisbane and had left immediately after the royal train, and five of them had arrived safely – the four Crossleys and a Studebaker – the three other American makes failing dismally. H.R.H. and the Admiral got into Major Bert Bell's two-seater Hudson, which led the party and went at a most tremendous speed, considering the state of the roads, thereby leaving all the other cars, except a very brave Crossley, behind. It was a most amazing drive, the cars skidding about dangerously in the thick layer of mud which was the only indication of where the 'road' was supposed to run. Sometimes, when the brakes were put on, the cars would go down hill on their own.

Frequently the wheels were revolving at forty miles an hour while the cars were scarcely moving; and on no occasion would the cars answer to their helms properly; they acted just like ships, for after the wheel had been put over it took some while for the cars to gather way to turn round, and they would go on turning after the wheels were straight. However, wonderful to relate, everybody eventually reached the station without mishap. The party was met by the eldest Bell brother, who conducted them to the homestead of Coochin-Coochin station.

'Coochin' in the aboriginal language means 'black swan', and the repetition signifies 'plenty black swan'. The flags which the Bells were flying on their staff was, accordingly, a red one with two black swans thereon.

The party did not arrive until a quarter past six, when it was quite dark, although the distance was only 14 miles. As soon as they arrived the Bells made them feel quite at home. Even before dinner the party had settled down to make a noise with the jazz drums belonging to the house. As the luggage had not yet arrived, none of the newcomers changed for dinner, which pleased H.R.H. very much, as he was able to keep on his precious puttees, much to the gratification of the ladies.

After dinner the party danced to a gramophone and the jazz drums, H.R.H. dressing up in coloured bow ties obtained at Brisbane, which were immediately pulled off.

SUNDAY, 1 AUGUST   The local parson had given out on the previous Sunday that H.R.H. would attend Divine Service. In this, needless to say, he was mistaken; and luckily the Bells had pointed this out to him soon after he had said it. The day turned out wonderfully, with blue sky and a dazzling sun. After breakfast, which was a movable feast, between eight-thirty and ten, the party went out and inspected an emu and three whip-tail kangaroos in a small enclosure in the front of the house.

Everyone then trooped off to inspect the horses, the majority of which were of the usual rough station type, though some of them looked very fine even in their unkempt condition. Shortly before eleven, the party mounted, and rode off to a paddock a mile or two away. Here they split up, and in twos and threes started mustering the cattle.

Most of this mustering had to be done on the face of a hill with much fallen timber about. All the horses were well trained in this type of work, and if they were given the slightest encouragement when any

cattle were sighted they would be off like a streak of lightning down
the face of the hill, putting the wind up the less experienced riders of
the party, who had to hold on like grim death. The view from the
summit of one of these hills was magnificent, as the grass-covered
plains were bounded on all sides by mountains.

By lunch time practically the whole herd of cattle had been collected. They were driven to a convenient spot, where the Bells told
their guests that they could leave the cattle and have lunch. The
non-riders, who had arrived by motor car, had started a blazing fire
and laid out places for luncheon on the ground. The cattle very
conveniently stayed where they were while the party had lunch, this
being quite one of the cleverest accomplishments. The meal consisted
of beef-steak which had been grilled over a fire, tea made in a billy,
chicken and enormous hunks of bread and butter. Captain Legh,
however, was more thirsty than hungry, and dashed to a bottle labelled
'beer'. Pulling out the cork he proceeded to pour the contents out,
when suddenly an exclamation was heard from him, 'Good Lord, it's
milk!' However, there was both beer and whisky, as the Admiral's Secretary soon discovered, and towards the end of luncheon he was invited
to mount 'Wander', a mount which had been originally relegated
to H.R.H., but which had been turned over to the Flag Lieutenant,
after Aileen had seen how well H.R.H. rode at Brisbane. As soon
as he was in the saddle H.R.H. gave the horse a good smack and it
cantered off, with the Secretary hanging on for all he was worth. He
got on very well until, being carried under some trees, the branches of
which were very low, his spectacles were knocked off. 'The perishing
beast then took charge,' as he himself put it, but luckily stopped when
it got among the other horses. The Secretary had no idea which string
to pull to make it stop. He was received, on his return, with a ringing
cheer, for he had upheld the honour of the Navy. A search party was
next organized to look for his spectacles.

After this everyone mounted again and drove the herd to a large
open space, where they could commence cutting out suitable bulls.
After the Bells had cut out one or two steers, H.R.H. and the Admiral
tried their hands, and of the visiting party these two were certainly in
a class high above the others. Everyone tried his hand, however, and
an average of quite half a dozen bulls apiece were cut out.

The Bells were trying to separate the bulls which were in the best
condition from the rest of the herd, and they would point out a suitable
bull to one of the party, who would have to follow it on horseback

into the mob until right close up to it. He would then gradually edge it out of the mob, by keeping his horse in such a position that the steer would always be going away from him. The critical moment came when the bull was on the very outside of the mob and would try and make a dash to get back into the mob again, when it was the rider's business to force him right out and keep him there. Most of the horses were so well trained that once they understood which animal their rider was after all he had to do was to sit tight and not come off when the horse swerved round to the right or left in its endeavours to keep the bull going in the right direction.

This game went on till nearly sunset, by which time the herd was divided almost exactly into two. It then merely remained to move the original lot back to their paddock before the party cantered home to the house. H.R.H. cut out the greatest number of animals during the day. He seemed to be for ever at full gallop, making hissing noises through his teeth, presumably to frighten the bull. The only real danger in the game was that if a bull got too hot by being chased he was liable to turn and attack the rider, but nothing of the sort occurred this day.

On return a queue lined up for hot baths, and at dinner the Bells looked with keen expectation to see the Staff sit down very carefully and gently, and were quite disappointed when each one sat down as heavily as usual declaring themselves to be neither sore nor stiff.

Several car loads of deputations came over about tea time from Beaudesert to inform the Admiral that the road was quite good enough for H.R.H. to motor over on the morrow as arranged in the official programme, but the latter very wisely held out, and said that it was in too bad a condition to send H.R.H. over. They were not in the least annoyed at this, in fact one car load came back three times after they had said farewell, to have another drink with their 'Dear Old Admiral'.

H.R.H. wrote a personal letter to Mrs Collins, who was getting up a dance at great personal expense for him, explaining profusely why he could not come.[1]

The party put on dinner jackets for dinner, H.R.H. and most of the Staff wearing bow ties of the most extraordinary colours, which

---

[1] Whatever Mountbatten or the Admiral may have thought, extreme offence was caused. The Prince's putative hosts believed that he had 'found the Bell girls more to his liking and did not want to leave them'. Fifty years later a sense of grievance still persisted.

were the rest of those which had been got in Brisbane for the occasion, and one or two of the wiser members of the party had made-up bow ties on, so that those who tried to pull them off were very badly sold. Some very quiet dances were indulged in first, but by-and-by some couples tried to cut other couples out, and several people were scouring the place looking for the unfortunate State Organizer to cut him out, as they said it was rather out of place to have a live 'steer' running about the house loose. Various people were thrown through the window from the verandah, where everyone was dancing, into the drawing room, and in the end war was declared between the Admiral and H.R.H. on the one hand, and Colonel Grigg and Captain Legh on the other, and it was not until long after 1.00 a.m. that the party finally retired, battered and bruised far more from the dancing than from the riding, to bed.

MONDAY, 2 AUGUST   The day was every bit as pleasant as the preceding one. After breakfast the official Coochin-Coochin stunt was done. First H.R.H. shook hands with Princess Susan, Mrs Brown and a small boy aged ten, who were the only three blacks on the estate, the others having all trooped off to Brisbane, where they had celebrated H.R.H.'s arrival far too well to see him again in their own home. These blacks have been adopted by Miss Aileen Bell, and are quite devoted to her. Susan then sang some songs, which were very strange and weird. She was just like a child about it, and when asked for an encore by H.R.H. in the little canteen, she did not want to sing again as there was not a large enough audience, but when some more people trooped in she readily started up once more.

After lunch the party rode back to where they had left the other herd, and there dismounted. The cattle were driven in single file between two sets of rails and posts to the dipping bath, which is a long bath not more than three or four feet wide but over six feet in depth, and is filled with a brown and evil-smelling liquid. Most of the cattle were quite used to this, and, closing their eyes, dived headlong into the bath, coming out all brown at the other end. Others had to be poked on from behind. This dipping is done to overcome the tick, one of the most dreaded cattle pests in Australia. Like nearly every other Australian pest, this has been introduced into the country, in this instance from South America. The brown liquid, which contains a mild solution of arsenic, burns these ticks and poisons them, so that they eventually have to let go and drop off. Under the present conditions, however, it is impossible to eradicate the pest altogether, although in parts of America this has been successfully done.

After dinner the party started dancing, and, although only two or three short dances were indulged in, this was fatal; for it made them very late in starting out for Boonah, which had to be reached by 8.30. All the girls and the three Bells accompanied the party, the latter driving them in their own cars, which was really better as they knew how to manage the extraordinarily slippery roads. Presently the lights of Boonah came into sight, which meant that the pleasant visit to Coochin-Coochin was drawing to a close.

At Boonah a great turn-out had been unofficially arranged, the lights which had been seen coming from a triumphal arch. In a way, it was one of the most wonderful departures from any station, for H.R.H. and the Admiral leant out over the rear platform cracking a stock whip and blowing a hunting horn to the enthusiastic multitude.

TUESDAY, 3 AUGUST   The train was due to reach Brisbane at 7.20, but owing to the fact that orders had been given that the train was not to increase speed to make up time, and time was being lost at each stunt, Brisbane was reached an hour and a quarter late at about 8.40. H.R.H. drove to a wool shed, where he arrived punctually at 9 o'clock. The party were taken up to the top in a lift, where an overpowering smell of sheep again greeted them. They were conducted, first to a dressing room, and then, between rows and rows of tables, to a platform, where supper was laid for them. Within two minutes of the arrival the King's health was proposed and drunk. This was followed immediately by the welcoming speech of the President, to which H.R.H. replied. He had only a few headlines jotted down as notes, and hardly referred to these, and, without doubt, this speech must be classed as one of his very best efforts. It certainly was wonderfully well received.

WEDNESDAY, 4 AUGUST   At 10.10 a.m. H.R.H. left Parliament House by motor for the Central Station. The route was so thickly lined with people that progress was very slow, and it was not until ten minutes after the train was due to depart that the station was reached. The crowd of notables on the station to say farewell to H.R.H. was likewise so enormous that it took seventeen minutes to say good-bye. Naturally, the railway authorities, knowing that H.R.H. would not want the train to make up time, began to get the wind up, and made three attempts to start the train, thwarted by the Flag Lieutenant, who stood on the observation platform and turned on the Westinghouse brake at each attempt. Eventually, nearly half an hour late, the train departed.

For a mile or two outside Brisbane, practically the whole track was lined by cheering crowds, and it really was a remarkable departure.

The train reached Toowoomba only twenty minutes late at 4.20. The party embarked in cars, and drove off with a mounted police escort to the Queen's Park. The route was lined by returned soldiers, who, as soon as H.R.H. had passed, formed up and marched to the grounds to the strains of a band. They timed their arrival to coincide with the reading of the addresses, so that the big drum entirely spoilt all chances of anyone hearing what was being read.

Toowoomba possesses a pet view, which is, apparently, shown to all great men. Great was the disappointment when H.R.H. flatly refused to be shown it, as he wished to go straight on to the Simla Red Cross Convalescent Home, which was on the programme as coming after the view. This he succeeded in doing.

When the Mayor came in to announce dinner ready, H.R.H., by way of making polite conversation, pointed to the photograph of a woman in scanty eastern attire and said, 'Who on earth is that woman in that extraordinary get-up?' to which the Mayor replied, 'That is my wife.'

At 7.20 the party went down to dinner, only five minutes late! Dinner, which was being given by the Mayor and Councillors, went off quite well, without any speech-making. After dinner H.R.H. shook hands with the diners and the hotel staff. As he was about to leave, a great commotion was observed near the door, and a little Chinaman, who was apparently the cook, was pulled in by two of the maids and made to shake hands with H.R.H.

The train was billed to leave at eleven, but H.R.H. arranged for a special extension up to 11.45. A small crowd collected round the rear car of the train when H.R.H. arrived. A sergeant of police, who was rather 'shot away', stood up and made conversation to everybody, paying compliments all round for quite ten minutes. The train finally moved off, leaving the crowd behind, cheering their best; but the police sergeant stood on the platform, and sang 'For he's a jolly good fellow' with a fine deep bass voice; after which, still standing on the platform, he imagined that he was leading the crowd in their cheering. As by then the crowd was so far off that only faint independent cheers could be heard, the effect of the sergeant's voice was three loud 'hip-ip-ip-ip-ips' at the correct intervals, followed by no regular cheering. After this exertion he wished H.R.H. good-night, and dropped off. Everyone then turned in.

THURSDAY, 5 AUGUST   The train, which had been stationary part of the night, moved off in the early morning, eventually stopping again for an hour for everyone to dress and have breakfast, proceeding on at 10 o'clock to Stanthorpe, which was reached at half past ten.

At this place a white opossum was presented to H.R.H. They are as rare among opossums as albinos are among human beings, and very few of the Australians themselves had ever seen them. In fact it was said to be 'one of the only six' in Australia; but then, as the Admiral is always saying, 'One should never believe what one is told and only half of what one sees.'

The train was not officially supposed to stop, even for water at Guyra, but a telegram had been received saying that there were many diggers collected there, and accordingly H.R.H. and the Admiral arranged that the train should be stopped for thirty seconds, to enable the former to shake hands with the diggers. It was raining when Guyra was reached, and owing to the train unfortunately overshooting the mark and stopping opposite the Mayor and Councillors instead of opposite the diggers, H.R.H. fell into the hands of the Mayor, who insisted on making a speech, though it must be admitted that he hurried as hard as he could, and fairly poured out a string of words into H.R.H.'s ears. After this he insisted upon trying to present his Councillors and the Red Cross workers, but the Admiral's arrival put an end to him so that H.R.H. was free to move off and shake hands with the diggers.

FRIDAY, 6 AUGUST   At 9.35 the royal train proceeded, arriving at Valley Heights shortly after 11 o'clock. There were some shy people standing at the other side of some palings, and H.R.H. stepped out and asked them why they did not come over, to which they replied that they were not allowed to. When he beckoned them, however, there was a wild rush to get round him, and he talked to them for a few minutes; after which, accompanied by Sir Godfrey, he got on to the locomotive, and the train left.

Wallerawang was reached while the party were having lunch, at about 1.30. A good number of people collected round the carriage window and watched H.R.H. having lunch, which so disturbed him that he got up and went out, crossing the railway bridge and talking to some of the people, and inspecting the local war memorial. By this time the train had finished watering, and as soon as H.R.H. turned up it proceeded.

At 3 o'clock the train arrived at Kelso, where the party was met by the Mayor of Bathurst with four horses. H.R.H. started for a ride, accompanied by the Mayor. H.R.H. started off at a sort of hand gallop, his excuse being that he could not hold his horse. As a matter of fact, three out of the four horses were stronger than their riders. The party were followed by a few cars, who were, however, firmly told that H.R.H. did not wish them to accompany him, and for about four or five miles the cavalcade galloped along unattended. This ride was by way of being known to nobody, but it was soon found that the route had been made well known, and at every turn there were motor cars to greet H.R.H.

In this manner the party eventually arrived at Bathurst, after a strenuous ride of seventeen miles. The Flag Lieutenant, who is a wonderful horseman on a cantering horse, had found himself on a horse that preferred to trot, and he consequently spent a very uncomfortable two hours, although he so tired the horse as to induce it to stop on one or two occasions, and was then able to 'shoo' it on to such an extent that the poor beast was forced to canter until it had joined its stable companions.

SATURDAY, 7 AUGUST The train stopped for water at a place called Gilgandra for about twenty minutes. A noisy returned soldier, with one or two men and several women and children, rushed round the train cheering and yelling 'We want Teddy', and knocked on all the windows without discovering which was H.R.H.'s. Not that it would have made any difference, as it would take a good deal more than that to wake him up. However, they succeeded in waking practically every other occupant of the train, and when finally the train proceeded out of the station without H.R.H. making any appearance, they proceeded to 'count him out' in the Australian fashion, i.e., to start with one and count up to ten, which is a way they have of finishing off unpopular speakers, and which they even did to unpopular generals during the war when trying to address their troops. Needless to say, H.R.H. knew nothing about it until he was told later in the morning.

The party reached Wingadee Station. Outside some buggies, or sulkies as they are more properly called, were drawn up, containing the women folk, and on each side of the small drive were drawn up the thirty-odd station hands on horseback. They followed the party up as far as the homestead, where everyone dismounted, and H.R.H. went round and shook hands with the men.

Wingadee Station, which is situated in the middle of a large plain, consists of about 19,000 acres and is the property of the Australian and New Zealand Land Company. This is a very rich Scotch company, having its head offices, curiously enough, in Edinburgh. In normal times there are some 80,000 sheep on the station, but the drought and the flood had left them with only 15,000.

After some refreshment the party went over to the ladies' room where much too strong tea was drunk. All were then shown their rooms. Of course, the boiler, as at Wanganui, must needs burst, and the water had to be heated in petrol tins over a fire built in an old iron tank in the open. The man who looked after this was perfectly deaf, as H.R.H. discovered after he had been trying to make conversation with him for five minutes. The other sanitary arrangements were distressingly poor.

About an hour after arrival, the party rode out to see the wool-shed where all the shearing takes place, though, of course, no shearing was taking place at the time, as the usual strike was in progress in this district. This entailed another three-mile ride, there and back, and after this everyone had hot baths in the muddy water, as the inside of the petrol cans in which the water had been boiled did not appear to have been any too clean. Just before dinner the electric lighting failed, and did not come on again until after dinner was over.

SUNDAY, 8 AUGUST   H.R.H. rode out with some of the station people to see various paddocks and sheep, as well as to examine an artesian well. The temperature of the water on coming up is well over 100°F, and is said to be excellent for rheumatism. Many beautifully coloured parrots were seen about, notably the lovely red and grey galahs.

The Admiral and P.M.O., as well as the riding party, inspected some fine stud rams just before luncheon. The faces of some of these animals were so completely covered with wool that they could hardly see, while great folds of wool-covered flesh hung down from their necks.

After luncheon, at which everybody, save H.R.H., who was suffering from indigestion, ate heartily, the entire party, with the exception of the P.M.O., mounted and rode out about six miles to a paddock

above: Mountbatten rounds up the final lunch party in Australia. Aileen Bell is on the right, with her brother Bert behind her (19 August 1920).

below: A relic of German rule in Samoa. Natives give H.R.H. a military-style salute (25 August 1920).

above: H.R.H. and Mountbatten with a surf-board instructor in Honolulu (30 August 1920).

below: An enthusiastic crowd greets H.R.H. in British Guiana (21 September 1920).

where some kangaroos had previously been sighted. Two specially trained kangaroo hounds and some sheep dogs made up the pack for the hunt. These kangaroo hounds are of a cross breed between greyhounds and wolfhounds, and are very fast and fierce creatures. Very soon three kangaroos were sighted in the distance, and the 'dogs', as the pack are always called here, were put forward. The kangaroos turned round and started off in gigantic leaps. The pack split up after a short while, but the overseer led the field after the larger of the kangaroos, which was of the Bluefly type. This animal led the party an amazing run, over flat, but in places treacherously boggy country. There was only one jump, and that an irrigation ditch which was scarcely noticeable. After a good three- or four-mile gallop the dogs became tired and the kangaroo got away, being one of the fastest, the station hands declared, they had ever followed.

A quarter of an hour's respite now followed, very welcome to the horses, when suddenly a flock of emus was sighted some twenty-five strong. The emu is a 'protected' bird, and permission had not been granted H.R.H. to hunt them; but, luckily, none of the party knew this. Everyone, therefore, started off in full cry after this flock, which turned and went down near a wire fence. One of the kangaroo hounds made a tremendous leap for the throat of one of these birds, and seizing firmly on to it, brought it down head over heels and killed it, to H.R.H.'s intense relief, for he had been under the impression that this particular emu was deliberately chasing him. In the meanwhile the entire party split up after separate birds. Most of these, however, got away, as there were no dogs. After that, one led the party a tremendous long run, stopping every now and then to get his wind, and if any dog or human being came near him he would kick out with his tremendous great legs which, if anybody had been near enough, would have proved exceedingly dangerous. He was a most game bird, and would always set off as soon as he had got back his wind, with a great steady stride. The riders, however, could now keep near enough to him to touch him if they so wished. Eventually he got into a clump of trees, and made his one mistake, for he stood in the middle of a pool until driven on, and then went off to another pool of water where one of the kangaroo dogs, making a leap, caught in him the hind quarters and killed him. To speed his death several of the party broke branches off the trees and hit him over the head. After this they plucked feathers out and stuck them in their hats.

MONDAY, 9 AUGUST   Gilgandra was reached at 10.25, and this was the place, it will be remembered, that had been passed on the Saturday morning and where H.R.H. had been 'counted out'. They fully made up for this by their amazing enthusiasm, which beat even official stunts along the line. H.R.H. first shook hands with the returned soldiers, the man in charge being the very man who had counted H.R.H. out. The Admiral had a few words with him on the subject, sizing him up as though he had been a defaulter and, subjecting him to a merciless cross-examination, extracted the following facts: Although Mr Miller was President of the local Returned Soldiers' League Branch, he himself had never been in the war. Nevertheless, he admitted that he knew perfectly well what 'counting out' meant. He admitted that he had been the leader in the counting out, and that it was he who had deliberately written the account of the shameful incident to the papers. These simple facts were repeated in a quiet tone by the Admiral, so that they sunk in not only to Mr Miller but also to several interested bystanders, and it was interesting to note how Mr Miller's moral self gradually shrunk until it disappeared altogether and an abject apology was received.

The Mayor, notable for his immense bulk, led H.R.H. to a small platform overlooking an opening where were gathered quite a large crowd of people. He made a perfectly hopeless speech, but it is only just to him to mention that the fact that he had been asked not to make a speech was probably preying on his mind. Wherever he moved on the platform there were many cries from school children telling him to get out of the light as they wanted to see the Prince. This was no easy matter owing to his great size, and as soon as he moved to another position he was greeted with more shouts from another quarter. At the end of this speech the crowd did an amazing thing: they started with ten, and then went on to nine, eight, etc., down to one; in other words they counted H.R.H. in again. This is the first time that any of the Australians travelling on the train had ever heard of anybody being counted in.

TUESDAY, 10 AUGUST   The train drew in at Miowera railway station about 7.20 a.m. The actual siding at which the train was stopped was marked only by some gravel strewn alongside the line, though further up a small wooden hut had a large board up to say that this was Miowera. This small hut is the one and only building in the whole of Miowera. The train was going to be used as a depot for some of the

Commonwealth Officials and for the servants, so the locomotive was detached and a dynamo car was connected up to provide the lighting. Wooden ladders were fixed to each doorway, reaching down to the ground, and the waste pipes of wash places had tin chute covers fitted.

H.R.H. was expected to leave the train at ten, but it was ten past eleven before the first move was made. Everyone walked over to the shearing shed, about half a mile distant, at which one gang of shearers who, marvellous to relate, was not on strike (though it should be explained that this was no fault of theirs as their demands had just been acceded to) were working. The party was shown every process, which was certainly very interesting, and merits a short description. The sheep to be sheared are mustered in a paddock and then driven down to big pens near the sheds. From these pens they are driven up a bottle-neck opening, at the end of which a man is stationed who operates two gates, which close two pens and admit each sheep into the open one of three pens according to its classification. This man has to be very quick at his work, for though the sheep are slow enough in the pens, when they come to the narrow part they proceed at a wild gallop, so that it is difficult to distinguish their ear marks, which are the only means of identifying to which pen they belong. The animals frequently get caught by the gates, which would not occur if they went at a more sedate pace, but truly the sheep is a very foolish animal. The sheep are next driven to pens inside the shed and divided up amongst the shearers. At this particular shed there were sixteen men shearing. Each shearer takes out a sheep and carries it bodily to where his cutters are. He then sits it up, and while holding it with the left hand, works the shears with the right. All shearing here is mechanical, the power in this case being provided by a steam engine. The shearer first runs his shears over the sheep's belly and the inside of the legs, a very delicate and difficult operation, especially as some of the sheep are truculent and apt to kick. The face is then shorn, and finally the back, which is the easiest part. The sheep seem to sustain remarkably few cuts.

As each sheep is finished it is pushed down a polished wooden chute, which leads to the outer pens, where they stay until the end of the day, and are accounted for to each man's credit. The present rate, just granted to them, is 14/- a hundred; and as a man can shear anything up to 200 a day, their earnings during the shearing season are very large, and are reputed to be spent almost entirely on drink. The sheep looks most absurd after they are shorn and shiver considerably, and, if the night should be wet or exceptionally cold, many of them perish.

The present breed of sheep out here carry four times the wool of their predecessors of 20 or 30 years ago, the average weight yielded by each sheep being 13 lbs per annum. Naturally, the mechanical shears, which vibrate very much, become difficult to hold towards the end of a hard day's shearing, and become blunted very quickly, especially if the wool has sand in it, and two men are employed by the shearers to keep their cutting blades sharp. Four boys are employed in picking up each fleece as it is shorn, and putting it on a table. Here men called wool rollers remove the rough edges from the fleece and roll up the solid fleece into a bundle, which they carry over to the classifying table, where two expert classifiers are at work. These are very superior gentlemen, dressed in clean white overalls. They must know their job thoroughly, for by the feel of the wool they have to classify it, and according to their judgement the price to pay for a particular fleece is settled. A packer now gets hold of the wool, taking it out of each compartment in turn. A large canvas bag is placed in a wooden box, the sides of which are held together by a patent fastening. The packer puts the wool to be packed into a box similar to the lower one. When this box is full he travels it over to the lower box, pulls the bottom of the upper box out and runs a mechanical ram down, which presses the wool into the lower box. This operation is repeated two or three times until the sack is full of tightly pressed wool. Before the ram goes down for the last time a piece of sacking to form the top covering for the sack is fastened to the underside of the ram.

While the ram is well down spikes are stuck in, which pin the covering to the sides of the sack so that the wool is kept in place. After the ram has been removed the top is sewn up and the bale is taken to be weighed. They weigh on an average 4½ cwt. The name of the station, class of wool and number of package is then stencilled on.

WEDNESDAY, 11 AUGUST   At half past nine a small buck-jumping display was given in front of the house, two rather vicious horses being ridden by two of the best riders in the district. They gave a truly wonderful exhibition, but as it was only a preliminary one they did not ride their horses to a standstill, but jumped off after a sufficient display. The first rider rode without reins.

Fairly punctually at ten H.R.H. mounted. He overheard the four photographers, who had somehow managed to creep in, though all except Brooks had come as far as Miowera without permission, arranging to motor out on this expedition. He at once put his foot down and refused to allow them to go. He had not ridden many miles, however, before the party in the motor cars overtook the riders, and to everyone's, especially H.R.H.'s, astonishment, Mr Everard Cotes, of Reuters, was observed in one of them.

The ride out was most pleasant, and occupied fully three hours, as the distance to the lunching place was 22 miles from the homestead. Shortly before the lunch place was reached the kangaroo dogs were unloaded from one of the motor cars and the party prepared for a hunt. There were five dogs on this occasion, all of the same cross-breed – greyhound and wolfhound.

The procession now moved off with intervals of some fifty or a hundred yards between them. First came H.R.H., then the huntsman and pack, followed finally by the rest of the field. When, after half an hour's ride a couple of kangaroos were sighted, they were startled by the advance riders and had got well into their stride before the dogs could be brought up to go after them, so that, unfortunately, they escaped. The going was very treacherous as there were many rabbit warrens about and the paddock, which had once been forest, was covered with fallen timber. All the trees in this paddock had been ringed, and were dead; and but for the wonderful skill of the bush horses there might have been several nasty falls. After about an hour of this the party worked round to where a fire had been built for luncheon. Some excellent mutton chops and cutlets were being grilled by an old man of sixty, who, having been rejected three times by the Australian Medical Boards, had shaved his beard and dyed his hair and joined up under an assumed name, and had seen much service in France.

Sir Godfrey and Captain Legh had shot a duck on the way over in one of the cars, and had great yarns to tell about the number of kangaroos and emu which the riders had not seen. Some of the men who had been mustering the sheep in the paddock had come across four baby emus during the forenoon. They were only three or four days old, but were already bigger than bantams, and were most sturdy upon their legs. They did not appear to have feathers at all, but seemed to be covered with hair. Unlike the markings of the grown-up emu they were camouflaged by nature with black and white stripes, so that at the distance of a few yards they were almost invisible. These were presented to H.R.H., and the Admiral, to everyone's astonishment, after due consideration came to the conclusion that they might survive the journey and could therefore be taken.

After luncheon the party re-mounted. Very soon three kangaroos were sighted, and this time the dogs got well away after them, the riders following pell-mell. H.R.H. followed the dogs after one kangaroo, while Colonel Smith and the Flag Lieutenant (who had secret hopes of shooting a kangaroo with an automatic pistol he carried in his pocket) followed one of the kangaroos which had no dogs on its track and which separated from the others. The former party, after a good run, arrived in time to see the kill, the dogs bringing down a kangaroo and worrying it to death.

In the meanwhile the latter two lost their animal, but by walking slowly at right angles to their previous direction they soon came across him once more with two or three others. They started him off again and were gaining on him rapidly when a dog arrived and the kangaroo, who was feeling rather tired, tripped over a branch of a fallen tree. The dog was at its throat in an instant, followed by two more dogs who suddenly appeared, and it was not long before they had finished this one off as well. Although it is great fun while the hunt is in progress, it is not a pleasant sight to see a kangaroo being worried to death, as they turn up great pathetic eyes at one and never utter a sound. The tail was cut off, and, as no one else wished to keep it, the Flag Lieutenant kept it. Not five minutes after this an old-man kangaroo, standing quite five feet in height, was sighted. The dogs immediately gave chase, but the old-man had not gone a hundred yards before he turned round to fight for his life. He was obviously the third one who had been chased previously, as otherwise he would have run considerably farther. He gave three violent kicks with his hind feet, but the five dogs were too much for him, and they all fastened on to him practically simultaneously, so that he was pulled over and left almost powerless. Nevertheless, he took much longer to kill than the previous two.

THURSDAY, 12 AUGUST H.R.H. and the Flag Lieutenant mounted and rode off to the small racing track, three or four miles away. It was a 7-furlong course, and was a very typical bush track such as is used for these meetings. In the first race there were four starters, the four mentioned above. H.R.H., who had the inside billet, won very easily; the Flag Lieutenant, who was on a fat military horse, being left yards behind to swallow the dust and clay sods which were being thrown up by the others. There were five more races, all of which H.R.H. won. The unkind observer would at once say that as he was always given the best horse, and as he rode the lightest weight, he would be bound to win; but in quite two cases out of the six this was very decidedly not so, and the betting among the local people was very much against H.R.H. winning the last two races, the last one especially, for he was not given the best horse nor the inside billet, nevertheless he just won both of them, and the local riders attribute this entirely to his skill in nursing his horse at the right moment and starting his spurt at the right moment, and, in fact, to sheer good horsemanship. They were really very pleased to see him win the last two races.

In the middle of dinner H.R.H. and the young lady on his right were getting on quite nicely together and started drawing pigs with their eyes shut. When it came to H.R.H.'s turn he preferred not to close his eyes, but to look up. He turned to his hostess and said, 'I will look at you and get an inspiration.' His hostess was delighted, and looked her very best. H.R.H. did not see the joke for some considerable time. The pig was far from being a good one.

After dinner H.R.H. stated that as he had beaten Leslie McLeod[1] in all the races that afternoon, he would challenge him on foot to the station when the time came for him to depart. This he readily accepted, and four competitors were entered – these two, Sir Godfrey and the Flag Lieutenant. The P.M.O. went round collecting their hats and offering to sell them to anybody as cast off clothing; and at 11 o'clock the four 'madmen' lined up, the rest of the party getting into three cars ready to follow. Presently the word to go was given, and the party started off in fine style down the drive in front of the house. H.R.H. set a madly fast pace over the treacherous roads. There was no moon, and it was quite dark save for the headlamps of the following cars, which managed to light up the road fairly successfully, making the hollows seem much bigger than they actually were. The party in the cars laughed and cheered and generally disturbed those who were trying to run. Everybody overshot the right-angled turn to the left, which had to be taken to get to the station, H.R.H. and McLeod overshooting the mark farther than anybody else. In the meanwhile the Admiral had leapt out and started running furiously to overtake the others, which he succeeded in doing in about thirty seconds. Leslie McLeod dropped out shortly after the Admiral joined in and Sir

[1] Son of the manager of the homestead where the party was staying.

Godfrey, seeing this, got into the Admiral's place in the car. The Admiral had not run a quarter of a mile before he again returned to the car, as the finishing post, the railway gate, hove into sight. This left H.R.H. and the Flag Lieutenant only in it, who now spurted and went all out for the last fifty yards, nearly falling in the exceedingly treacherous ground. The result was a dead heat, though H.R.H. thinks he was a nose's length in front.

FRIDAY, 13 AUGUST   Blayney was reached about twenty minutes to four. This being a junction the station platforms were enormous; and on the near platform there was a small canvas-covered dais, on one side of which were the school children and on the other the returned soldiers, the general public standing on the 'down' railway lines, so that everyone would have obtained a very good view had it not been for the inordinate number of notables gathered upon the dais. An Indian Army Officer, complete with turban and chain shoulder straps, was in charge of the returned soldiers. He was a local man, and having been twice rejected in Australia, had gone to India and joined up in the ranks, eventually having gained a captaincy in the 15th Lancers. It was very cold here, but Blayney is considered to be the coldest place thereabouts, and in the distance, just before Blayney was reached, snow-capped mountains could be seen from the train.

At 9 o'clock Newnes was reached, and here the train stood for the night. Being near the summit of the Blue Mountains the air was very sharp.

SATURDAY, 14 AUGUST   The night was bitterly cold, and in the early hours of the morning the train moved on, reaching Sydney about 10.10 a.m. The party drove straight to Man-o'-War Steps, where they embarked in the barge and proceeded on board the *Renown*. After luncheon H.R.H. and the Flag Lieutenant went ashore to the races. They had a very bad day, losing vast sums of money between them.

SUNDAY, 15 AUGUST   Shortly before five H.R.H. went up the harbour in the barge some eight or nine miles to Yaralla, the home of Miss Walker. At Yaralla a large party collected. Everyone went in and changed for dinner, H.R.H. and the Staff wearing dinner jackets. After dinner the pianist from the Wentworth came in and played some dance music, which he insisted on playing terrifically fast, and great difficulty was experienced in making him play slower. The evening was proceeding perfectly normally until an apparition appeared with the top of a large clothes basket on its head, a warming pan in its hand, and wearing a skirt and pinafore. This turned out to be the Admiral disguised as a Chinaman. Mrs Verney, the niece of the lady of the house, who had dressed the Admiral up, then caught hold of the Flag Lieutenant and dressed him up in a weird rig, which mainly consisted in the rest of the washing basket jammed completely over his head, after which the Admiral insisted upon playing 'follow my leader', or, as Mrs Verney put it, 'the man from Cook'. Everybody joined in, and presently the entire party were spread out throughout the house crawling under beds, squeezing through windows, and generally doing quite the maddest things imaginable. The worst tangle, however, occurred in Colonel Grigg's room, where a bed had been made up for him to spend the night. H.R.H. and the Admiral started a fight, in which some of the others soon joined. Colonel Grigg, regardless of the fact that it was his own bed, seized the mattress, blankets, and sheets, and threw them over the scrappers. After that everybody started getting out sponges and throwing them at each other. One by one the party escaped from this room and the pandemonium spread all over the house. Tablecloths, towels, sheets and sponges were next seized on, dipped in water and thrown about, a few people even going so far as to throw squeezed oranges. The dominating character was the Admiral, who could be seen laying out about six ladies at one go, and then rushing at H.R.H. with shouts and screams. Eventually one of the Walker twins took a bucket of water and tried to throw it at the Admiral, but only succeeded in completely drenching the unfortunate Miss Walker's very valuable oriental carpet. Her nerve then gave way completely, and with tears in her eyes she implored everyone to spare her carpet. After about half an hour peace was gradually restored, and the party collected their gear, including H.R.H.'s jazz set, which had been brought, and took their departure.

WEDNESDAY, 18 AUGUST   At 9.30 a.m. H.R.H. and the Flag Lieutenant went ashore in the barge and drove to the Centennial Park for the last time. They were met by the horses again and they trotted round to Randwick Racecourse, where H.R.H. rode two or three 3-furlong sprints on race horses. After a final visit to the steward's room, during which it came on to rain, H.R.H. departed by motor for Man-o'-War Steps and returned on board, where he changed into a frock coat for the Official State Luncheon.

The State Luncheon was got over really quite quickly, and all the lunchers were got off by 2.15; after which an endless array of deputations and Mayors arrived with gold medals and daughters which they wished to present to H.R.H.

Everything was upside down, and the barge took ten minutes in coming alongside, so that H.R.H. had to wait on the Quarterdeck. Eventually, however, he got ashore at Admiralty House Steps, entered a car which was waiting, and motored to the Anzac Hostel, where he saw some twenty inmates. After this they drove to the ferry, which accommodated the motor, and they crossed over, sitting in the car, to the other side. They then drove to the Royal Naval House, which had been responsible for entertaining the men of the *Renown*. They next visited the Imperial Service Club, a returned officers show, and had tea there.

Mr Le Souëf, of the Taronga Park Zoo, sent two little ring-tailed opossums on board during the day to replace the two which had died at Melbourne. They have been christened 'Good-o' and 'Dinkum'. A lady wallaby, considerably bigger than 'Digger', was also sent by him; but as she fought 'Digger' she had to be sent back.

The Official Federal Dinner took place in the evening, and after this quite an amusing little dance, which lasted until 2.00 a.m.

The dress for this dinner was ball dress, much to H.R.H.'s disgust, as he considered it very pompous for one so young as himself; in fact, so much did he feel this that he wore mess dress in order to go on the Quarterdeck and receive the Governor-General, having to rush back and change into ball dress before dinner. After dinner everyone had to change into mess dress for the dance, as this dress had been laid down for the dance.

THURSDAY, 19 AUGUST   At about 10.20 a.m. H.R.H. visited the boys' training ship, *Tingira*. He inspected the boys on the upper deck, and shook hands with the Petty Officers, after which he made a short speech. In the meanwhile the rest of the Staff had gone over in the Staff motor boat, *Craiglea*, to Admiralty House Steps, where they were later joined by H.R.H.'s party, all then going up to say good-bye to the Governor-General. The Flag Lieutenant went on to Man-o'-War Steps, and there picked up a party consisting of Margaret Allen, Mollee Little, Aileen and Dolly Bell, Peggy Macarthur, the Captain's 'bit', and Miss Dangar. Bert Bell was the only male. They arrived on board about half past eleven, just before H.R.H. returned in the barge with the Weigalls. The 'pieces' were put under cover while the ship proceeded out, and H.R.H., accompanied by the Admiral, went to the 'special bridge' to wave to the crowds.

As *Renown* got under weigh, all the ships in the harbour sounded their sirens, and H.M.A.S. *Australia* manned and cheered ship and fired a 21-gun salute. As a matter of fact the sirens considerably interrupted the cheering. *Renown* only just managed to make the 8-point turn to port near the Heads.

After lunch everybody moved up to the reception deck and danced. Captain Barker took some cinema pictures of the dancing, and Brooks some snapshots.

About half past three it was discovered that the band, which had played without a murmur, had not had dinner; so the party broke up and retired to various rooms for the afternoon, re-assembling for tea in the after cabin. One thing which worried the Admiral rather, was the fact that the Weigalls, having to catch a train, had to leave in the *Australia*'s picket boat at a quarter to three, leaving the young ladies on board unchaperoned, but the respectability of H.R.H., the Admiral and Bert Bell combined was considered to be as effective as that of one lady chaperone.

The party were eventually taken off by the *Australia*'s picket boat at 5 o'clock, which had by then returned after landing the Weigalls.

And so ends the account of H.R.H.'s tour in Australia.

The Journey Home

FRIDAY, 20 AUGUST The day was remarkably fine and pleasant, though there was still a slight swell on. Everyone seemed rather despondent at leaving Australia, though pleased also at the idea of having actually started on the homeward journey.

SUNDAY, 22 AUGUST The cinema show was put off after dinner, and H.R.H. went down to the Wardroom for a 'Grand Jumble Sale', as the invitation put it. Everyone sat round the three sides of the Wardroom, and then entered the Commander and the Paymaster Commander dressed respectively as the Reverend Elihu Miggs and Mr Bubb Wunnie, the famous auctioneer. The Reverend Miggs addressed a short sermon to those present, and then the auction began. A sweepstake had been formed, with 2/- tickets. These had been drawn during the afternoon, and the auction was for the purpose of re-selling these tickets to the highest bidder, half the money given for the ticket going to the owner and the other half into the pool, which was to be divided among the winners. Instead of naming the owners of the tickets they were described as various articles to be sold in the auction sale. H.R.H. was described as 'a piece of Georgian furniture', the Admiral was 'a wet sponge' and 'a crumpled bow tie', Colonel Grigg as 'cuttings from *The Times* giving the history of the Grenadier Guards', Sir Godfrey as 'a straw hat from Harrow', Captain Legh as 'the ladies' "*vade me-cum*"', the Admiral's Secretary as 'a prematurely old man', and the Flag Lieutenant as 'a bull used for stalking by girls'. The tickets sold at from 5/6 to twelve guineas, H.R.H. very gallantly buying so many as to ensure losing unless getting the four winning tickets. The sum of £70 was spent during the evening, but the first prize will only be about £17.

MONDAY, 23 AUGUST At 7.00 a.m. the ship anchored in the same billet at Suva. As it was an unofficial visit, the Governor of Fiji had been asked to come off in plain clothes; but, as he had not got the message in time, he did not turn up at all, having had to go back and change into plain clothes as soon as he had reached the landing stage.

Shortly before 10 o'clock H.R.H. and all the Staff, except Captain North, who was still on the sick list, landed. After the guard had been inspected the party drove direct to Government House. The day was very pleasant and not nearly so hot as in April. The party went down to the grounds just outside Government House, where the Mayor was giving a garden party. H.R.H. stood under an enormous tree with hanging branches heavy with foliage. The most lovely sprays of lilac blossoms hung from the tree in various places, and completely took in all those who did not see the bright yellow and bright pink sprays hung in various other parts of the tree, which proved to be made of paper and hung there by the Mayor's daughter. The garden party was really a sort of popular reception of the white population, there being not more than four or five hundred people present. While this was in progress the native band played selections from their repertoire. They played very slowly indeed, in a mournful and 'tinny' air. After H.R.H. had shaken hands with quite fifty people they played the 'God Save'. This was quickly followed by the 'Robber's Chorus' from 'Chu Chin Chow'. Then came the Russian Imperial National Anthem, and then 'All people that on earth do dwell'. At this point someone went and told the band that hymn tunes were rather depressing at a garden party, whereupon they played 'Mademoiselle from Armentières'. In the meanwhile, some of the local enthusiasts tried to explain away the atrocious playing of the band by saying that native lips were not formed to produce the best results out of brass instruments.

TUESDAY, 24 AUGUST   The ship sailed at 7 o'clock. The day was fine with a nice cool breeze, so that it was not too unbearably hot.

TUESDAY, 24 AUGUST   This day was added in owing to the ship crossing the 180th meridian (International Date Line).

WEDNESDAY, 25 AUGUST   Shortly before 9.00 a.m. the ship anchored just outside the harbour of Apia, the capital of British Samoa. It had been intended that H.R.H. should land in a special native boat, but this had to be abandoned owing to the heavy swell which was running. As none of the ship's boats were hoisted out, the official landing had to be made in a local motor launch.

Eventually everyone managed to jump into the aforesaid motor boat, and no sooner had she shoved off than her engine stopped and she rapidly drifted astern. This produced yells from the Captain to the Officer of the Watch for a boat-rope, which was eventually procured, so that she was prevented from drifting right out of sight. Luckily, within five minutes they had the engine going again, and cast off the rope. The boat now began to roll and pitch and jump about, discomforting some of the party so much that they had to leave the stuffy little cabin and take refuge in the open stern sheets. In trying to get out these people were thrown from one side to the other and on top of the other occupants. Luckily H.R.H. had insisted on the military members removing their spurs before landing, but even so Captain Legh nearly transfixed Sir Godfrey with the spike of his helmet. Those who did go and sit outside got drenched with spray, in spite of wearing burberries. Inside the harbour it was fairly calm, and some half-dozen fautasis – which are long 30-oared native canoes – were well able to keep up with her at a speed of at least seven or eight knots.

Ashore there was a large congregation of natives round the landing stage, leaving an open space in the centre where returned nurses had fallen in, with whom H.R.H. shook hands. The natives had some difficulty in recognizing H.R.H., and kept asking people, 'Which is he? Which is he?' Presently, however, as he stepped forward alone to shake hands with the two principal Chiefs they recognized which was he, and cheered. The former of these chiefs is the son of the late King; but as no native Kings are allowed now, he and the other chief have been made fautuas, or chief native advisers to the Administrator. On this island, Upolu, there are about 150 white residents. All the Germans, except thirty-five who are married to Samoan women, have been deported; and these thirty-five are reputed to be the most law-abiding of all the white citizens in Upolu![1]

From the landing stage H.R.H. walked to the Court House, along an asphalt road which was rather sticky from the heat. He sent for the schoolmaster, who turned out to be a German, apparently excessively loyal to Britain, for after H.R.H. had spoken to him he ran among the school children shouting 'Cheer-*r*, cheer-*r*'. H.R.H. mounted a dais in the small Court House, and the white officials and their wives were presented to him.

The party next embarked in some very dilapidated cars and, ac-

---

[1] Samoa had been part of the German Pacific Territories until 1914 and had been administered by New Zealand since then, under League of Nations mandate from 1919.

companied by a mounted police escort, drove about a mile along the sea-front to a native village. At the outskirts the cars stopped and everyone disembarked. Two native 'jazz boxes' of enormous dimensions were being beaten, producing a most weird hollow noise. They are made of great logs of wood about 18 ins in diameter, 4 ft long, and hollowed out in the middle like a canoe. H.R.H. was taken by the chiefs out of the main road, which was lined on either side, two or three deep by natives who smelt strongly, but not too unpleasantly, of coconut oil.

On the ground they had three or four tapa cloths laid for H.R.H. to walk on. These are very fine cloths, made of the bark of the tapa tree, and various patterns are painted on them with a native red stain. When H.R.H. came to the end of the four mats he was about to place his foot on the gravel, when a shriek of horror went up from the natives and one of the chiefs pulled him back. It turned out that the horror was expressed at the idea of his foot touching the ordinary soil, and presently the tapa mats in the rear were removed and placed in front of him again. This performance was repeated many times before the dais was reached.

The native band played the 'God Save' when H.R.H. eventually arrived and the ceremonies then started. First of all kings' kava was made. Twenty important chiefs were seated cross-legged on the ground in one row, dressed in bright petticoats and wearing magnificent head-dresses, or twigas. These are made of human hair bleached in lime and are decorated with coloured parrots' feathers round the top and little mirrors in front. On the top of the head five pieces of wire bound round with coloured wool and about 18 ins high are stuck vertically upwards. In the centre sat a great big chief named Faumuina, and it was he who made the kava. He had the most enormously powerful arms, which glistened with coconut oil. Some three or four more chiefs were doing a sort of 'jazz roll' up and down in front of the sitting ranks and in between them. These were there to excite the other chiefs and make them brave for battle, and to keep away those not participating in the making of the kava. In their hands they had fearsome-looking weapons, which were like long knives with a hook curling upwards. They are called neifu otis, and are used in war for cutting off heads, and lifting them from the ground with the hook at the end afterwards. Luckily the chiefs did not, as they should have done, chew up the kava root and spit it into a bowl; but merely pretended to spit into a corked bottle, which was passed round. After the kava root had been pounded up and mixed with water, the grains of kava had to be removed from the big wooden bowl in which it was being mixed, and this was done by pieces of stripped bark from the fau tree, with which the chief who was making the kava cleaned out the bowl several times, wringing the juice out and throwing the fau over his head to a chief who was there to catch it. Eventually the drink was ready, but one man had to make five journeys from the big bowl to the cup, filling it with only a few drops at a time, before H.R.H. was given the cup to drink.

The party retired to the Fono House for lunch. This was a hut with a large dome-shaped thatched roof standing on wooden pillars. Captain Legh was immediately taken charge of by a small native girl with very little on. He did not seem to object. The remainder were looked after by either native men or women, and sat down cross-legged on the ground. The only drink that was provided was coconut milk drunk from the shell.

After this the party went to two more native houses, in the first inspecting some women at work making various native mats and baskets, and in the other house seeing some men's work. The entire floor space in this hut was taken up by a party of men who were playing a weird sort of game which consisted of throwing the tops of coconuts, highly polished, along strips of matting until they touched one another; but it was impossible to follow the rules.

After this the party were conducted to a house containing a lot of German furniture, in which some of the white people provided tea and refreshments, which consisted mainly of whisky, lemonade and sandwiches, and was a polite way of giving the party some European food, after the strange native meal.

This completed the official programme for the day, and the party once more embarked in cars and drove three or four miles inland to Vailima. This was the home of Robert Louis Stevenson, but when the Germans came they added on to it and made it into the home for their Governor. It is now used by the Administrator as Government House.[1] H.R.H. changed into flannels and set off to walk up to the summit of a neighbouring hill, where Stevenson had been buried. This would doubtless have made Stevenson laugh very much, as the only reason that H.R.H. went up to see his grave happened to be because he was buried on a hill and H.R.H. wished for some exercise. The usual time

[1] Colonel R. W. Tate, who was responsible to the New Zealand Ministry of External Affairs.

allowed to get to the summit is half an hour, but as H.R.H. did not wish to be late in leaving the shore, he managed to walk it in less than fourteen minutes. The party had tea with the Administrator and Mrs Tate. The house is full of relics of the German days; a picture of Bismarck hangs over Stevenson's favourite fireplace, and another picture of the Prussian Guard marching past the Palace of Berlin hangs outside the Administrator's bedroom.

MONDAY, 30 AUGUST   The ship arrived at the harbour entrance of Honolulu shortly after 9.00 a.m. The ship's berth was No. 9 pier, and, owing to her great length, she succeeded in using up four berths. There was also some difficulty in turning her, as one of the tugs was rather useless, and produced some choice language from the Pilot and the Captain. At 10 o'clock, however, the ship was secured; and immediately the Governor's and General's Aides and a U.S. Naval Commander paid official calls, though their chiefs very kindly refrained from doing so, as this was an unofficial visit on the part of H.R.H. The way they lapped down their whiskies and sodas reminded everyone that this was a 'dry' country.

THURSDAY, 9 SEPTEMBER   Shortly after 7.00 a.m. *Renown* entered the picturesque harbour of Acapulco and let go her anchor. The harbour is surrounded on the three landward sides by tall hills, appearing a strange bright green in the morning sun. At eight o'clock a 21-gun salute was fired, with the Mexican flag at the main, and the oiler *Fortol* came alongside the port side.

The Intelligence Department of the Staff was somewhat ill at ease in Mexican waters, as they were in considerable doubt who the present President was, or whether a revolution was in progress in Acapulco. It luckily turned out that the revolution had temporarily ceased whilst the Presidential elections were taking place.

The earliest visitors on board were the Health Officer and the British Vice-Consul. The next excitement was caused by the approach of a boat flying the Mexican flag, from which emerged five copper-coloured gentlemen, three of whom were in the most wonderful comic opera uniform with enormous cow-boy hats. No one on board had the slightest idea as to the nature of this deputation, and it was only after several of the members of the Staff had in turn engaged the party in polite conversation that their identity was discovered. It was the Military Commander of Acapulco with his Aides, accompanied by two civilian interpreters, and they had come to pay their respects to H.R.H. As no notice had been given of this call, H.R.H. happened to have no clothes on at the moment, but he eventually appeared and talked to the visitors, who then departed quite pleased with themselves.

The British and American Consuls came on board to lunch, as did the Captain of the oiler, a gentleman whose dialect caused much speculation. Several guesses were made as to his origin, some being convinced that he came from South Wales, others being equally certain that he was a Hun. However, it transpired in the course of conversation that he was a native of the northernmost part of the Shetlands.

H.R.H. went ashore shortly before two. He was met at the landing stage by a crowd of Mexicans of every conceivable colour, who did nothing but gape, and did not attempt to follow as H.R.H. struck off at a brisk pace across the plaza and down the main street of the town.

Acapulco has a population of just under 5000 and is a poor though picturesque-looking town of typically Mexican appearance. Hardly any of the houses are more than one storey high, though this may perhaps be due to the fact that the whole place was completely wrecked by the great earthquake of 1909. The inhabitants are almost entirely full-blooded Indian or 'mestizo' stock, and very few purely Spanish types are seen.

H.R.H. and his party walked through the local market and looked at some enormous sombreros, the Mexican national headgear, promising the storekeeper that they would buy some on their way back to the ship later on in the afternoon.

They then walked on through the outskirts of the town, which became more and more primitive and abounded with the most amazing type of smooth-haired, long-snouted pig. The Flag Lieutenant took a great fancy to these animals, and stopped continually to take photographs of them, his ambition being to get a picture of H.R.H. stroking one, though in this he was unsuccessful.

The explorers then got into a narrow rocky path, winding between native huts, and were getting rather lost when a rascally looking Mexican came up, and after a violent outburst in Spanish, with which Sir Godfrey was made to cope, took charge of the party. He led them on until eventually they reached an unusually well-laid metalled road, which ran between thick vegetation parallel to the mountain range.

H.R.H. started off at a terrific pace, and the rest of the party, now reinforced by three small boys, straggled along behind. From these Sir

Godfrey elicited the information that the road on which they were walking was really the permanent main line from Acapulco to Mexico City! During the recent revolution the rails had been torn up for some distance out of Acapulco, and when things quieted down the inhabitants had very sensibly come out and removed all the sleepers for firewood. The local authorities thereupon adopted the wise plan of gravelling and rolling the track, thereby forming a first-class boulevard, which must certainly be the best road in the whole province of Guerrero.

After about a mile the road emerged through a rocky cutting on to the cliffs, whence a magnificent view of the sea was obtained. Several picturesque groups of Mexican women riding donkeys with grain sacks were passed, all going in the direction of Acapulco. The heat grew more and more oppressive. H.R.H. and Colonel Grigg got farther and farther ahead. All enquiries which Sir Godfrey made from his escort pointed to the fact that the objective of the advance party was the 'tunnel', but opinions as to its distance varied between 'two minutes' and 'two kilometres'. Captain Legh suddenly ordered Sir Godfrey to ask whether there were any snakes about. It took the latter about five minutes before he could remember the Spanish for 'snake', but he was eventually assured by the head guide that there was not a snake within miles of Acapulco. Captain Legh refused to believe this and insisted on the question being repeated later to one of the small boys who came up. This gentleman stated that the bushes were stiff with poisonous serpents several yards long, but that they did not come out till dusk. Whereupon Captain Legh looked anxiously at his watch and quickened his pace.

In the meanwhile the Flag Lieutenant ran ahead to tell H.R.H. and Colonel Grigg that the time was getting on. They both, however, insisted upon seeing the tunnel, so he accompanied them. The tunnel, when they eventually came to it, was about a quarter of a mile long, with such a bend in it as to make the centre quite dark. It was rather a weird experience. One could feel a draught playing on one's face, and all round one could hear bats squeaking and jibbering. Every now and then women with donkeys would pass, sometimes with no warning and sometimes carrying a torch, which threw up grotesque shadows against the rugged sides of the tunnel.

They were soon caught up by H.R.H. and the others, everyone being now soaked to the skin by the heavy rain which began to fall. On nearing the town they were met by the two Consuls in a car, who kindly offered them a lift, but it was thought better to walk the rest of the way.

By five o'clock the ship had weighed and proceeded out of harbour.

MONDAY, 13 SEPTEMBER   At 6.00 a.m. *Renown* entered the dredged channel at Balboa. The ship proceeded direct to the Miraflores Locks. Admiral Johnston, U.S.N., was expected here, but, owing to having fallen down and dirtied his new whites, he went back to change, and so missed the ship. The lock here having been negotiated the ship proceeded through the Miraflores Lake to the Pedro Miguel Locks.

The novelty of negotiating the locks had by no means worn off, and everyone watched the working of the eight electric 'mules' with interest. They consist of long and very heavy trolley cars with a cable drum in the centre from which a large wire cable is attached to the ship. They work four each side, and help to keep the ship in position and move her along. The most fascinating part to watch is when they climb the very steep slope between the locks, as each lock is just over 28 ft higher than the previous one.

The ship reached the Gaillard (Culebra) Cut shortly before ten, having entered the high level part of the canal shortly after half past nine. The little island which had been there previously – caused by the land slide – had been dredged away, and dredgers were still at work in this part. H.R.H. came up to watch the passage of the Cut, and breathed a sigh of relief when it was over, as he had entertained secret fears of another land slide occurring, which would delay the passage home.

It was not nearly so hot as on the previous occasion; but it rained a good deal. H.R.H. consented to go by the rickety light railway via the spillway to some landing steps on the banks of the Chagres River. This river, higher up, forms the main channel through the artificial lake of Gatun. It had stopped raining, and the day was lovely. The launch proceeded down river, and H.R.H. and the Admiral got the two tarpon rods out and trolled from the stern sheets. This river is a typical tropical river, the jungle coming right down to the banks each side and presenting an impenetrable growth. It is bright green with occasional dashes of lilac or white where some plant is in flower. Alligators abound in this river, and the party were on the look out for them, and thought they spotted one or two snouts stuck up out of the water, but they might have been logs of wood, as it was hard to see near the banks. On one overhanging branch an iguana fully four feet long was lying sunning itself; and various brightly coloured birds were flying about. Everyone took turns with the rods aft, but no success was met with at all. After about an hour and a half of this the party proceeded to the mouth of the river and fished in the sea. The foreshore extending from the left bank was lined with coconut palms, and on the right beyond an old Spanish fortress there was a little cove with a pleasant sandy beach. All round here pelicans were flying and swooping down after the fish.

They had hardly got beyond the old Spanish fort when the Admiral's line ran out with a shriek of the reel. He managed to play his fish successfully, and landed a 12½ lb 'jack' fish, or kabally. The next strike was secured by H.R.H., who got very excited, as he was uncertain as to the correct thing to do; but, under the Admiral's guidance, he successfully played the fish close up to the boat. As soon as the fish was near everyone congregated round and got in H.R.H.'s way, and each other's way, and in the way of the man with the gaff, so that, although this fish should easily have been gaffed at least twice, it eventually broke away under the boat. It was estimated to be at least four feet long.

FRIDAY, 17 SEPTEMBER   *Renown* arrived at Port-of-Spain, Trinidad, at 9.00 a.m.

The Governor, Sir John Chancellor, was not due to call till 10.00 a.m., but his boat was seen coming off sometime before that and created a little consternation. His Ex., however, was only allowing himself a margin, and politely hung about in the distance until the right time. When he came on board he presented his Executive Council with great promptness and efficiency and retired at once again to the beach, as H.R.H. was due to land without delay.

It was five miles to the jetty, and very hot. On arrival H.R.H. said that he wished to shake hands with all the returned men present. There were a great many officers from British units, as well as from the West India Regiment, many of whom had come to the island recently to start civilian life there. They included an unusually large proportion of officers from the R.A.F. There were also about 300 ex-service men. H.R.H. shook hands with all, which delayed the programme for nearly half an hour, but was better worth doing than anything else in the morning's ceremonial. The proceedings were watched by a large crowd of every conceivable complexion. Theodore Roosevelt on his first landing in Trinidad, appalled by the mixture of types, ejaculated that he had never seen such awful 'racial carnage' before. It describes very well the cocktail character of the Trinidad crowd, in which every human being seems to be a blend of many different ingredients – that is all except the pure-blooded negroes and the East Indians, the latter presenting the most distinct type of all. It was noticeable, though, that few wore caste marks on their foreheads.

From the Town Hall H.R.H. drove westwards into the country through sugar and cocoa plantations where the native and Indian population was very numerous. The East Indians live in picturesque villages of considerable size. One noticed two things – complete absence of Hindu temples, and a much higher standard of comfort than the similar East Indian community maintains in Fiji. All the native and Indian population had taken great pains to decorate the road through the villages. It was, therefore, a great pity that a rather prolonged rain storm made it necessary to drive with the hoods up, so that in many places the population did not see as much as they might of H.R.H. as he went by.

The party eventually arrived at Government House, which proved to be a cool large building in very beautiful grounds maintained as a special Botanical Garden looked after by experts from Kew. All were terribly badly in need of drinks and luncheon, as it was nearly 2 o'clock, and went in without changing.

'Digger' was sent for and arrived about tea-time.

Dinner was a large function of about 60 people, including a dozen or so women. The Governor made an excellent speech, in the course of which he related an apocryphal story regarding a letter supposed to have been written home to Queen Alexandra by the King when he was first out here as a Midshipman. His Majesty was supposed to have said that he had spent a night 'in the hottest room, in the hottest house, in the hottest island in the world'. H.R.H. denied all knowledge of this story in his reply, and explained that so far as he was concerned he found the climate very agreeable.

H.R.H. and Captain Legh went to the small bathing pool where they had bathed during the afternoon and cooled themselves down before turning in. They went to the room shared by Captain Legh and the Flag Lieutenant in the cottage, to dry themselves, and there found a tarantula spider, fully 6 ins across, sitting just above Captain Legh's bed. By the aid of a landing net and stick, specially kept for the purpose, the spider was secured and slain. In the room above, which the Admiral's Secretary was using, a lizard was found under his bed, and outside the back door of the cottage the servants discovered a toad of horrific dimensions. Throughout the night, moths of varying sizes, flying ants, flying cockroaches, and many other insects buzzed round the mosquito nets, and it only remained to find a boa constrictor (which was plentiful out here) in one of the beds to make the night perfect.

SATURDAY, 18 SEPTEMBER 'Digger' got lost in the bushes, but after some two hours was recovered, apparently none the worse for his escapade. He must, however, have eaten something which had poisoned him, for he was suddenly seized with convulsions, and, although brandy was administered to him, immediately after dinner he expired. With him goes much of the gaiety of the Staff, for he was a most universally popular pet, to whom everyone had grown so used and attached that it is hard to picture life on board without him.

Poor McKenna, the wine steward, who had looked after 'Digger' since he was a little 'Joey', was much upset at hearing the news of his death.

SUNDAY, 19 SEPTEMBER H.R.H. and the Staff accompanying him to Demerara took their departure from Government House. They proceeded by barge to H.M.S. *Calcutta*. As soon as they had all safely got aboard, she weighed anchor and proceeded. Everyone on board the *Calcutta* had been most kind in giving up their cabins to make room for H.R.H.'s Staff and retinue; though, of course, these cabins appear very small after *Renown*'s.

MONDAY, 20 SEPTEMBER Towards 10.00 p.m. the ship crossed the bar at the Demerara River, with only a few inches to spare. She proceeded slowly to Georgetown, the capital of British Guiana, which is situated in the province of Demerara, and eventually berthed alongside a very rickety wharf, belonging to Booker Bros.

TUESDAY, 21 SEPTEMBER At 9.45 His Excellency the Governor of British Guiana arrived to pay his official call on H.R.H. This official came in white uniform with helmet and plumes, and a single riband of St Michael and St George, but with no neck decoration or star. On arrival at the gangway he was received with all ceremony by the Admiral, Captain and Officers, and Guard and Band; but he took no notice whatsoever of the latter, and did not even salute. After five minutes with H.R.H., this gentleman departed, walking straight over the side and again completely ignoring the salute of the guard, or the strains of the music which were played in his honour.[1]

At 10 o'clock H.R.H. and Staff landed, the Prince being received under a temporary wooden structure on the pier by the afore-mentioned Excellency, who greeted him with his hands in his pockets, whilst the guard and band furnished by the British Guiana Militia saluted.

From the landing place, the procession proceeded through great crowds of the inhabitants, who were most enthusiastic, to the Policy Building. H.R.H. was conducted to a room where there was assembled a company of about 250 ladies and gentlemen of all nationalities, colour and creed. His Excellency then proceeded to instruct a large coloured gentleman, immaculately attired in a frock coat, to read the address, which was a very lengthy epistle, giving the fullest particulars of the progress, and statistics generally, of the colony. It was with the utmost difficulty that the Prince and Staff were able to achieve what the audience found to be quite impossible, viz., not to laugh. After this address had been replied to, H.R.H. proceeded to shake hands with every individual in the room.

The personnel of Government House consisted of His Excellency and his A.D.C. and a coloured young lady, who was presented to the Prince as his Private Secretary. As was explained by His Excellency, there appeared to be some doubt as to how the Prince and Staff would be looked after, as normally only His Excellency lived in Government House, and the Private Secretary lived in a house next door, and between them they had twenty servants, but he thought the arrival of such a large party would put the twenty servants a little out of joint, though he hoped for the best.

The Prince and Staff then changed into plain clothes, preparatory to driving to the races. His Excellency's plain clothes consisted of a change of coat and hat only; the coat being a form of white Norfolk jacket, and the hat a mongrel Stetson. The *tout ensemble* might be said to have been very similar to a Hun globe-trotter, and certainly no one could possibly mistake him for such an exalted personage as the Governor of an ancient British Colony.

On arrival at the races, the Prince was met by a gentleman who, as the party discovered afterwards, was the owner of the racecourse,

---

[1] Sir William Collet, whom Mountbatten charitably refrained from identifying, should have known better. He had been in the Colonial Service all his life.

President and Committee of the Jockey Club, official starter, clerk of the course, and, in fact, general chucker-out. This gentleman directed the Prince to a special stand in front of the grand stand, which had been apparently built for the occasion, and which contained five wicker arm-chairs with large pink cushions. The horses, four in number, were then produced, and with much difficulty H.R.H. was induced to sink down into a pink cushion and watch the first race. On closer inspection it was found that the horses, unlike most race horses, were only between 14 and 15 hands, whereas the jockeys, mostly black, weighed about 9 or 10 stone, and it may be added that the riding was of an indifferent description.

On glancing at the programme it was discovered that, although there were six races, the number of different horses down to run only totalled seventeen.

After dinner, which was a very long affair, the Prince drove to the Assembly Rooms and attended a ball given by the municipal authorities. At this ball there were about 300 people, practically all being black. There was a very good band, and the floor was excellent. The Mayor was a black gentleman, the Mayoress being a particularly nice person, who, by some extraordinary mistake, was quite white, although her sister was as black as your boots. The ladies danced extremely well, but the great objection was, especially with one particular lady dressed in black, that the dye came off their dresses on to one's white uniform.

WEDNESDAY, 22 SEPTEMBER   Shortly after eleven the party embarked in motor cars, the seats of which were painfully hot, and drove to the wharf. The guard of honour of police was again drawn up, and H.R.H. inspected them. He then bade farewell to the Governor and proceeded on board, while His Excellency retired to the further end of the jetty, where he stood awaiting the ship's departure in his usual attitude.

Sharp at seven bells *Calcutta* cast off her wires, and, proceeding cautiously, again crossed the bar successfully. A mirage was observed on the port bow in the shape of a promontory, looking solid enough until examined through a telescope, which revealed some of the trees hanging in mid air, and one piece of the land to be up out of the sea altogether. On consulting the chart it was discovered that no such promontory existed anywhere near the mouth of the Demerara River.

THURSDAY, 23 SEPTEMBER *Calcutta* passed through the Bocas de Dragos shortly after 8.00 a.m. and anchored near *Renown* at 8.50.

At 9.40 H.R.H. proceeded to *Calliope*. A wait of some twenty minutes now ensued for the barge to return. Ashore the Governor met H.R.H., and the party drove to the Fire Brigade Headquarters. Immediately on arrival a loud electric gong was rung, and forthwith some thirty black men with brass helmets slid down two poles from the floor above at great speed, and jumping on to their various motors and engines tore out yet faster. One somehow expected them to fall off like the Keystone Fire Brigade in the Charlie Chaplin films, but this was far from actually occurring, for they turned out to be most efficient, and in less than no time had the hoses playing, wetting everybody with the spray. They then all fell in and H.R.H. inspected them before re-embarking and driving to Government House.

FRIDAY, 24 SEPTEMBER At 3.00 a.m. *Renown* got under way and proceeded, arriving at 9.00 a.m. off St George's, Grenada. The Governor[1] called on board at 9.30. At 10.00 a.m. H.R.H. landed in the barge. The party then proceeded in Ford cars to the Court House. It was rather a case of 'the animals went in two by two', for the Staff and visiting officers were divided up one to each car with one of the notables of the island to accompany him. At the Court House addresses were exchanged with the islands of Grenada and St Vincent.

An hour's drive, up hill all the way, through the most lovely scenery, brought the party to a large house outside which some couple of hundred black people were gathered, all shrieking and yelling. The roads were very steep and with such treacherous twists that at every bad corner half a dozen black men were stationed to push the cars round and up, as the engines invariably stopped at the critical moment. From the stopping place the party proceeded on foot for about half a mile down a very muddy and steep path, doing their best to keep a foothold, but completely giving up trying to keep their nether limbs clean. After half an hour's struggle the party came to a small and very ordinary looking lake, called the Grand Etang, which was notable for two reasons – it lies in the crater of an extinct volcano some 2000 feet above sea level, and His Majesty The King, some 40 years ago, rowed on it.

[1] Sir George Haddon-Smith.

Struggling back up the slope and re-embarking in the cars, the party returned down hill to Government House in about a quarter of the time it had taken them to get up.

SATURDAY, 25 SEPTEMBER   At 6.00 a.m. *Renown* weighed and proceeded. At 9.15 *Renown* went in close to Kingston, the capital of St Vincent, to let the inhabitants obtain a view of the ship. It was owing to an infectious disease breaking out in this island that H.R.H.'s projected visit there had had to be abandoned.

At 1.00 p.m. St Lucia was reached, *Renown* anchoring outside the small harbour of the capital, Castries. At 1.40 H.R.H. and the Governor of the Windward Islands[1] left the ship officially in the barge. On the wharf the party embarked in Ford cars. This procession was run on entirely novel lines, on the principle that 'the last shall be first and the first shall be last', for the gentlemen of the press, photographers, etc., drove in a Ford bus at the head of the procession. Next came the Admiral's Staff, followed by the rest of the Staff in reverse order of seniority, finishing up with H.R.H., the Governor and the Admiral. This would have been more successful had the inhabitants been informed that H.R.H. was driving in the last car, though perhaps this merely worked them up for a paroxysm of frenzy when H.R.H. did arrive. An escort of very inexperienced riders added to the gaiety of the proceedings, and it was with some relief that Columbus Square was reached after a ten minutes' drive round the town. Here an address from the island of St Lucia was read by the Administrator. Children then sang the 'God Bless'. It was rather amusing to hear the way they pronounced various words; there was no twang as in Australia, but H.R.H.'s name was invariably sung 'Printsoffvells'.

On arrival at Government House the party removed their swords, and went for a drive to see 'a historical view'. Some twenty minutes driving brought the party to the summit of the hill on which Government House stands, or rather not quite to the summit, but to the bottom of a grassy road about 100 yards long set on the very steep incline leading to the actual summit, and this the pilot car attempted to take. It was far too wet and slippery, however, and half way up the car started slipping backwards down the hill, with the wheels going full speed ahead. The occupants leapt out and proceeded to try and push the car up, but it only continued its downward slide, churning

---

[1] Sir George Haddon-Smith again, in a different guise.

up mud and turf and smothering everyone, the Administrator most of all. After the view had been admired, H.R.H. inspected the naval wireless station, which, although kept very clean and efficient, contains an installation of an absurdly old and low-powered type. The cars went down hill very much quicker than they came up.

About 7.00 p.m. everyone shoved off in the barge and returned to *Renown*.

SUNDAY, 26 SEPTEMBER   At 5.30 a.m. *Renown* weighed and proceeded.

At 7.30 a.m. the ship passed close to the famous Diamond Rock off Martinique. Everyone in the mess had been studying the history of this rock, which had been commissioned as a man-o'-war and held by a hundred men for two years against the French. Nearly everyone turned out to see this diminutive island, which rises perpendicularly out of the sea and does not look as though it could possibly have contained the hundred men it did.

At noon, Sir Edward Merewether, Governor of the Leeward Islands, came on board to luncheon. Shortly before two H.R.H. landed officially in the barge. The official drive took place through the streets of the capital, Roseau. The natives were as wildly excited here as anywhere, pointing at H.R.H. and shouting, 'Lookateem! Lookateem!'

MONDAY, 27 SEPTEMBER   At 8.00 a.m. *Renown* arrived off Plymouth, the capital of the Island of Montserrat.

At 11.00 a.m. H.R.H. left in the barge, landing at ten minutes past eleven. On the pier where the barge went alongside, a guard of honour of a score of blacks was fallen in, apparently arranged on the principle of putting the biggest next the smallest, which looked incongruous. After having inspected this guard, H.R.H. walked down the pier and embarked in a Ford car. Government House was reached after a three-minute drive. Here H.R.H. shook hands with one returned officer and a dozen returned men. The black children, under some Belgian priests who could only speak French, sang 'God Bless de "Printsoffvells"'.

After this the party embarked and returned to the wharf, leaving immediately in the barge and returning on board, arriving by 11.40. This is by far and away the shortest official stunt for an entire colony that has ever been done, as it lasted only twenty minutes.

FRIDAY, 1 OCTOBER   At 7.00 a.m. *Renown* anchored in Five-Fathom Hole. It was possible to see the bottom for a long while before anchoring. At 9.20, H.R.H. and all the Staff embarked in the barge and proceeded to *Calcutta*. As soon as everyone was aboard, *Calcutta* proceeded down the north-west coast of Bermuda.

H.R.H. embarked in the Commander-in-Chief's barge, and steaming round in a circle came alongside the landing stage a few yards astern of the *Calcutta*, where the official landing was made. The party got into carriages and drove off. Motor cars are forbidden in Bermuda, owing to the narrowness of the roads and the terrific amount of white dust lying about.

About half-past five H.R.H., the Flag Lieutenant and the A.D.C. went down to the swimming place to bathe, H.R.H. being stung slightly by a black snakey creature called a whipmaray.

After an official dinner the party departed for the Princess Hotel to a ball given by the Colony. This is a magnificent hotel, opened specially for the occasion, but otherwise kept permanently shut until the Season, which starts in about another month or two. The place is then invaded by rich Americans, who squander money right and left, causing prices to soar excessively. The ball was a good one, but it was exceedingly hot, and by 12.30 the party had left for home.

SATURDAY, 2 OCTOBER   The Government House gardens are most delightfully laid out; and here, for the first time, the wonderful 'blue bird', symbolical of happiness is to be seen flitting about.

At a quarter to eleven H.R.H. walked down to the Ducking Stool Steps, where the Commander-in-Chief's barge was waiting.[1] The party embarked and proceeded to the U.S.S. *Kansas*, girding themselves with swords before arriving alongside. The ship was manned, and as soon as H.R.H. set foot on the gangway buglers blew various blasts accompanied by rolls on drums. Directly H.R.H. got to the top of the gangway the 21-gun salute started, so that he and the Staff, who were spread out over the whole length of the gangway, had to stand to attention until this was finished. The party were conducted by Admiral Hughes[2] to his after cabin, 'to give time for the crew to get to their quarters', as he put it. Shortly afterwards the party proceeded on deck once more, and the bugler was, as usual, ordered to give 'one blast'. The Americans have a simple method of dealing with men who fall in

[1] Rear-Admiral Everett was acting Commander-in-Chief.
[2] Rear-Admiral Hughes, known to everyone as 'Walrus'.

incorrectly dressed or in a dirty rig – they put them in the rear rank, and this rank is, apparently, never inspected; at least, H.R.H. was not allowed to do so on this tour of inspection.

After luncheon, which was a fairly short affair, H.R.H. drove to Admiralty House, where he planted a tree, and everyone looked round the grounds. Paymaster Lieutenant-Commander Ricci, Admiral Everett's Secretary, alias 'Bartimeus', told the party that he had just written a new book called *Unreality*.[1] This is his first attempt at a novel; and the love scenes between the hero (who is the Flag Lieutenant at Admiralty House) and the heroine occur in this garden; so the party looked at it with special interest.

H.R.H. and the Flag Lieutenant played a single at the Government House tennis courts, the first two sets being very closely contested, each winning one, though H.R.H. won the match with the third set.

SUNDAY, 3 OCTOBER At ten minutes to ten everyone set out in carriages for 'Prospect Park', where a Drum-head Service was being held in the open. The *Renown* band played the hymns in the band-stand near by, without any music other than that provided in some local prayer books, which incidentally turned out to be wrong, so they finally had to play according to some music which the Bandmaster had written out overnight.

After luncheon, which was attended in plain clothes, the party set out in carriages. Presently the Devil's Hole was reached. This is a most extraordinary rock bowl, set about fifty feet back from the sea, filled with clear water direct from the sea, to which it is connected by a subterranean passage. The pool is alive with all manner of fish, principally groupers, of between 20 and 30 pounds weight. The manager gave H.R.H. a dead squid tied to a fishing line, and as soon as this was thrown into the water every fish in the place made one dart at it, colliding with each other and snapping viciously in their effort to get the bait. H.R.H. dragged it up, and with it came a tremendous fish, which presently let go and dropped back into the water. These fish are so voracious that they will attack anything. There is a tale concerning a lady who is supposed to have brought her baby in her arms when she came to see this pool. She got so excited that she dropped the child in, and it was immediately set upon by the fish and dragged down out of sight – for the bowl is a good thirty feet deep. Again, a large dog is

[1] L. A. da Costa Ricci, alias Lewis Ritchie, alias Bartimeus, wrote many successful books with a nautical setting. *Unreality* was published later in 1920.

said to have fallen in once, and to have been dragged under almost immediately never to re-appear. The only shark they had had died just previously. Several turtles were seen swimming round, and some of those prettily coloured blue angel fish. Some biscuits were handed round to be thrown in, and after these the great fish would rush, with a snap of their jaws and a whisk of their tails. It was a fascinating and rather gruesome sight.

Presently the party moved on to the Crystal Cave. Everyone descended a passage lit by electric lights, until they came to some steps which led still further down. A hundred feet below the surface they came to the most wonderful subterranean lake inside a big cave, some 250 feet long, silent and mysterious. The depth of the water varied between twenty and thirty feet, and a pontoon bridge had been constructed along the entire length of the lake, while the whole thing had been cleverly wired with electric lights. The sight was really amazing, for myriads of stalactites hung down from the low dome-shaped roof, varying in diameter from three feet to a thirty-second of an inch. They were of a salt-white colour, and glistened with moisture, and at the far end there were two or three fairy grottoes, which were really marvellous to see.

The Admiral came on board for a few minutes to take a final farewell, and then the tug returned to Bermuda, while the *Renown* weighed and shaped course for home to the accompaniment of the band playing 'Rolling Home to Merry England' and 'Take me back to dear old Blighty'.

WEDNESDAY, 6 OCTOBER   The Admiral continued his inspection, doing the Engine-Room Department during the forenoon. H.R.H., who seems to like the heat of the nether regions, also went down and followed with the Senior Engineer in the wake of the official party.

The entire Gun Room, with the exception of three unfortunate junior snotties, who were on watch or other duty, dined aft with H.R.H. After dinner everyone proceeded to the Gun Room. The junior snotties first performed the Haka, which they had been taught by Captain North and the Flag Lieutenant. For this they were stripped, but wore armlets and skirts of tow. They then did an evolution: 'Letting go the anchor'. The evening then settled down to a typical Gun Room one with H.R.H. at the drums.

FRIDAY, 8 OCTOBER   The Admiral inspected the Gunnery Department of the ship during the forenoon, H.R.H. following him round unofficially.

The rig was half whites, but the party's trousers were anything but white by the time this inspection had been finished.

SUNDAY, 10 OCTOBER   At 8.00 a.m. two destroyers joined up as escort and took station astern. A couple of hours later six more destroyers joined, three forming on either bow each side.[1] The weather was misty and there was a very strong breeze, but luckily no fog. At 6.00 p.m., within a few seconds, *Renown* and escort anchored. It is worth noting that out of the twenty-seven places visited by *Renown*, the Navigator has only been fifty-four minutes out in his reckoning, which is an average of two minutes a place!

After anchoring the Duke of York, Prince Henry and Wing Commander Greig[2] came on board to dinner, and spent the night on board. H.R.H. talked for a few minutes to the Commanding Officers of his escorting destroyers before dinner.

MONDAY, 11 OCTOBER   At 7.45 a.m. *Renown* weighed and steamed down the lines of destroyers, who manned and cheered ship as she passed. Aloft she presented a curious spectacle, for the Admiral's Flag and the Standard were flying from the fore and main respectively, the Trinity House Flag (H.R.H. being an Elder Brother) at the starboard yard-arm, the entering signal from the port yard-arm, and a paying-off pennant, 450 feet long, trailing far out into the sea from the mainmast where it had been hoisted quite incorrectly, but very effectively, alongside the Standard.

The morning was exceedingly misty, but people of Portsmouth were able to obtain a good view as the ship passed in, and crowds had collected, who cheered. The fort fired a 21-gun salute, and as the ship berthed alongside South Railway Jetty the band finished off their selections by playing 'Here we are again'. The officers then changed into frock coats and swords, H.R.H. said good-bye to the men, and shook hands with the officers. Guards of Honour next arrived, the naval guard from the barracks trying hard not to be put off in their

---

[1] One of the destroyers was H.M.S. *Wishart*, which Mountbatten was to command in 1934-5.
[2] Wing Commander Louis Greig was Comptroller to the Duke of York and his partner in winning the Royal Air Force tennis championship.

above: Renown dressed overall and manned.

below: The clink of teacups at a typical garden party: Government House, St Lucia (25 September 1920).

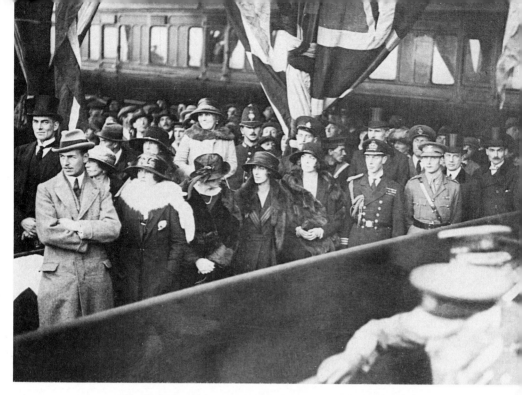

above: The departure for India, watched (from left to right) by Harold Wernher, Nada Milford Haven, Zia Wernher, Louise Mountbatten, Edwina Ashley, The Duke of York and Prince Henry (26 October 1921).

below: Captain North, Mountbatten and Sir Godfrey Thomas exercise with pogo sticks as *Renown* nears Gibraltar.

above: H.R.H. being wheeled by Mountbatten in the King's Messenger Race in Malta (2 November 1921).

below: In the Crater at Aden, with evidence of the parsees' loyalty in the background (12 November 1921).

above: Arrival at the Gateway of India in Bombay. H.R.H. shakes hands with the Viceroy, Lord Reading (17 November 1921).

below: Nautch girls resting after a dance in the palace at Bikaner (2 December 1921).

slow swinging step by the quick step played by the 60th Rifles' Band for the military guard which was provided by that regiment.

The Commander-in-Chief, Admiral Hon. Sir Somerset Gough-Calthorpe, next came on board, followed a few minutes later by the Marquess and Marchioness of Milford Haven and Lady Louise Mountbatten.[1] These parties gradually returned ashore, until finally, at 10.15 a.m., H.R.H. disembarked from a steep and slippery scarlet covered brow. An address (the last this trip, to the Staff's great grief!) was read by the Mayor of Portsmouth, and after H.R.H. had read his reply, the party embarked in the train, which left at 10.30 a.m. to the accompaniment of the most genuinely sounding cheers heard this trip – to whit, the farewell cheers of the ship's company of *Renown*.

A couple of hours' run brought the train to Victoria Station. As soon as the train stopped Their Majesties The King and Queen entered the train and greeted H.R.H. H.R.H. was the first to leave the train, followed by Their Majesties and his two brothers. Most of the Royal Family, Cabinet and Chiefs of the Services were present.

Two semi-state carriages had been provided. H.R.H. received the most tremendous ovation from the crowd, and having driven via Parliament Square and Trafalgar Square to Buckingham Palace, he remained to luncheon there. A great crowd had collected outside, and he made a short speech to them after lunch; having to make another one to another crowd from his rooms at St James's Palace on his return there.

The trip is over. The party are already beginning to feel homesick for the old ship. The tour has been such an amazing success that 'hot-air' words in this irresponsible diary would be superfluous and out of place.

To finish up with the usual statistics, the ship steamed another 4 miles from Spithead to South Railway Jetty; but as the distance given for the day before had allowed for these 4 miles, it leaves the total sea distance travelled by H.R.H. 35,653 miles, of which 34,811 miles were steamed on board H.M.S. *Renown*, 795 miles on board H.M.S. *Calcutta*, and 47 miles on board H.M.A.S. *Anzac*. The overland distances already given came to 9844 miles (not including any of the distances driven in the West Indies, etc.), and this brings the grand total number of miles travelled by H.R.H. on his tour to 45,497 miles. The time actually spent at sea since leaving Sydney the last time is 37

---

[1] Mountbatten's parents and his sister, the future Queen of Sweden.

days 2½ hours, and the total time spent at sea during the trip, 84 days 14½ hours, of which all except 2 days 4½ hours were spent on board H.M.S. *Renown*. The oil fuel consumed since leaving Sydney is 16,622 tons; making total oil fuel consumed for the trip (with H.R.H. actually on board) 35,796 tons. Seventeen towns or places were visited on the trip back; making total number of towns and places visited 208. The trip occupied 210 days.

II

India,
The Far East
and Japan

26 October 1921 to 21 June 1922

The original plan had been that the Prince of Wales's tour of Australasia should be followed almost immediately by a visit to India and Japan. Strong protests by the Prince and various other factors led to the modification of this plan; the Prince was to be allowed a year at home before setting off again.

Mountbatten was determined to form part of the team again, and was lobbying all and sundry before Renown had even reached Australia. The Prince was strongly in favour of the idea – 'David wants me as a friend,' Mountbatten told his father. The official reason was that at first it seemed as if Admiral Halsey would not be accompanying the party and the Prince thought it essential that Captain North should not be the only naval officer on his staff. By the time Halsey was reinstated it was taken for granted that Mountbatten would be on the tour, this time as 'a pukka Flag Lieutenant!'

For the Indian leg of the tour the Prince's entourage was reinforced by Lord Cromer, son of the great proconsul, banker turned courtier, and a man of considerable experience and common sense. Halsey, North, Godfrey Thomas, Legh and Dr Newport survived from the Australian team; Sir Geoffrey de Montmorency of the Indian Civil Service was attached to provide some local expertise; and the Hon. Bruce Ogilvy took the place of Lord Claud Hamilton. Mountbatten was now an established member of the party and encountered less resentment than on his first expedition: 'I can assure you that things couldn't be going better,' the Prince of Wales told Lady Milford Haven, 'and that he's getting on very well with the rest of the staff who are *not only nice to him but recognize him as my personal A.D.C.'*

Possibly alarmed by the near-disaster that had befallen Mountbatten's record of the Australasian tour, Halsey did not suggest that an unofficial diary would again be desirable. Nevertheless, Mountbatten decided to keep one for the satisfaction of himself and of his closest family. 'I am making it very full and personal, just like a letter,' he told his mother. The chronicle which resulted was less studied than his previous effort and, being intended for a much more restricted circle, considerably franker. It is still a young man's production, with all that that implies in the way of brashness and intolerance, but the Mountbatten of October 1921 was wiser and more generous than he had been twelve months before.

Events of great importance to him happened between the two tours. His father died suddenly in July 1921, shortly after visiting his son aboard H.M.S. Repulse. Lord Milford Haven had been ill for some time and had never fully recovered from the shock of his enforced resignation as First Sea Lord, but to his son he was still the repository of infinite wisdom and authority. Mountbatten's brother, Georgie, Earl of Medina, now became Marquess of Milford Haven. Mountbatten would have felt the loss more severely if he had not, a few weeks earlier, met an intelligent, beautiful and dynamic girl called Edwina Ashley, who, to add to her other attributes, was known to be heiress to her grandfather, the great financier Sir Ernest Cassel.

By the time the journey to India began Edwina and Mountbatten were, if not engaged, then not far away from it. Mountbatten told his mother that he was reasonably sure Edwina would be prepared to marry him, and only the fact that his father had so recently died inhibited him from formally proposing. He undertook not to take any further steps until he was back in England, but his resolution wavered when Edwina announced that she was coming out to India to stay with the Viceroy, Lord Reading, and would be in Delhi at the same time as the royal visit.

The Journey Out

WEDNESDAY, 26 OCTOBER 1921   Aunt Louise[1] came and fetched me at St James's Palace in her car at 11.15. After having driven all round London we eventually reached Victoria Station punctually at 11.45. Most of the Talent in the Country had already assembled at Number 7 Platform. Nearly all the family were there, already busy kissing each other 'Good Morning'. About 5 minutes later David arrived with Bertie and Harry, followed shortly afterwards by the King and Queen. The latter were both very charming to me, condoling about Papa and enquiring about Mama. Presently the 'Good Bye' kissing started, though in this case not entirely confined to the family! and then we all got into the train. Bertie was accompanied by Louis Greig and Harry. It is with deep regret that I have to record on the first page of this little diary that a very mild cocktail proved rather too much for the 'Young Duke' and his hilarity knew no bounds throughout the journey down. However, it kept us all amused at a time when some of us anyhow were feeling rather sad. Luncheon was served in the train, immediately after passing Horsham. At this place David leant out of the window and waved to all the little Blue Coat boys. He threw *The Times*[2] at them and the ensuing scrap for little bits, as souvenirs, may be imagined.

The train arrived a few minutes before 2.00 p.m. Matters were so well arranged that practically no delay took place before proceeding onboard.

The Naval School of Music, who have provided the band for this trip, have had a new uniform invented for them by the so-called 'Welfare' Committee. It is somewhat reminiscent of the old Hungarian Band Uniform, having light blue facings on an ordinary Marine's tunic. However they played very well. The 'alert' was sounded by a dozen

---

[1] Mountbatten's great-aunt, Princess Louise, Duchess of Argyll.
[2] At the similar point on the last trip it had been the *Mail*. A higher tone was evidently now being struck in the royal party.

buglers from the Regimental Drum and Bugle Band which we have on board, and sounded most effective.

The next hour was spent in leave takings. Nada had brought a party to see me off – Edwina, Louise, Zia and Harold,[1] and I now went to the jetty to fetch them onboard. I took them up to my cabin, into which they all managed to squeeze somehow or another.

Presently Bertie and Harry drifted along and invited the whole party to go into the After Cabin. I was much touched at so many people coming to see me off until I discovered that their real reason for coming onboard was to read such weekly papers as they did not take in.

David came in for a few minutes to talk to them, but spent most of his time writing letters. At 3.30 my party went ashore. The wind had held up the tide and consequently our departure, originally fixed for 3.50, was delayed twenty minutes. Eventually we slipped our wires and to the strains of 'Auld Lang Syne' went ahead. David and I stood on the Reception Deck, aft, until we were clear of the jetty, when he went to his little bridge up forward, but I stayed aft and watched my party through my telescope till they disappeared from view among the crowd. I then went up and joined David aloft.

We certainly had a grand send off. All the foreshore was black with people and many steam boats and tugs followed us out crowded with enthusiastic well-wishers. As we shoved off *Victory* and all ships in harbour fired a 21-gun salute. At Spithead we fell in with *Dunedin*, a light cruiser who is to escort us. She took up station 4 cables astern.

David dispensed with the band for dinner as no one was feeling in the mood for music. It is rather terrible to think that it will be eight long months before we get home again. However I do realize how very, very lucky I am to be coming on this wonderful tour and I don't suppose there can be one fellow in the whole service who wouldn't change with me like a shot if he were given the chance.

THURSDAY, 27 OCTOBER There was a slight swell running in the 'Bay' but the ship did not move very much. Most of the usual recreations indulged in at sea were started today, such as squash, deck hockey, clay pigeon shooting, etc. I layed out one of the jig-saw puzzles I had brought, which helped to keep some of the party occupied. The

---

[1] Nada was Mountbatten's sister-in-law, now Lady Milford Haven. The others were Edwina Ashley; Louise Mountbatten; Zia, Nada's sister; and Zia's husband, the millionaire Harold Wernher.

greatest success, though, was scored by the 'pogo' sticks. Nearly everyone, including David had a go, mostly with indifferent results, except as regards blisters on the hands, which were splendid in every case.

FRIDAY, 28 OCTOBER The sea went down completely during the night and the weather has become noticeably warmer. We sighted the coast of Portugal during the forenoon, and about lunch time a Portuguese Man-o'-War passed us without taking any notice of the Standard or Ensign. However as there appears to be a pleasant little revolution in progress in that country and the Navy has so far played a leading part, this was only to be expected.[1]

After dinner we had the 'jazz band' in for the first time, and they really proved the greatest success. They consist of piano, saxophone, banjo, trombone or water whistle, violin and drums. David played the drums himself for the last two tunes – 'My Mammy' and 'Humming' – and very well too. It made my feet itch to dance to listen to the band and reminded me so of the happy week-end we spent at Dunrobin in December.[2] In fact I felt quite 'home-sick'.

SATURDAY, 29 OCTOBER We were met by a flotilla of destroyers early this morning, who joined up with *Dunedin* to escort us in.

At 10 a.m. the Governor, Sir Horace Smith-Dorrien, paid his official call. At 11 a.m. David and the whole Staff landed officially. We proceeded at a slow pace through Main Street, which was crowded, mostly with Gibraltarians. Their form of respectful welcome is not to shout and cheer, as in Australia, but to remove their head-gear and bow. I vaguely remembered Main Street from having lived out at Gib in 1906, when Papa had the *Drake*, but I could not recollect at which hotel we lived. We then drove via the eastern beach and Catalan Bay to Monkey's Quarry, which is the site for the new Admiralty Oil Tanks. We got out, while the cars were being turned, as the road ends here and looked at a cave, which I seem to remember having seen some fifteen years ago. The Rock is an amazing place, especially at the North End, where the cliff rises sheer to many hundreds of feet. Near the frontier gate a respectful crowd of Spaniards were drawn up, kept back by the Spanish Gendarmes. These Gendarmes wear a very queer

---

[1] A dress rehearsal for the coup that in 1926 overthrew the government and brought Dr Salazar into office.
[2] At which Edwina Ashley had been present.

rig, with a hat just like Napoleon is always depicted as wearing. Shortly before 1.00 p.m. we took our official departure.

As soon as David had shifted into khaki and the N.O.s had removed their epaulettes we all went ashore again. David proceeded straight to the Convent for lunch with the Governor. The rest of us drove up to the Rear-Admiral's House, the Mount, for lunch.

After lunch the others joined us at the Mount, where they made David plant a young palm. Thence we proceeded by car along a very dusty road, to the detriment of our frock coats, to the Buena Vista Barracks where two companies of the Middlesex were fallen in for David to inspect. While there I met a lieutenant of the Regiment, who seemed to know who I was as he informed me that he had been the first British Officer to enter Ekaterinenburg, three days after the ghastly murders. He said he had himself seen the relics of Uncle Nicky, Auntie Alix and the children, and later the remains of Auntie Ella.

After the inspection we drove to the Alameda Parade Ground, which I remembered quite distinctly and here the usual school children stunt took place. All the usual features were there. First David walked amongst them, then they sang the 'God Bless' and the 'God Save', finishing up with a grand march past. Unfortunately the Colonial Secretary was wearing a uniform much more similar to the clothes of a 'fairy tale' Prince having, among other things, ostrich feathers in his hat, with the result that a number of children were firmly convinced that he and not David was the Prince of Wales.

At 6.00 p.m. we all returned and shifted into mess dress. At 7.45 we gave a dinner party of 34 people, which caused me a lot of trouble. I got no thanks either, as David cursed me afterwards for putting the Spanish Governor[1] next to him, which I had been told to do. We sailed at 10.00 p.m. for Malta.

SUNDAY, 30 OCTOBER The Admiral is taking out a most delightful little Sealyham. Its real name is David, and I always call it this but David insists on calling it Dickie. Anyway the Admiral was airing his dog on the reception deck early this morning when he beheld what must be quite the most drastic way of teaching a cat clean manners. One of the ship's cats had apparently messed some sailor's favourite piece of brightwork. The infuriated matelot calmly lifted up the offending feline, walked to the side with it and dropped it overboard!

---

[1] The Governor of Algeciras, José Villalba.

Charles of Belgium,[1] who is a snotty onboard, came up to see me today. He is quite a nice boy but, my word, he is a stopper. He came to my cabin in the afternoon watch and stopped till well on into the last dog. However I gave him some papers to read in the end and carried on work on the Malta Programme.

David came in to see him for a moment and rendered Charles completely speechless from fright.

David must have consumed an unusual number of cocktails tonight, as when I came in later on I found him actually writing a letter (a thing he rarely does and only then under the greatest provocation). This one was to the Queen of the Belgians to tell her how her son was getting on onboard.

MONDAY, 31 OCTOBER   I sent out six invitations for dinner today, and among others I sent one to Charles of Belgium. Presently he came up to my cabin and asked to be excused for tonight as he wasn't feeling very well. I therefore sympathized with him and struck his name off the list, substituting another. It was only later that I heard that Charles's shirt was dirty and he had not had time to have it washed!

TUESDAY, 1 NOVEMBER   The clocks were put on half an hour early this morning, but as no chits were sent round to the Staff about this, we were all at least half an hour late for breakfast. In fact by the time I appeared on deck we were half way up the Grand Harbour of Valletta. Most of the big ships of the Mediterranean Fleet were present, except Georgie's[2] ship the *Cardiff*, who must needs be at Constantinople. The usual calls were paid commencing at 9.30, but as this is not an official record I do not intend to lumber up these pages with monotonous accounts of 'calls', etc. I will just mention, however, that the C-in-C (de Robeck)[3] brought George,[4] who is a snotty in the flagship, over with him. David at once put him (George) on his personal staff, so that he could be with us the whole time.

A drive along the harbour and up through Floriana to Valletta followed, with occasional stops to allow the numerous groups of school children to get the 'God Bless' off their chests.

[1] Prince Charles was second son of King Albert I, and acted as Prince Regent from 1944 to 1950 while his brother, King Leopold, was in exile.
[2] Mountbatten's brother, the Marquess of Milford Haven.
[3] Admiral (later Admiral of the Fleet) Sir John de Robeck was Commander-in-Chief of the Mediterranean Fleet and also High Commissioner in Constantinople.
[4] Prince George, later Duke of Kent.

The procession then moved down Strada Reale, the main and least narrow street in the capital, Valletta. The streets were packed with enthusiastic crowds. The splendid part about the Maltese is that they do not shout and cheer very much but clap to show their appreciation, and this is incredibly restful after the yelling crowds of Australia.

We all formed up on the main staircase of the Palace and removed our head-gear. The procession then walked along the corridor to the ball room, which was acting as a temporary abode for Parliament. The Governor[1] first read the Authority from the King for David to open the Parliament (signed by Winston Churchill[2]) and then David delivered his speech, declaring the first Parliament of Malta to be formally opened. The whole proceedings were interspersed by continual and lengthy fanfares from the Royal Malta Artillery, which didn't really assist matters very much. As soon as the formal declaration had taken place, all the bands played the 'God Save', all ships fired a 21-gun salute and finally all the inhabitants went quite mad and rushed round cheering like lunatics. All the Maltese are inordinately pleased at the idea of having their own Parliament, though I am certain that most of them don't in the least understand what a Parliament is yet.[3]

Charles of Belgium turned up at 12.55 and reported to me, as I had undertaken in a weak moment to pilot him through the lunch given by the local club, the Casino Maltese, to which we had all been invited. I had warned him when he came over to see us a month ago that he would require a respectable outfit of plain clothes and so was much annoyed to find him wearing uniform boots and gloves with his old grey suit. Shortly after 1.00 we all walked over to this 'Casino'. They had not thought of providing any place for our hats so we had to leave them on the floor of the hall. Lunch was served at one of the longest tables I have ever seen. As was to be expected, they had asked half as many people again as could possibly sit down in comfort. To get in at all, one had to stand in front of one's chair till all the people in the immediate neighbourhood were ready, then, at a given signal, everybody pulled their chairs up and sat down together. Once in position there was no chance whatever of moving one's body, though by great feats of skill one managed to work one's hands so as to get

---

[1] Field Marshal Viscount Plumer, veteran of Ypres, Passchendaele, and other blood-soaked fields.

[2] who was briefly in charge of the Colonial Office.

[3] The Maltese were perhaps best left in ignorance. Their 'Parliament' had only the most limited responsibility for local affairs.

on with the food. However a purely native show like this is very good 'propaganda', which one must not forget in passing judgement.

After half an hour's rest at the palace we all embarked in cars once more and proceeded to the Governor's country residence, San Antonio, which possesses the most lovely gardens. A garden party was held here, which George and I found so terribly boring that we went into the orangery and ate oranges.

We had brought the two Welsh Guardsmen out with us, still in full dress, while we were in plain clothes. They drove back in the car immediately behind mine. Presently we came to a party of libertymen, ashore from the fleet, lounging about. They took no notice of David or of us, but when they saw the orderlies, with their scarlet tunics and bearskins, they at once straightened up and saluted smartly!

We returned to the ship where we shifted into naval ball dress and landed again at 7.30. Some of the staff dined with the Lieutenant Governor; I belonged to the palace party and sat next to the Prime Minister.[1] After dinner we drove to the Opera House and sat through two acts of Aida. It was well given but to my mind it does not compare to any of Wagner's operas. Afterwards David and the staff went on to a dance given at Admiralty House, but, as I don't want to dance just yet so soon after Papa's death, I returned to the ship.

WEDNESDAY, 2 NOVEMBER   At 10.00 a.m. all the Naval Party proceeded in the barge to Sheer Bastion Steps and then walked along the Dockyard Tunnel to Teccarteen Steps, whither the barge had already proceeded. The whole route was lined with some 4000 Maltese Dockyard Maties, who clapped and cheered incessantly.

We looked over the new Fleet Education Centre, and were much impressed by the various classes we found at work there. It was only afterwards that I privately heard that as no regular classes were working that day, the Commanders of neighbouring ships had to hurriedly tell off classes at 'Both Watches' to fill up the various class rooms.

Lunch took place at Admiralty House, 51 Strada Mezzodi. As we used to live at 42, I was especially interested to be going to lunch next door. I remembered everything fairly well, though the street seemed considerably narrower. This is probably due to my having grown considerably since 1908. I sat next to Miss Tyrwhitt, the daughter of

[1] Mr Joseph Howard.

Georgie's Admiral,[1] and asked her to be my partner, in a polo and golf ball contest, which one could not enter without a lady as partner. Immediately after lunch we all drove off to the Marsa, where a gymkhana was being held.

The first event was this competition, for which I had entered. I was mounted on a very nice black pony, and we had to hit a polo ball through three goals. As soon as the polo ball was through the last goal the lady holed out with a golf ball. We ran this off in heats and I regret to say that I was a good last in my heat. What is more my wrist ached considerably before we got half way round.

Perhaps the most amusing contest of the day took place at the finish, after tea. This was called the King's Messenger Race. We entered a Staff Team, David being the King's Messenger. He first had to run 20 yards in a sack, then mount a mule bareback, which was held by Captain North. After riding with great difficulty in a more or less straight line for 100 yards the beast was caught by Montmorency. David then jumped into a stretcher, in which Godfrey and Bruce carried him for 50 yards. Joey Legh was holding a pony for him and he cantered on for another 50 yards. Here George caught the pony while David literally flung himself into a wheelbarrow, which I was holding. I wheeled him for 20 yards and then tipped him out. We were the first barrow in our heat across the line, but in the 50-yard sprint that followed the Destroyer Sub-Lieutenants' team caught up. Even so we might have won but for the Admiral's scrupulous honesty. The Admiral was driving our Carozzin and refused to start until David had actually got inside, while the before-mentioned team drove their Carozzin out to meet their King's Messenger. However, we came in a good second.

THURSDAY, 3 NOVEMBER   We sailed about 9.00 a.m. The fleet once more manned ship and cheered as we passed, also firing a 21-gun salute.

The whole foreshore, wherever such a thing exists, was black with people, as were also the two barraccas. They all made a great noise as we passed.

It was a nice fine day with a stiffish breeze, which helped to keep the ship cool.

[1] Rear-Admiral Sir Reginald Tyrwhitt, at that time commanding the third light cruiser squadron. His daughter Mary was in due course to become Director of the Women's Royal Army Corps.

FRIDAY, 4 NOVEMBER   We had one of the 'Press-Knights' aft today for dinner, a most charming man representing the *Daily Express* – Sir Percival Phillips.[1] Apropos of these 'Press-Knights', it is worthy of mention that the other one, Sir Herbert Russell,[2] complained bitterly in the Ward Room, after he had been up to dinner, that the Padre was put on David's right while he (a knight of the British Empire) had been put on the left. To make matters worse, Janion (the Admiral's late Secretary who is taking passage out in us) addressed him as 'Steve' and smacked him on the back, whereupon Sir Herbert drew himself up and demanded to know who was being addressed. On being assured that he himself was referred to he stalked out of the Mess.

SATURDAY, 5 NOVEMBER   Another fine and cool day. Shortly after 1.00 p.m. we entered the narrow entrance to the harbour of Port Said. By 1.30 we were secured, head and stern, to buoys off the Suez Canal Company's Offices.

We drove in cars through the picturesque town to the Governor's residence, where some police horses were in readiness. Port Said used to be a filthy place, but it has improved enormously under the British regime. I was fascinated by everything I saw, as I had never been as far east before. The men nearly all wear a long garment, like a coat and skirt in one, called a 'gallabeah' I believe. Of course one has seen pictures of the yashmaks the women wear, but I had never noticed that they use a piece of wood, not unlike a clothes peg, to support the front of the veil. It fits over the nose and to my mind spoils the effect of the yashmak. However, to proceed, we mounted at once and set off at a brisk canter towards the point, some miles off. I rode a very nice little arab, with rather a queer short canter, which was quite comfortable, when one got used to it. Once or twice we nearly ran into some quicksands, but on the whole the going was good. There were several natives paddling in the surf, pushing what looked like a plough before them, or pulling it. It turned out that they were shell-fishing, and I hear that it is a highly unprofitable industry, so why they do it I cannot imagine.

---

[1] A journalist of American birth, distinguished mainly by the length of his entry in *Who's Who*.

[2] The Reuter correspondent, whose book about the tour, *With the Prince in the East*, is a miracle of obsequious pomposity.

There was a big dinner tonight, which gave me a lot of trouble. Many prominent Egyptians, with unpronounceable names, appeared, who all kept their fezzes on during dinner. After dinner a further boat-load of prominent citizens and notable sheiks came off. And so to bed, feeling somewhat weary.

SUNDAY, 6 NOVEMBER At 6.45 a.m. we slipped from our buoys and proceeded up the Suez Canal. I regret to say that as I did not turn out till 8.45 I do not know what the upper reaches are like. As the canal has presented an almost unvarying panorama of sand, palms and deserted British ammunition dumps for the rest of the day, I do not think that I can have missed anything thrilling during the first two hours. All the same it is a most interesting experience to pass through the canal, all the more so when one has already passed through the Panama Canal, which is very different, the latter passing through hilly country, with three locks at each end, while this canal passes through the flattest country imaginable.

I was afforded my first view of an Egyptian desert, and was surprised to find that it undulates considerably, whereas the only other desert I have ever seen, the Nullarbor Plain, in Australia, was flat as my hat. The canal is 86 miles long, as opposed to the Panama Canal which is only 45, consequently it meant taking two days to pass right through, and we anchored for the night in the Bitter Lake, about 5.00 p.m.

A 40-knot Thornycroft hydroplane, belonging to the Canal Company, shot past the ship and David had a signal made to her to ask if she would give him a trip. He and the Admiral then went round the lake and later, when it was dark, Bruce, some of the ship's officers and myself went in her. It was a wonderful sensation and I was lucky enough to steer.

MONDAY, 7 NOVEMBER We weighed and proceeded at about 9.30. It is beginning to get considerably warmer, but the heat is not yet oppressive. The yellow sand against the blue of the sky is a really lovely combination, and the waters of Suez Bay, which we reached about 1.30, added the finishing touch, a sort of bright blue-green, which I have never before beheld off a picture postcard.

Our stay at Suez had been made entirely unofficial to the supreme grief of all the local officials, and we were therefore able to land without delay. The Thornycroft speed boat had been placed at David's disposal and we therefore landed in that, which considerably added to the joy of going ashore.

TUESDAY, 8 NOVEMBER We landed in the speed boat, lunched in the Officer's Mess at the Base and set off almost immediately afterwards for a long hard ride. On the way back we came to some jumps, which we went over. David lent me his horse for part of the time and I must say it was a beautiful jumper though none of the other horses were much good.

We sailed at 5.00 p.m.

WEDNESDAY, 9 NOVEMBER Today was infinitely the hottest day of the trip so far. Everyone has been lounging about, trying to make up their minds to do some work. I tried hard and regret to have to say that I failed, until sunset. Talking of sunsets, I have rarely, if ever, seen quite such a beautiful one, as we had today.

We have all started wearing helmets. They have rigged the sea water baths again, only much better and deeper ones this time. It was a great relief to plunge into one of these great canvas baths.

Joey gave David a hit on his right wrist whilst playing squash with him the other day, and playing polo at Malta on top of it has made it rather bad, so that he has to have it massaged. He has not been able to play squash lately either and so to help him get exercise and to relieve the boredom of just running round the reception deck I rigged up some jumps, by laying basket chairs on their side, and we hurdled over these.

THURSDAY, 10 NOVEMBER Another stiflingly hot day. Even the sea looks lazy, and has a heavy, almost oily appearance. David was allowed to play squash with his left hand today and I played with him. I am pretty bad at squash (as at most things) but David's left hand was so erratic that I had no difficulty in beating him, although we were not really playing for points. Afterwards I floated in the big bath, which was most pleasant.

I forgot to mention the other day that Captain North caused consternation among the poorer members of the Staff by announcing that he was taking 150 shirts ashore with him. He explained that one could not do with less as the Indian dhobies use dirty water to wash clothes in and all one's shirts go yellow. They also have a much simpler way of tearing shirts, it appears, as they simply use a brick to scrub the fronts with.

We are all busy learning Hindustani and I am bringing out a leaflet in conjunction with Montmorency, our tutor, of simple phrases, etc., such as *'Button kamiz men legado'*. This means 'Put buttons on that chemise', in other words, 'Put studs in that shirt'. We even talk it at dinner.

FRIDAY, 11 NOVEMBER   It was very pleasant sleeping on deck and now I cannot imagine why I did not do so days ago.

The Padre held quite a nice little service, with just a few prayers and an address. At 11.00 the bugle band, with muffled drums, sounded the Last Post and then we had the two minutes' silence observed everywhere throughout the Empire on Armistice Day. At the close the Reveille was sounded and we had another hymn. Altogether a fine service, although the bugle band was not up to its usual standard.[1]

SATURDAY, 12 NOVEMBER   At 5.45 a.m. David and I had to shift our camp beds between decks as they had to rig the main derrick guys for hoisting out the barge. This gave us an unexpected opportunity of seeing Aden and its island in the rosy light of dawn. The volcanic mountain crags looked magnificent, silhouetted against the glowing sky, and even at that hour in the morning it made one feel quite poetic. Funnily enough I had mentally pictured Aden as a town built on the fringe of a low, flat desert and it was an agreeable surprise to find it a sort of second Gibraltar.

We landed officially in the barge at 9.15. The party then drove off in motor cars, the seats of which were painfully hot. Inside the big hall there are a number of pillars, and at each of these stood a fine big Indian Cavalryman, with lance complete. Four of the leading arab rulers were then received by David. First came H.H. Sultan Sir Abdul Karim bin Fadl bin Ali, K.C.I.E., The Abdali and his small son. They were both magnificently attired in purple, scarlet and gold robes, though the effect was somewhat spoilt in the case of the little one owing to his wearing patent leather button boots, with calf uppers. A third gentleman followed them, who looked very similar, save that his garments were not so gorgeous. David waited nervously in the middle

---

[1] The diary gives little hint of the Prince's sometimes almost suicidal gloom. On this day Mountbatten told his mother: 'David goes through his black phases more often than ever now – poor chap!'

of the room, while all three made deep bows, touching their foreheads with both hands at the same time. He then came forward and shook hands with the father and the son, after which he tried to do this with the third person, who however retired with much shakings of his head. This was lucky, as it turned out to be the native interpreter, and had he allowed David to take his hand in the presence of the Chiefs it would have been an insult to them.

Next came the oldest man I have ever seen, Sultan Husein bin Ahmed, The Fadli. He is reputed to be 109 years old, but as he was only 101 when the *Malaya* was out here last year I fear this is an exaggeration. Nevertheless it is quite credible that he is over 100 as he needed an officer to support him and looked very old and wizened. During the war he could not make up his mind whether to be British or Turkish in his sympathy, so he himself remained in his own territory while he sent his son to the Turks and his grandson to the British at Aden. As his country comes under the sphere of our influence we have, not unnaturally, objected to his son becoming regent, and it was his grandson, a very fine-looking fellow, who accompanied him this time. The son is naturally not over-pleased with his father, though Sultan Abdul Kader, The Fadli, which is the name his grandson rejoices in, is delighted.

We now drove back in reverse order, David coming last, past the landing steps to the Crescent. Here there were some 1500 troops on parade, which David inspected. It was here that I saw for the first time that nice old custom of the Indian Officers, when they come up for presentation. Each officer half draws his sword and presents the hilt to David as a token of his allegiance. David then touches the hilt to signify that he accepts the allegiance and that the sword may be returned.

We now formed up, two by two, and advanced in reverse order to the Reception Shamiana. This was a raised platform, covered by a richly hung awning, in the centre of which stood a gigantic high-backed throne, in which they evidently expected David to sit. Needless to say he did not do so. A peculiar feature of the platform was that it was built so as to include a statue of our mutual great-grandmother.[1]

Addresses were exchanged and then we all motored back to the Prince of Wales Pier, where the Guards were still drawn up. We returned to the ship in the barge.

[1] Queen Victoria.

I met a most delightful old parsee at lunch, who knew Papa. He is quite a character here and is said to own half the place, but the two things that I liked best about him were his hat, which was a black (with white speckles), shiny, weird-shaped affair, supposed to resemble the hoof of the sacred cow, and his name, which he spelt Hormusjee Cowasjee Dinshaw.

We motored to the Crater where another part of the town lies. This is in point of fact the oldest part and is Aden, proper, the modern part being called Steamer Point. Aden is really a small rock peninsula connected to the mainland only by a narrow sandy isthmus. The Turk actually got to within 5 miles of the place during the war. The winding road leads up to an artificially cut mountain pass in the side of the great crater. This pass is spanned at one point by a bridge carrying the strong wall built to protect the original British part from raids.

We stopped where the path leads to the Tawela Tanks, and here the 1st Yemen Infantry were drawn up on parade. This is one of the few, if not the only, British regiment recruited from the arabs. They looked very smart in khaki, with shorts; their head-dress is peculiar to themselves, as it consists of a puggaree wound into a point on one side, with a green and white striped piece of cloth hanging down on the other.

While David was inspecting them I looked about and saw a banner, which had been hung out by the parsees, bearing these words: 'Tell Daddy We Are All Happy Under British Rule'.

The most interesting part however were the Tawela Tanks themselves. To quote the inscription on a recently erected tablet: 'These Tanks, regarding the origin of which nothing is accurately known, were accidentally discovered by Sir Lambert Playfair in 1834. They were completely hidden by rubbish and debris from the hills but were opened out and restored by the British Government. The aggregate capacity of all the tanks exceeds 20,000,000 gallons.'

The lower circular tank (called the Playfair Tank) is quite enormous. Like all the minor ones, this tank has not been hollowed out of the rock, but has had dams built all round a natural ravine, so that one walks along the top, as at the Mappin Terraces in the London Zoo, and gazes down into the pit. To complete the illusion we found two small lion cubs chained to the railings. They were most amusing little fellows, with great fat podgy paws.

It was very hot and so I did not struggle to the very top, though nearly everyone else did and I thought them all mad, till I saw some fellows discreetly wiping their mouths. It was only then that I discovered (and too late) that they had built a temporary 'bar' here.

We returned to the ship which sailed at 5.30 for India.

SUNDAY, 13 NOVEMBER   David and I had again slept out and I was woken at a very early hour by a rush of water under our beds. I sat up and looked round in time to see a hose being quickly pulled up behind the side awning of the superstructure, while still pouring forth a stream of water. It turned out that the end had been let down by mistake by a man who could not see what was the other side of the awning. I was pretty angry as my spare blanket, slippers, book, etc. were of course soaked. I had just got off to sleep again when the sun started to shine straight into my eyes. I turned round and it burnt the back of my head.

At this point David and I reluctantly removed our bedding to our cabins, and we both over-slept and were nearly late for church at 10.30!

MONDAY, 14 NOVEMBER   Everyone had started packing today and all the passages are littered up with luggage. We have all had labels issued to us, each one having a distinctive number. As there are 26 on the Staff in India and I am the junior one my number is pretty low. As a matter of fact the 10 Indian Princes don't count in this system but as David does this makes my number 17. Even so, these numbers run to 71, though all our servants have the same numbers as us.

Then each piece of luggage is numbered in a consecutive series belonging to any particular person. I do not know how many pieces of luggage I have, but I see this typewriter case has 27 on it!

We have also had Volume 1 of the *Official Programme and Order Book* issued to us and this contains over 200 pages of small type. It contains detailed lists, timetables, train plans, instructions, etc., and should prove most useful. I was put in car 11 while David was in car 5 in the broad guage train so that we were 6 cars apart. In the other two-metre guage trains I was left out altogether.

Finally the Admiral hit on the brilliant idea of my using David's sitting room in all the trains, thereby being near him and making room for my servant.

TUESDAY, 15 NOVEMBER   It was noticeably cooler today, thank goodness. Packing continues and you walk through the superstructure at your own risk. I have verified the amount of my luggage. There are 30 pieces in all, of which 3 are cases of ammunition and 4 belong to my servant Hiscock. There must be some three or four hundred cases in all to be landed from the ship. Thank goodness we don't have to pay any excess luggage fares.

WEDNESDAY, 16 NOVEMBER   Tomorrow we arrive in India. I am not by nature incurably romantic but there is something rather wonderful, rather thrilling, at the idea of setting foot for the first time in a country which genuinely belongs to the Far East. India is a country one has heard about, read about, even dreamt about, but up to the present I have found it hopeless to attempt to conceive what it is like in real life. The next four months ought to show me. We are going to traverse India from west to east, and then from south to north, with a trip to Burma wedged in between these two tours. Finally we double on our tracks and return to the west – Karachi.

In a way I feel sad at leaving the ship and I know how tired and irritable we shall all be in four months' time.

India and Burma

———— ◁▦▷ ————

India in 1921 was in such disarray that many of those best qualified to express an opinion felt that the Prince of Wales's visit was ill-advised. The Montagu-Chelmsford Report, which had reiterated that the aim of the British Government was to establish India as an independent democracy within the Empire, should have improved the atmosphere, but the Indian National Congress Party, inspired by Mahatma Gandhi, saw no evidence that there was any serious will to turn these pious intentions into reality. The unrest that ensued led to the introduction of trial without jury for those accused of political crimes, and, in April 1919, to the massacre at Amritsar.

In 1920 Gandhi and the Congress Party, in alliance with the Muslims, launched a movement of non-cooperation with the Government. Gandhi ruled that the Prince of Wales's visit should be boycotted, though this should be a passive gesture of disapproval, without any violence or even overt signs of hostility such as 'hartals' – strikes and closure of shops. Lord Reading, the Viceroy, knowing how thin the margin was between violent and non-violent opposition, contemplated recommending that the tour should be called off, but concluded that this would be a confession of impotence so damaging as to make it essential to take the risk. There was some debate as to whether the tour should start in Bombay, traditional arrival point for any distinguished visitor but the scene of much recent disturbance; on this point too the Viceroy resolved to stand firm.

Only about 60 per cent of the Indian subcontinent was 'British India' proper, under the direct rule of the Viceroy and the Indian Government in Delhi; the rest was made up of princely states which owed allegiance to the Crown but enjoyed a fair degree of independence in everything except foreign policy and were administered by their feudal rulers with the advice of – or sometimes under the control of – a British Resident. The Prince of Wales was to spend almost as much time in the princely states as in British India, but it was in the latter that political disturbance was anticipated. Burma was an anomaly, a colony under the Viceroy yet in practice administered on all but the broadest issues of principle from Rangoon. It was subject to the same nationalist pressures as India, but the atmosphere was more relaxed and no one expected that the Prince would encounter any marked evidence of hostility during his visit there. The same was true of Ceylon; though the control of Delhi and the influence of Indian politicians was stronger than in Burma.

THURSDAY, 17 NOVEMBER 1921   We anchored in Bombay Harbour at 6.30 a.m. I dressed in white full dress at once, as there was a lot to do.

At 9.00 H.E. The naval C-in-C came onboard. He left after ten minutes and then the Viceroy, accompanied by Lord Rawlinson[1] (the military C-in-C) and 7 of the Ruling Princes attached to the staff, paid his official call. The Ruling Princes were dressed in their full state clothes and looked magnificent. The Maharaja of Patiala was wearing some of the most magnificent jewels I have ever seen in my life. He wanted to see Charles, as he had just seen the King and Queen of the Belgians, while he had been over in Europe. I went down to get him and he was not fallen in with all the other officers, so I sent down for him. After ten minutes he appeared looking very frightened. He was wearing a jacket instead of a tunic, as his tunic was at the wash he explained to me. He is quite incorrigible about his clothes, but of course it makes him more like a true snotty.

The Staff then split up, the more junior members, including myself, going in the picket boat while David and 10 others, including the 7

[1] General Lord Rawlinson was to die four years later while still Commander-in-Chief, as the result of a surfeit of cricket followed by polo.

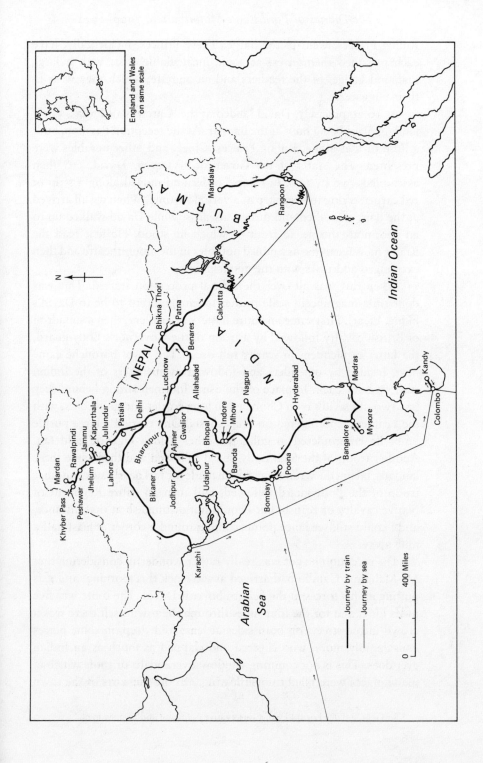

England and Wales
on same scale

N

BURMA

Mandalay

Rangoon

Indian Ocean

Bhikna Thori

Patna

NEPAL

Benares

Calcutta

INDIA

Lucknow

Allahabad

Khyber Pass

Mardan

Peshawar

Rawalpindi

Jammu

Kapurthala

Jullundur

Jhelum

Patiala

Delhi

Lahore

Bharatpur

Gwalior

Ajmer

Bikaner

Bhopal

Indore

Mhow

Nagpur

Hyderabad

Madras

Jodhpur

Udaipur

Baroda

Poona

Bombay

Bangalore

Mysore

Kandy

Colombo

Karachi

Arabian
Sea

——— Journey by train
——— Journey by sea

0   400 Miles

Ruling Princes, went in the barge. These Princes, incidentally, have each provided themselves, at some incalculable cost, with a large diamond badge, of the feathers and an aigrette, which they wear in their puggaree.

At 10.20 precisely, David landed at the 'Gateway of India', a new landing place being built at the Bandar. At the reception Pavilion, built a little further along, Ruling Princes, Chiefs and other notables were presented. The staffs of the Governor,[1] Viceroy, David, etc. then assembled, two by two, in reverse order and moved along a strip of red carpet, trying to keep step at a very slow time. When we all arrived at the dais, we halted and turned inwards, while David walked up to an enormous throne, in front of which he stood. He first read the King's message to the assembled notables in the amphitheatre and then exchanged addresses with the municipality.

When this was all over the official procession started. This was done on a magnificent scale (rather too magnificent to be to David's liking, I fear). First came an entire battery of artillery, then a squadron of British cavalry followed by a troop of the Governor's Body-guard, the latter resplendent in scarlet full dress. The royal barouche came next, headed by out-riders and followed by members of the Indian staff on horseback. In place of the usual footmen sitting behind they had two of David's own Chobdars in long scarlet and gold coats, with the Feathers embroidered on their chests. One carried a large purple umbrella embroidered in gold, the other held a gigantic gold fan. Another troop of the Sikh Body-guard followed and then came three landaus, facing the wrong way which made me feel nearly sick. Another troop of the Body-guard followed, and then an entire Regiment of Native cavalry or British, but I could not distinguish at that distance, and I could still see lance points coming round a corner at least half a mile away.

The reception he got was really rather wonderful considering that Mr Mahatma Gandhi had arrived at 7 o'clock this morning, and was putting all his forces in the field to boycott David. The route was five miles long, and for the four miles through the town itself there was a crowd in the streets on both sides at least four deep, in some places considerably more, who cheered and clapped as much as an Indian ever does. This is not counting windows, verandahs or roofs which in many places were filled to overflowing. On the outskirts of the town

---

[1] Sir George (later Lord) Lloyd, Conservative politician and businessman.

the crowd dwindled down to one deep and less, which is only to be expected.

The drive finished up at Government House, which is situated the other side of Back Bay at Malabar Point.

The Non-Co-Operationists, enraged at the failure of their propaganda, chiefly due to the efforts of the parsees who are very loyal, started rioting this afternoon at Byculla, a part of Bombay. Rumour has it that they have killed several parsees and police and that they have suffered even greater casualties themselves. Our pressmen who are living at the Byculla Club were besieged and had a bit of a scrap.

In the evening a big reception was held of some 2000 people or more with nearly all of whom David had insisted on shaking hands, which was all the more appreciated since it was unexpected.

FRIDAY, 18 NOVEMBER   David and I had breakfast in his rooms, and after that he spent a delightful morning receiving official calls from all those Ruling Princes of the Bombay Presidency having dynastic salutes of 11 guns and over. After this the Kumars of the Rajkumar College were presented. He finished up the morning by meeting the lesser princes in bulk.

Lunch was a more or less unofficial meal, after which everyone lazed about feeling too hot and tired to do anything else. At 4 o'clock we drove down to the Willingdon club to see the semi-finals of the Prince of Wales Commemoration Polo Tournament.

Dinner was the same as last night and a state ball was given afterwards. At midnight we left for the train to go to Poona.

SATURDAY, 19 NOVEMBER   As this day begins at midnight and I did not turn in till 2.30 a.m. I will commence by giving a description of the train. It is easily the most magnificent one that we have ever had, beating the Trans-Australian (and even the Canadian Pacific according to the others). There are eleven gigantic coaches, painted a creamy white, with David's arms in the centre of each one. The whole train is over 700 feet in length and is carrying about 100 souls, I should say.

The Admiral went down just before the ball and had several alterations made so that I get a cabin in No. 4 next to No. 5 which is David's car. Altogether one is so magnificently looked after that I only hope this won't spoil every other form of travel for me.

As well as Hiscock I have a very nice native bearer, who rejoices in the name of Kanickum. He is hard-working and talks quite good

English and spends most of his time bowing and trying to take my boots off. He is very polite to Hiscock and they get on well together. He refers to me as 'The Sahib' and calls me this occasionally, though more often 'Sir', and he has even tried to copy Hiscock and produces a guttural 'Meelorr'.

Each coach contains only four cabins, which may help to give some idea of their size. Mine is just twice the size of the cabin I had onboard P 31. It contains an unusually big couch which is converted into the bed for the night, a knee-hole writing desk (roll-top), a sort of chest of drawers, an ordinary chair, a leather arm-chair, two collapsible tables, stowage for 8 suitcases, racks, hooks, etc., also two overhead fans, 6 lights and finally there is a bathroom next door. As a matter of fact I do not use this bathroom, for though I only have to share it with the policeman, I am too long for the bath and David has an enormous one, which he lets me use.

David's apartments are so big and well fitted that it is hard to believe one is in a train at all. This is the broad gauge train but we are also going to have three more for the narrow gauge lines. We always have four trains at one time to move about. There is the royal train, which I have been describing above, the supplementary train, the 'press' train and the 'horse and car' train. In our train there is the most magnificent dining room, but I might go on forever raving about this 'dream' train.

We left Bombay 10 minutes late and the engine driver at once tried to make up time by shooting along at 55 miles an hour. The train began to rock most terribly and I must confess that even I had visions of another accident, but David, whose nerves were in a bad state after two heavy days, could not stand it at all and ordered them to go slower, in fact never to exceed 35 m.p.h.

I stayed with him till 1.30 and as he didn't feel like sleep he came along to my cabin and sat in my arm-chair till 2.30.

I saw him back to bed then but when he went to sleep I do not know, as he just hated the train and the rocking and I can quite understand it too. I glanced at the country, lit by moonlight as we passed and so fell asleep.

I was called at 7.30 by my two servants. I found that in spite of the aforementioned quantity of furniture there was room for both Hiscock and Kanickum as well as myself to move about.

We arrived at Poona at 9.30. The escort on this occasion really were interesting as they were drawn from various 'Private Armies'. We had the Gwalior Imperial Service Lancers, the Kolhapur Lancers and dozens of small troops of Indian State Irregular Mounted forces. Their get-up was wonderful. One party had pieces of armour and heavy studded shields, and all the colour schemes had run riot. They were commanded by Scindia (Maharaja of Gwalior) who wore the full dress (scarlet) uniform of a Lieutenant-General and rode behind the barouche. As may be imagined he perspired considerably, but he is really a splendid man and most loyal. The procession drove out to Shanwar Wada. The route was well lined, considering it was mostly through open country, but there were no great numbers. At one place native irregular infantry were drawn up with native bands, which produced the most weird and plaintive noises. Quite the most interesting part, though, was to see a number of State elephants drawn up near the route. One was a perfect giant, towering head and shoulders above all the others. They had silver howdahs and their foreheads, legs and trunks were painted with gold and silver and bright-coloured paints. There were also camels and many other weird sights.

Eventually we reached the Shanwar Wada and David laid the foundation stone of a war memorial to the Mahrattas who fell in the Great War. After this we were shown over the remains of the old palace of the Mahratta Kings. We mounted to the top of the outer wall and here cool drinks and guide books were handed round.

The procession now reformed and moved off to the site of another memorial, this time to Shivaji, the great mahratta, who in his time appears to have caused our government more trouble than all his neighbours put together. In true British spirit it had been arranged that David should lay the foundation stone to this memorial. The ceremony here was even more impressive, and after it was over the Maharaja of Kolhapur and his men handed round pan and attar and garlands to David and the Staff. Pan consisted, in this case of some betel nut, wrapped up in a leaf, which one is supposed to chew, but when I tried this one of our native orderly officers stopped me, warning me that it would make me sick. Attar or itr, as it is varyingly spelt, consists of some 50 horse-power scent, which is usually put on one's handkerchief, but this time they provided the handkerchief as well.

Each one of us then had a garland hung round our neck, made of gold and silver tinsel and ribbon, not unlike Christmas tree decorations, and, indeed I felt quite like a Christmas tree with it on.

David then did a very good thing; he walked round in front of all the stands, so that the people could see him. They rose to their feet and cheered themselves hoarse. I was told that immediately after we had all left, the crowd broke through to the dais and flung themselves on the throne touching it with their foreheads and kissing it. They have however a certain number of Western ideas as well, for they all tore the carpet to shreds to keep pieces as souvenirs.[1]

We were the guests of the Western India Turf Club at lunch and then drove in state down the course to the Poona Races, which were good fun, but not unlike other races.

After the races we changed from the state carriages to motors and drove via a long route to Ganeshkhind, the summer residence of the Governor. Ganeshkhind is a most delightful place, similar in appearance to an ordinary country house at home, this appearance being enhanced by the grounds, which are laid out in an English fashion. At 7.00 we drove to Kirkee station, which is close by, the route being lined by troops bearing torches. I was quite glad to see the train again after rather a hot and tiring day.

There is a travelling Post Office attached to David, called the Prince of Wales's Camp Post Office; this has a telegraph department. Wherever we go or at whatever station we stop at, a man solemnly gets out and stands with a placard in his hand. This worried David at first and when he finally saw him follow him to the War Memorial he came to the conclusion that it must bear some Gandhi propaganda words. He walked over to the native and read these words on the card: 'Prince of Wales Camp Telegraph Office'.

Telegrams have arrived giving news of fresh riots all day. It seems a case of the Parsees v. The Rest and God help all the poor innocent passers-by who get in the way and the police who try and make peace.

SUNDAY, 20 NOVEMBER   David and some of the Staff lunched at the Orient Club, which is the only combined 'Black and White' Club in the city; the rest of us lunched quietly at Government House.

We drove to Bombay Cathedral, where a moderately short evening service was conducted by the Archbishop. He omitted a sermon and instead substituted a number of specially composed prayers, mostly topical. The one I liked best (and which very nearly gave me the giggles) started 'Let us pray for Guidance for all those who are helping and arranging the tour of Edward, Prince of Wales'.

[1] The Prince's visit to Poona, and in particular the speech he made at the memorial to Shivaji, was extraordinarily well received and dispelled the last doubts of those who had urged the cancellation of the tour.

MONDAY, 21 NOVEMBER   Several of us, including David and myself, went down to the Willingdon Club and knocked polo balls about. While there we heard a 31-gun salute being fired. On enquiry, this turned out to be the salute announcing David's return from Poona, which according to regulations could not be fired on a Sunday.

We drove to the Maidan where a naval and military tournament was in progress. We first saw some amazingly fat and muscular Sindhi wrestlers. Then followed the usual type of display, including a naval field-gun display, which was very good. The most interesting thing though was trick riding by the 2nd Lancers.

David and all the naval members of the staff had dinner at H.E. The Naval C-in-C's house and afterwards everyone foregathered at the Byculla Club, where a dance was held. This being the rioting quarter of the town, British troops with fixed bayonets were posted at every side street. No attempt at disorder, however, occurred.

TUESDAY, 22 NOVEMBER   Metcalfe[1] was A.D.C.-in-waiting yesterday and has to go ahead by train to Udaipur today, so I was left to do A.D.C.-in-waiting today, although I am not usually supposed to do this job.

At 10.40 a.m. David and those of the Staff on duty went in uniform to the University, where amazing to relate they did not attempt to confer any honorary degree on David but contented themselves with reading addresses in English, Sanskrit and Persian.

After lunch at Government House we drove down to the Willingdon Club. We were supposed to drive in at the main entrance, but as no one had troubled to inform me I naturally directed the procession to enter by the usual entrance. Consternation followed as we were supposed to be the guests of Ruling Princes and Chiefs, who were all collected at the other entrance. Presently they arrived round in great hurry, and much out of breath.

We saw the final of the commemoration tournament played off. This was Rutlam v. Enthusiasts, the former winning after an excellent game by 5 goals to 3. An amusing incident occurred after the 5th

---

[1] Edward 'Fruity' Metcalfe was a young officer of the Indian Cavalry who was attached to the Prince to look after arrangements for polo and other equine diversions. He became the Prince's closest male friend and stuck with him until after the abdication. 'The nicest fellow we have,' Mountbatten told Edwina. 'Poor, honest, a typical Indian cavalryman.'

chukka, when a pipe band imagining the match was over marched on to the ground playing loudly. The players were furious and ordered them off the ground. The band however played on unperturbed and when they got to the end even turned round with a view to playing on the way back. This was too much for the players who charged down upon the band, causing the latter to flee.

We left in cars at 10.00 p.m. and drove through various parts of the town to the station, the crowds pressing round as thickly as in Australia so that David stood up in the car to let himself be seen. He also gave orders for the crowd to be let on the platform and consequently had a perfectly magnificent send off.

WEDNESDAY, 23 NOVEMBER   Owing to the tremendous ovation which David received in Bombay our departure had been late and consequently we did not arrive at Baroda until 9.00 a.m. We were met at the station by the Gaekwar himself. The usual official procession through Baroda City now took place, brightened considerably by the really rather attractive uniform of the Baroda state troops, who formed the escort and lined the streets.

We drove straight to one of the Gaekwar's palaces just beyond the city called Laxmi Villas, which had been lent to us during our stay. It really was quite magnificent and came up to my wildest dreams of the glories of Native India and of rich Maharajas. It is a gigantic place, well equipped inside, being only twenty-five years old, but externally it is a replica of the older type of Indian architecture, with carved arches and turrets with cupolas.

My room had been arranged quite near David. It was really a suite of sitting room, bedroom, bathroom and dressing room. In the sitting room four enormous silver plates were piled with every imaginable fruit and nut. These apparently were a 'dali' or gift from the Gaekwar.

The sanitary arrangements for the natives are priceless but unfortunately not suitable for description in these pages. Luckily for us the usual means are provided as alternatives.

Next followed the Ceremony of Mizaj Pursi (Health Enquiry). First four of the Gaekwar's principal officers drove up and enquired after David's health. What the answer was, I don't know, but itr and pan was shed upon them by one of our staff and they departed in their gorgeous clothes in an American car.

A deputation of the four principal officers of state now drove up and were received by Captain North and myself. They had come to

above: One of the Crossley motor cars passes back into British India during the visit to Nepal (14 December 1921).

below: The first tiger killed, with the five guns who were present (from left to right): Piers Legh, Admiral Halsey, H.R.H., Mountbatten and Colonel Worgan (14 December 1921).

above: The scene at Baghai after Mountbatten shot his tiger (16 December 1921).

below: The procession on arrival at Rangoon (2 January 1922).

above: Getting out of the train at Mandalay and being received by the umbrella bearers (5 January 1922).

below: H.R.H. afloat in his somewhat rickety barge in Mandalay (7 January 1922).

above: The palace at Mysore illuminated for H.R.H.'s visit (20 January 1922).

below: Arrival at the palace at Gwalior (8 February 1922).

conduct David to Nazar Bag, but when our party started to get a move on the poor old deputation seemed to get left behind. The route to this other palace, which is in the heart of the town and slightly smaller, was lined with troops and His Highness's artillery in their queer full dress fired a 31-gun salute, nearly into the cars, as we left.

At Nazar Bag we were conducted into the 'Throne Room' and David and the Gaekwar at once sat down on a silver and purple sofa.

Then in turn all the Baroda officials, including British officers in the Gaekwar's service came forward. The natives all went through queer motions, stooping low and lowering and raising the extended palm and arm very quickly. This I afterwards learnt signifies that they are shovelling up metaphorical dust and pouring it over themselves to show their humility and unworthiness.

Each one, this time including whites, then offered narzars of 5 gold mohurs (money) to David, usually on a handkerchief. This signifies laying all one's wealth at the Prince's feet. It is not meant to be accepted, and it would apparently cause consternation should this be done. David had merely to touch the mohurs and remit them. Itr and pan was then distributed. The pan was very grand, each individual nut being wrapped in gold or silver paper. It was a very difficult feat to hold the leaf so that the nuts did not roll off. Added to this there was a large conical bouquet for everyone, on which the itr was placed. As one had to control a sword, hold a helmet and gloves and try and avoid tripping over the long gold and silver garlands that were put round our necks the departure was less dignified than the arrival. Before finally going we were shown the state jewels, the value of each being attached in ticket form, as in a shop. A rope of pearls, priced at about 10 lakhs[1] caught my fancy, but as it turned out that a lakh is 100,000 rupees, I came to the reluctant conclusion that this was too expensive.

A so-called garden party took place after lunch, which was really more in the nature of a variety entertainment. The State elephants were all out, painted with the most lovely colours. I had a ride on the biggest of the lot. They carry silver 'accommodation' ladders, which are let down so that one can climb into the howdah, which in this case was silver. It seemed quite a long way up, but presently the whole front part rose in the air to my intense surprise, throwing us all back. As soon as we had got used to this slant the rear part came up throwing

[1] A lakh was worth approximately £6800 in 1921.

us forward. We were now miles above the ground and I realized that the elephant had been getting up from a kneeling position. It was very much like being at sea in a small boat when the great creature began to walk. The mahout, who sat across the elephant's back, steered him with two pointed ankuses.

After this we inspected a solid gold gun mounted on a silver gun carriage. There was a silver limber and the team were two of those hump-backed oxen, richly caparisoned. This was said to be worth 2½ lakhs. There was another all-silver gun near by.

There were lots of side shows, fighting cocks, acrobats and rustic scenes from Kathiawar. Altogether my head was in a whirl at the wonder of it all. In the midst of these strange scenes we came across boy scouts and girl guides.

THURSDAY, 24 NOVEMBER   Up betimes and to horse. Twelve of us rode, the remainder motored out 9 miles to a cheetah hunt. I saw a long-tailed langur monkey jump up into a tree as we passed and at least a dozen of the pretty little striped squirrels. Indeed, I found one sitting on the table of my sitting room yesterday eating the Gaekwar's nuts.

I was lucky enough to get a billet on one of the cheetah carts, though I must confess I felt nervous when I saw how thin the rope holding the cheetah in the back of the cart was. It purred or growled angrily when I got in and lashed its tail so that it actually tickled my nose. There were three cheetahs in three of these two-wheeled carts drawn by hump-backed oxen, and two of them had leather eye-pads, to blindfold them.

This cart went in and out of holes, jolting and throwing us about in the most startling manner. We missed three good chances of letting our cheetah go owing to the crass stupidity of our old driver, who, together with the cheetah, belonged to the Maharajah of Kolhapur, and wasn't taking any orders from Baroda. He seemed obsessed with the idea of getting up to within 30 yards of a herd before letting his animal go. All he succeeded in doing was in driving all game before him. Eventually tired of this we split up, the Admiral joining up with my cart.

Presently we came on a large herd of deer. The grass and under-growth was so thick that we had got to within 60 or 70 yards of them before they noticed us. I counted 5 fine heads and quickly consulted the Admiral who agreed to shoot; we, therefore, asked the old man to stop. Stop, he did, but his pride was so hurt that we preferred shooting to watching a hunt that he at once slipped his cheetah, which went bounding along far more like a dog than a cat, and indeed they say that a cheetah really belongs more to the canine family.

He stopped every now and then and presently we lost sight of him and the herd who had all scattered. We followed and discovered the cheetah holding the smallest baby in the whole herd, with his teeth in its throat. One of the attendants then disembowelled the unfortunate little animal, and drawing a ladle of blood off, held this under the cheetah's nose. This at last made him leave go, and while he was greedily lapping up the blood, he was blindfolded and secured.

David shot a doe, but no one else got anything. One of the other cheetahs got a fine buck. We returned by car and had lunch as soon as we had changed, leaving by train at 2.15.

I typed away hard at this diary until 8.30 p.m. when we reached Rutlam, where our luggage was transferred to the narrow gauge train, in which we embarked after dinner.

FRIDAY, 25 NOVEMBER Everything is so much smaller and more uncomfortable, but then the width of the rails is only 1 metre. David and I had breakfast in my temporary bedroom and at 10.00 a.m. we arrived at Udaipur. As David has had his red tunic made so tight that he can never hope to be comfortable in it he is sticking to whites as long as he can. This certainly is more comfortable, but the problem of getting clean tunics is becoming acute. I have had to order more and get on to the dhobi to hurry up my washing.

The Maharaja is very ill and his heir, the Raja Kumar, who is incidentally a dwarf and a cripple, had to deputise for him. The scenery and people were totally different. One might have stepped back into the Middle Ages. The route was lined by irregular troops, liegemen of the local chiefs. Many of them had no form of firearm, and none had uniform, except the actual guard of honour. Some wore breast plates and other pieces of armour. All carried shields and either a long curved sword, the scabbard of which they held loose in their disengaged hand, or some form of venerable flint lock. These muskets varied in length from about 2 feet to quite 7 feet. No two men attempted to hold their arms in the same way.

Elephants and state horses in their full rig were out, too. At the end of the route, all the women were collected in wonderful dark-coloured clothes of every hue.

We drove straight to the Residency, where we are being put up.

At 4.45 we proceeded by motor boat to the small island of Jagmandar on the big artificial lake, on which the borders of the town stand. The boat was gaily decorated and hung with lamps. We did not appreciate the decorations too much as the lamps dripped on nearly everyone's clothes.

The city and palace look too attractive from the lake. The palace is built on a hill side, with great white walls supporting the front face. The whole district is mountainous and dry, so that cactus and shrubs form most of the vegetation.

We had tea at Jagmandar, which besides being a pretty little place is historic to us, since the Maharaja allowed our fugitives to shelter there during the Mutiny.

After this we went on by boat to Khas Odi, where there is a deep arena, aurrounded by ramparts. From the ramparts we watched them throwing fodder down. They have made a habit of this for some time and all the pigs in the place have got to know of this, consequently there were at least 300 of them there. I regret to say that even when there is famine in the town the pigs are not neglected – there are times when I do sympathize with the Bolsheviks.

However it was very interesting, especially to see some of the older boars, with big tusks, go round looking for trouble in order to attack a smaller pig, which would run off squealing. I have never seen so many 'bullies' as among these pigs.

We now went to the top of the arena and presently a steel door was raised and with much shouting and poking from behind a magnificent leopard bounded in. Another door was quickly raised and, with much grunting, a large boar was pushed in.

At first nothing happened, both animals being frightened. The natives threw stones and this roused the boar who rushed at the leopard, ripping him with his tusks. The leopard scratched back but jumped clear as soon as he could. In fact the leopard was a most surprising coward. The pig did not leave him much peace, though, and at last the leopard leapt on the pig and bit it twice in the neck, causing the old boar to squeal loudly. Then the boar turned on the leopard again and charged him and ripped him, till the poor beast lay apparently lifeless. By throwing stones and tin cans on strings at the boar they got him off and shut him up. They now threw a stone at the leopard, who immediately bounded up and stalked away, apparently no worse off.

SATURDAY, 26 NOVEMBER   After breakfast we changed into shooting kit, David and I wearing shorts. We afterwards regretted this as our knees became terribly sunburnt. We motored out the short distance to Pichola Lake and then waded out into the marshy part of the lake, to go snipe shooting. We had a very good morning, frequently wading knee-deep, which was rather pleasant on such a hot day. Altogether we secured five and a half couple of snipe.

SUNDAY, 27 NOVEMBER   I was called at 5.45 a.m. and dressed in shikari kit, taking my .375 magazine rifle. We drove out about a couple of miles to a hill called Sajangarh. Here we left the car and proceeded on foot. It was bitterly cold as the sun had not yet risen, and I was well wrapped up. As the sun got up I found that I soon had to discard woolly waistcoats, etc.

For nearly an hour we tramped in silence without catching sight of the game we were after – chinkara, an Indian gazelle. Eventually we sighted some and through the glasses I could distinguish a couple of fine heads. I fired and missed. This, quite apart from any question of my own skill, apparently is the usual fate of the first few shots at chinkara by any novice. In fact Captain North fired quite a number before he got one yesterday.

We moved on a bit and then started again. This time the shikari motioned me to go quietly and presently I espied, at least 200 yards off, two gazelles. I could not see very well through my glasses, but one had no horns, and the other did. I came to the conclusion that the former was a doe and the latter a buck. I accordingly fired at the buck. It took me several shots before I brought the chinkara down. When we got down I was disappointed to find that the head was a very small one.

The shikari at once took a strip of his puggaree off and wound it round the dead animal, which he proceeded to carry on his head. It made him all bloody, and as I did not want the body I mentioned in Hindustani that it was a very small chinkara. I then motioned to him to put the body down. He apparently thought that I really did know Hindustani after all and poured forth torrents of it. The more I shook my head and shrugged my shoulders the louder did he talk. It really is very trying to be out for long with a man with whom one must converse, but with whom one possesses no tongue in common. The shikari continued to carry the gazelle on his head, and I afterwards learnt that the natives here consider them a great delicacy. I was surprised to learn later that it was a doe after all. Luckily it is not the close season and does are being shot, but I never realized that some of the does have horns.

When I got back I had breakfast with David, and happening to mention that I had got a chink he told me that the Staff were not allowed to shoot on Sundays, by the King's special orders. I was worried at having done so, without knowing, and still more as I had made all arrangements to have another try at a crocodile. I therefore went and saw Lord Cromer, who was annoyed, but admitted having omitted to tell me of H.M.'s wishes. He very nicely allowed me to carry on with my mugger shoot but made me promise to take every precaution that no one found out.

I saw the others off to the little Scottish Mission Church, and as soon as a car returned from there, commandeered it and set out with my .400/.450 double barrel express rifle and drove the car myself out to Badi Talao.

It was terrible driving, along a narrow, undulating, twisting track, sprinkled with cattle, donkeys, goats and old women at the most unexpected corners. After five miles we got to the edge of a lovely big 'tank'. The shikari and I set out on foot along the most treacherous going conceivable. My guide swung along at great speed, whilst I stumbled after him with enormous difficulty, frequently slipping and tearing myself and my clothes. After an hour of this we got to a ridge overlooking another arm of the lake. My shikari peeped over and returned with the news that an enormous mugger was sunning himself some two or three hundred yards off, on the banks of what he assured me was an island. It would have been impossible to get nearer had it really been an island, and so taking his word for it I stayed where I was and had a shot with my sights at 300. The shikari vows I hit him, only too far back to instantly paralyse him. The crocodile turned completely over and fell back into the water. This, I was later assured, happens nine times out of ten.

The Resident, from the shikari's description, is sure that the mugger was killed, and will have the lake watched, as the creatures sometimes come up again after a day or two. I was furious to find as we walked on that there was a small isthmus connecting the shore with this 'island', out of sight from my position.

I did not get back to the car till 2.00 p.m. and I have never known what it was to be thirsty before. My tongue could hardly move and I could not produce one drop of saliva.

I had lunch and three long drinks on return. We left by train at 6.30 p.m.

MONDAY, 28 NOVEMBER   This was the first occasion on which David allowed cloth full dress to be worn, and the Staff looked very brilliant disembarking from the train at Ajmer. In fact they quite rivalled the finale of a pantomime for colour.

The reception which David had here was good, but not so good as at other places. It really does begin to look as though the only doubtful part of the tour is going to be British India.

We proceeded to Mayo College and were met at the gates by a mounted escort from their O.T.C. Mayo (named after the Viceroy who did most to found it) is the Eton of India, with far stricter entrance rules. Only Ruling Princes and their relations may send their sons to this college. There are some 80 boys of all ages from about 10 or 12 to over 20. David, after receiving an address of welcome from the Principal, gave prizes to over half the boys, in fact only 37 did not get them.

On the whole there appears to have grown up a wonderful public school spirit in the College, though of course each one has a far grander room to himself than anywhere at home, except possibly at the Varsity, as I noticed on looking round afterwards. The uniform of their cadet corps is wonderful: a sort of white frock coat and breeches with large patent-leather boots and spurs; a big, curved sword (nearly as big as the smallest trooper); and a puggaree. We had a big dinner at the Residency, before returning to the train.

TUESDAY, 29 NOVEMBER   We arrived at 8.30 a.m. at Jodhpur station. The one day in cloth full dress had proved too much for David and we braved the elements in whites. It is all right for the Army officers as David has ordered them to wear blue 'overalls', and it is really the legs that feel the cold when they are in white trousers.[1] David horrified the Admiral by suggesting that the Naval officers should wear blue gold-lace trousers with a white tunic, to fall in line with the army. Needless to say this arrangement is not to be carried out. However by 9.30 it was quite warm and by 11.00 one was thankful to be in whites.

Today I had a complete day off. I ordered a camel and went for

[1] King George V did not consider it in the least 'all right'. 'I am surprised to see that you and your staff are wearing blue overalls with your white tunics,' he wrote. 'A most extraordinarily ugly uniform.'

an hour's ride. They have a large quantity of these animals here and they do nearly all the work, including watering the roads, with water skins strapped each side. It is all right while the old camel is ambling along at a decent speed but the moment he slows down the motion becomes like that of a dinghy in a heavy swell and it makes one feel a little sea-sick. A native sits on the saddle in front of the hump and you sit on the second saddle behind the hump. The saddles have stirrups but are heavily padded, like an arm-chair.

WEDNESDAY, 30 NOVEMBER   I was called at 5.45 a.m. and left at 6.30 for Raikabhag Station. We left by a small special train and proceeded about eight miles to a place called Banara.

Here there were horses waiting for us. They always arrange pig-sticking in heats, either three, four or five spears making up one heat. We had three heats of four spears, two sahibs and two natives in each, the two latter merely being there for assistance and not attempting to get 'first spear'.

As soon as everyone, including the fifty or sixty beaters, were mounted we formed into a single line abreast, the whole line covering at least half a mile, with the three heats distributed at intervals, my heat taking the left-hand wing.

The whole line now advanced over fairly smooth and level country, the sandy soil being covered by low bushes. We proceeded like this for half an hour and then lost sight of the other two heats and their beaters as they went to the right of a hillock, which we passed to the left. It appears that just then a sow got up and was soon speared by both heats. As a rule sows and 'squeakers' are not ridden, but they had told us to go after everything on this occasion, and this inclines to confirm my suspicions that no real arrangements, or as they call them over here 'bandabasts', had been made for our party. Anyway I rode for nearly four hours without seeing the smallest sign of a pig. However I saw plenty of other game, such as black buck, chinkara, foxes and partridges.

In the evening there was a state banquet in the mess tent. This is easily the biggest marquee I have ever seen in my life, being 35 ft high, 150 ft long and about 60 ft wide, with heavy chandeliers hanging from the ridge rope. It was a queer sensation walking about on the carpet inside, as they had had to put sea sand underneath to prevent the white ants from eating through.

THURSDAY, I DECEMBER   This morning we left at 7.00 a.m. and proceeded to a place called Bouria.

The ground we were to ride over was far more treacherous than before, as in many places there were large slabs of flat slippery rock strewn round with smaller chunks of it, and the whole country was covered with nullahs, a sort of wide and deep ditch. These nullahs are terribly treacherous and fairly put the wind up me, as I remembered how Papa came to grief in one when he was out pig-sticking 46 years ago. They are frequently 5 ft deep by 8 ft wide, but they vary considerably, some have sloping sides, some perpendicular. The really wonderful part is how a good local horse will scramble in and out of a nullah at full gallop and how they keep their feet on these rocky slopes.

There was no lack of bandabasts here, and soon half a regiment of native cavalry dismounted, started to beat the hills. Presently a big boar was observed to break away and David's heat were soon lost in a cloud of dust. David had a most extraordinary piece of bad luck; one of his reins broke while he was in full gallop after this pig. It took him two hundred yards before he could pull up his horse with the remaining rein. David altogether had rather bad luck today, though he had one very lucky escape when an infuriated hog charged him from quite a good distance off. David calmly waited for it with his spear but the pig somehow slipped past and still more miraculously failed to bring the horse down.

We rode round to the further side of the hills, which was a precipitous rocky face, with ledges running diagonally along it. Presently we saw a sounder (mob) of pig working away from the beaters along one of these ledges. Lower down there was a hyena, which broke away first, and our heat pelted off in full pursuit. I can't remember when I have been so frightened. The horse took complete charge and proceeded at an almost incredible speed, nearly as fast was the hyena, who lay well ahead. Metcalfe was pressing the hyena hard, but presently it jinked across his horse to the left and came near me. I lowered my spear and was making desperate efforts to get at the hyena when it jinked again, this time to the right. I anticipated that the next alteration of course would be to port and accordingly worked to the left myself, but in this I was altogether too clever as I got the wrong side of a stone embankment and had to dismount to lead my horse down. In the meanwhile within twenty yards of me the others had caught up and were finishing off the hyena. After this we cantered back to where we had started the run from.

Our next run was after a pig. By now I was beginning to feel less terrified and didn't mind negotiating nullahs so much, in fact it was not long before I was taking a fierce joy in the difficulty of the country we had to get across. This pig ran along a stone wall at the top of an embankment and would not come down so Hanut Singh very pluckily went up and faced its charge, leaving his spear stuck through its back, as the point had come out the other side and he could not get it out again. In the run that followed I would have got a 'spear' but for the pig jinking right across my horse, and one is warned against spearing then as it is obviously certain to bring one's horse down over one's own spear. We all had a thrust at the end including myself.

As soon as we got back to the hill we observed, on the only side on which I had not yet been, three pig being chased by one heat. Our heat galloped to the assistance. I again nearly got a spear but eventually the pig got back to the hills and was lost. Just as we were giving up this side in despair we saw some men gesticulating on the summit. Following their line I saw a large sounder making away and at once signalled with my spear to the others, all of us then giving chase.

Prithi Singh offered to ride a pig with me and accordingly picked out a rideable boar out of the sounder for me to follow. I had several shots at him, but always seemed to miss him, nevertheless a nameless gentleman assured me afterwards that I had technically scored a 'first spear' as he saw the blood on my spear and the mark on the pig, before anyone but me had had a go. This, he assured me, would have counted in the Kadir Cup. I suppose he was right but I must admit that I felt just a little unsatisfied and was therefore delighted when on the way back to the station I spotted another pig. We all gave chase and ran for a furlong along the bottom of a nullah after it.

It ran along the embankment our first pig had followed and was there joined by a second boar. The first one now jinked right back and everyone behind thinking I had not noticed this shouted to me to come back. I was furious as I was on the tracks of this new pig and one is not supposed to ride a pig alone for fear of accidents occurring where no assistance is available. I saw no one was following and therefore shouted as loud as I could. Prithi Singh heard me and followed. By this time I had lost the pig, but we cast ahead and sure enough in five minutes time picked him up again. The boar now broke away from the wall and I followed hard, Prithi very considerately keeping behind me the whole time. We had quarter of an hour's hard riding now, with the pig jinking and running in circles and charging, in fact using all his cunning to get away.

My horse was absolutely pumped and it was all I could do to keep him at a gallop, as one cannot properly spear at any other speed. At last my chance came and before I realized I had touched the pig with my spear, the head had come out the other side so that I could not withdraw it and had to leave it in.

Poor Prithi Singh had a dangerous job trying to finish him off as the pig, now so dangerously wounded, made desperate efforts to charge and the spear in his back made it difficult for anyone to approach. Eventually the pig fell over on its side and Prithi dashed up and finished it off with his spear.

It was not a particularly large boar, but I must say I did feel pleased at having at last got a pig. The Resident has promised to have the heads of those pig our party got mounted and sent to the *Renown*. Altogether 11 pigs were accounted for by our party, though nearly all by Indians. It was one of the best mornings I have ever spent anywhere, but I did feel stiff afterwards.

This day is a red letter one for me, as besides getting my first pig I played in my first game of polo. I played in two chukkers, the 8th and the 11th. The average handicap of the other players must have worked out at something over 5, and there was certainly some of the best polo in India being played here this afternoon, which considerably added to my bewilderment. I spent the whole of the first chukker trying to learn my place in the field and never really got near the ball. I was playing on the Maharaja's side against David, and, of course, it was due to the latter that I was playing at all. In the last chukker, to my own intense surprise, I actually hit the ball three or four times. Anyway I loved it and hope to get lots more.

After a quiet dinner we left by train for Bikaner.

FRIDAY, 2 DECEMBER   We arrived at 10.00 a.m. at the city of Bikaner, capital of the state of Bikaner. David was received by the Maharaja, Sir Ganga Singh and the Maharaja Kumar Sadul Singh, or Hiroud as his father calls him. I had met them both at Wolfsgarten with Uncle Ernie some fourteen years ago[1] and had played with Hiroud. I am bound to admit that I completely failed to recognize him as he looks

---

[1] 'Uncle Ernie' was Ernst Ludwig, Grand Duke of Hesse, and Wolfsgarten a palace belonging to the royal family.

so much older than 19 and has added a considerable amount of flesh since I last saw him.

We walked on gold carpets to the carriages. Our 'cavalry' escort this time was the Ganga Rissala Bikaner Camel Corps. I don't think I have ever seen so many camels at one time, all trained to perfection. They padded noiselessly behind our carriage, gorgeous in their full dress trappings. The men wore white frock coats with scarlet facings and carried a modern service rifle at the trail in the right hand. The streets were lined with infantry and the park roads with regular cavalry.

We are living at Lallgarh, the town palace. Some of us are inside, I for one having a room actually opening on to David's, which is nice, but the remainder are in tents, as at every other place.

The state banquet was got over tonight. Afterwards we went out and saw a fire dance being performed. The men who perform avoid being burnt by 'faith' they say, it being a religious ceremony, but all my faith did not prevent me from burning my fingers on a live charcoal one of these men had spat out of his mouth. There is a big heap of red hot charcoal in the centre and the devotees dance round holding bits in their fingers and running over the middle occasionally. In the hall of the old palace we saw a sword and spear dance, one man hopping about on genuine sword blades (sharp) and spear-heads and nails and saws without cutting himself. We also saw some 40 Nautch girls dancing and singing.

SATURDAY, 3 DECEMBER All of us except David and the Maharaja, who followed later, left Lallgarh at 9.00 a.m. by motor for the country palace at Gujner some 21 miles out. We stopped two thirds of the way out at Kodamdesar, which we reached at 10.00. Hiroud then assigned us to our various butts, giving me a good one near David, which actually was bad as I will explain later. These butts, of which there were 18 so that there was one for everyone, were disposed round a small 'tank' or pond. We had not been in there long before our game appeared – demoiselle crane.

They fly in groups of about 40 and usually at a tremendous height, descending cautiously over the tank. The slightest thing will scare them away and we had instructions to keep complete silence, which, with the exception of our host we all did; nor were we to fire till David had had a shot. This last restriction somewhat handicapped those butts nearest him, as by the time he had fired the birds has usually passed my butt. I did however succeed in bringing down one, which had something like a six-foot span, from wing tip to wing tip. The total bag was only 28 for 18 guns, as they are very difficult shooting.

We now drove on to Gujner. Gujner is really a palatial shooting box, right in the middle of the most wonderful shooting country. I am in the house, but there is as usual a large camp in the grounds. The grounds are prettily laid out, reminiscent of those at home.

In the afternoon we had a duck shoot. I was in one of the home butts, but owing to the low state of the water I had to drive round and row out in a punt, my loader and cartridges coming in a second one. These natives have no idea of handling the smallest craft and we had several collisions and ran ashore twice before reaching my butt. It proved a regular starvation corner as the birds all flew too high by the time they got to us. After dinner we played fives on the Maharaja's best billiard table.

SUNDAY, 4 DECEMBER   In compliance with the King's wishes there was no shooting today, although this had been originally arranged. David and I had a bit of a lie in.

After lunch we lazed about and at 3.30 David took me on at tennis. So even were we in the first set that it lasted for 24 games, David eventually wearing me down. He was then joined by Harvey and I was joined by an old Oxford Blue and we beat the other side. David continued playing but I went off with the Maharaja to watch the pigs being fed. They were much closer than at Udaipur, being on the same level as the spectators with only a low wall separating them.

After each boar had eaten his fill he went and lay down nearby on his side and allowed the jackdaws to come and pick the ticks off.

MONDAY, 5 DECEMBER   We left at 7.00 a.m. as we were due to shoot imperial sand grouse. Hiroud Singh drove me there in his Rolls Royce. He and the Maharaja are being very nice to me, far too nice in some ways. For instance at dinner last night David naturally went out first, followed by the Maharaja; everyone then waited for the Maharaja Kumar, precedence being the life and soul of India, who came over to me and said, 'You go next.' He refused to take no for an answer so I hurriedly explained in as low a voice as I could that I had chucked my social position for this trip and simply went as an A.D.C. Hiroud then said, 'Oh, but not with us, my father wants you to go out second.' I finished up by saying, 'For goodness sake go on, you are keeping everybody waiting.' Luckily none of the Staff overheard this little scene, but it was very unpleasant.

The grouse started coming over soon in large numbers but very fast, so that even our best guns who were not used to this type of grouse were missing every shot. Most of my line of butts got between twenty and thirty birds and only my atrocious shooting prevented me from securing the same. I got eight, and I was shooting too badly to enjoy my morning. David got 65 or I should say 32½ brace. The Admiral got 43½ brace, but the Maharaja topped the list by miles with 69 brace. Altogether over 500 brace of imperial sand grouse were accounted for.

At 11.30 we had 'brunch', which is a local term for a mixture of breakfast and lunch, and at 1 o'clock David insisted on taking me for an hour's hard walk along the dusty high road. We had some difficulty in getting in as neither David nor I had passes and the sentry so far from recognizing David regarded him with marked suspicion.

WEDNESDAY, 7 DECEMBER   At 9.30 a.m. we arrived by narrow gauge train at Bharatpur. Throughout the tour by rail I have noticed line watchers and I have now enquired deeper into the matter. It appears that six hours before our train is signalled the neighbouring villagers have to tie up all cattle 1000 yards at least from the railway line as the line is an unfenced one. They have to supply an inner cordon of watchers stationed every 100 yards along the line alternate sides of it. From dusk onwards throughout the night they have also to have a light in their hand, usually a rough torch lit hurriedly from the little fire they have made to keep themselves warm throughout the bitterly cold northern Indian nights. There is so little wood and inflammable material lying about the desert-like country that they use dried cow dung, which they laboriously collect, to make their little fire with.

Not infrequently one sees an entire family out with the father who is 'line watching', and the more prosperous ones have a camel to take them home again after their six-hour spell is over. There is also an 'outer cordon' of guards at every station, however small, so that the minimum number of men to the mile required is 180, and it frequently takes over 3000 unfortunate shivering natives to guard a single night's journey for us. Their only reward being that if they carry out their duties properly they will not be evicted by their sardar.

Another astounding thing I noticed in Bikaner as we drove through the streets with Hiroud is that his future subjects all yell 'Kamha', or some such word, by way of greeting. Hiroud tells me that this is a derivation of the old Hindustani for 'Pardon', which perhaps is the clearest proof of how feared the old Maharajas must have been.

One more digression before picking up the threads of the narrative again. At Udaipur an old warrior was on duty outside the gates of the Residency, sitting, all dressed up in his queer old armour, on his shaggy little pony. One of our press men, who could speak Hindustani, got into conversation with him and learnt that he had already been on duty outside the Residency for 21 hours on end, being fed by his two attendants when hungry. On further enquiry it transpired that the old man was on duty for the duration of our visit and did not expect to leave his post for the next two days. I scarcely credited this story and appealed to the Resident for corroboration; he however was not in the least surprised to hear this, and, while being unable to vouch for the truth of this particular case, he explained that the whole country round about was still run on these medieval lines.

And now to get back to the station at Bharatpur. The Maharaja was there to greet us, dressed in a lion tamer's uniform, which we afterwards discovered was the uniform of his body-guard, which he had hurriedly designed for our visit. In fact he has re-dressed his entire state army in new and wonderful full-dress uniforms.

The Maharaja of Bharatpur (he is only three years older than me) is a most go-ahead and original man. He was at school at Wellington and has a great knowledge of engineering and electrics. In this respect he reminds me of Georgie and indeed his room was one mass of gadgets, cinemas, etc. all rigged up and run by himself. Give Georgie £250,000 a year and his rooms, cars etc. would not be unlike Bharatpur's, though I must admit that they would be more sensible, for this chap's imagination has run riot and we saw some of the queerest things that he has invented or arranged.

Overhead we were escorted by aeroplanes from his air force, the only native one in India. The Maharaja himself is an expert pilot and mechanic and has nine machines, Avros and de Havillands.

At the station there was a fleet of Rolls Royce cars, most of them quite new. I saw at least ten different ones, including a luggage lorry. He also has two of the most magnificent modern Daimlers, which cost him £9000 and £12,000, and although I think he was swindled I have never seen more marvellous cars. He had wanted to lend them to David for the tour, but they could not be accepted owing to our contract with Crossleys. The big limousine used to be on exhibition in the show rooms opposite the R.A.C. in Pall Mall and I had often admired it there.

This state has produced the most bizarre spectacles of all. In one place there was a complete sedan chair, slightly larger than a Pickford's furniture van, slung between two enormous elephants. In another there was a team of six elephants, gorgeously caparisoned in blue and gold with the Prince of Wales's Feathers embroidered on their pad cloths. These had been intended to draw the solid silver coach, in which the Maharaja had wanted David to drive. We subsequently saw this team actually at work on the polo ground drawing the silver carriage at a good speed. There was also a local 'Holy Man', whom I mistook for the court jester, since his get-up was ridiculous. He had smeared his face and hands with yellow, he wore a large gold gown and on his head had a sort of kakoshnik of peacock feathers. In his hand he carried a broom made of peacock feathers which he waved over our heads from the back of his elephant.

The palace we are living in is called Moti Mahal and is a mile or two away from the town. The carpet in David's room is light blue velvet with much heavy gold embroidery in it, valued at 70,000 rupees. The bed is supposed to be worth 10,000 rupees.[1]

Nearly all these things are made in the state, which possesses fine and up-to-date work shops of every description.

The baths, however, were so new that the water had not been laid on.

I left at quarter past twelve with a so-called shikari, who in reality was simply a soldier with some slight knowledge of the country and little of anything else. We motored out in one of the Maharaja's cars. After a five-mile run the shikari spotted a black buck in the distance, so we stopped the car and proceeded to stalk the buck on foot. It was exceedingly difficult work and when after half an hour I had wriggled on my tummy to within range I of course went and missed. After this we worked deeper into the jungle and presently came across some woodmen, one of whom accompanied us as guide. The tracker led me up to a clearing where I could see something moving about and my shikari whispered the only English he knew in my ear, 'Shoot, Sahib.' I snapped over the safety catch and crawled forward. Presently I found myself looking into the most foolish face I ever hope to see. It was not unlike a figure of eight and at the top were two small and fat horns.

---

[1] About £4800 and £700 respectively.

The face was munching away with a kind of sideways motion, and then as it turned I saw it had a body like a cow and was trying to wag its tail. Now I have never seen a nilghai, but I have always heard that they look like a pantomime cow and so I came to the conclusion that this was one. I crawled back and said 'nilghai' to the shikari who nodded excitedly and said, 'Shoot!'

Now I luckily knew that Bharatpur is a Jhat state and that the Jhats worship all form of cattle, even nilghai, so I made motions of praying to the nilghai to explain to my guide why I did not shoot. Of course he did not understand, but it turned out later that I was right not to shoot as complications would have inevitably ensued.

I wanted to go after black buck but did not know the native name for it so I made a face like a black buck, held up both my arms for horns and pointed with my foot in the direction we had seen our first buck. Wonderful to relate they understood and the tracker got me to put my hand on his shoulder so that he could indicate when to stop and go on without speaking. He led me up to a herd, who however got wind of us and cantered away while I blazed away at the leaping bucks, missing of course.

They were running in a circle so I cut across the diameter and got to within 100 yards of two fine buck, who were still running. I knelt down and whistled and they both stopped and looked my way. I then shot the larger head, though it took two shots to kill him. My shikari had no knife and no apparent knowledge of skinning. Luckily I remembered how they had skinned stags' heads at White Rock in New Zealand and so set to work myself with the assistance of the shikari. When it came to actually severing the head from the neck I had great trouble in finding the right place and foolishly let my companion have a go. He literally hacked away with my knife, striking bone every time and ruining my blade. I soon stopped him and then twisted the head round and round till it came off.

When I came to measure this head I found it was about 26½", as near as I could make it with very rough means. This is very very good as the record for this part of India is only 27½".

After a quiet dinner at the palace we motored out to a big open ground where stands had been erected, and footlights and overhead circuits arranged, the latter entirely designed and wired up by the Maharaja himself. The pageant that followed was wonderful, infantry, cavalry, camel corps, elephant batteries, motors, etc. went by like toys at Hamley's Christmas fair.

THURSDAY, 8 DECEMBER   David, Fruity, Bruce and myself went down to the polo ground before breakfast to knock a ball about. The Maharaja was there and had a new wonder to show us. This was what is known as the Regimental Brake. First come 8 horses, then 8 camels and finally 14 elephants, all harnessed together in pairs. One would expect them to be drawing at least a battleship, but no, when the end of the team comes into view a small yellow brake is discovered.

The elephants are perfectly paired off, first come a pair of babies, followed by a slightly larger pair, each pair growing in size until finally one comes to the last two which are about the biggest in the state. The whole team of 30 are wonderfully trained. We saw them at a walk and at a trot and taking corners and never once were the traces slack between any of the animals.

Lunch took place in a large Shamiana erected near the butts, and after it I accompanied David home. I asked the Maharaja for permission to take my shikari, who had been loading for me during the forenoon, and have another stalk after black buck. He very kindly offered to take me himself to his mother's preserve. Accordingly he fetched me at the palace in one of his many new Rolls Royces. This one was a delightful two-seater, all silver body, with a comfortable dicky seat in which he took two of his staff, behind.

The Maharaja now showed me how he chases black buck in a Rolls Royce over the most impossible country. We went through the big loose hedges, over the sloping banks, in and out of large holes, twisting and turning among rocks, now at 50 miles an hour, now at 5, and never changing below 3rd speed. If Rolls ever need an advertisement they ought to have an account written of what that car did. The springs were so wonderful that one felt no jar but the whole car heaved and rocked like a boat at sea. Every now and then Bharatpur would tug at my sleeve and say, 'There's a big one, Sahib, have a shot,' and I would obediently stand up and of course miss, but I did not candidly expect to get anything out of that car, and though it is fun there is not very much sport about it.

It had been arranged that on our way to the old palace for the state banquet we should drive very slowly, so as to give David time to admire the many wonderful illuminations, decorations and street entertainments provided for him. Just before we started, however, Lord Cromer informed me confidentially that word had been received from police spies in the city that certain seditionists had made a plot to attack David's car as it passed through the narrow streets of the bazaar, probably with bombs. They were evidently relying on the fact that David always travels in the first Crossley and that we would be going slowly, so Lord Cromer sent me out to re-arrange the cars, putting David's fourth. Only the Admiral and the police knew besides me, and I had received orders to keep my mouth shut. We were all told off for cars and I had the doubtful honour of going in the first Crossley – the decoy royal car. We were preceded by the Commissioner of Police in the pilot car and David's car was followed by the touring Daimler. The other occupants of my car were unconscious of a possible attack. I found some comfort in fingering the 'six-shooter' in my pocket. When we came to the ugly quarter of the town the entire procession leapt forward at 50 miles an hour and so we got through safely to the palace.

Of course there may not have been a word of truth in the rumour we had heard and since nothing happened we like to believe that this is the case. After the banquet and an excellent amateur conjuring performance, we left by broad gauge train.

FRIDAY, 9 DECEMBER We arrived at 10.00 a.m. at Lucknow and drove through moderately crowded streets to the new Council Chamber, where addresses were exchanged with the Legislative Council. Thence we drove straight to Government House, where our camp is and where we are living.

There was a medium-sized dinner party followed by a dance, at which I danced seven dances and then retired to bed. I am afraid that I prefer native states to British India.

SATURDAY, 10 DECEMBER After lunch we motored to the racecourse. All the races were being ridden by gentlemen riders, and David rode in four of them, winning two and coming in second in the other two; a remarkably fine performance, especially in the second race which he won from a large field by good horsemanship. In fact so pleased were we all with his second win that a large party of the Staff, myself included, went and backed him for the next race and lost.

SUNDAY, 11 DECEMBER After lunch David visited the Hosainabad Immambara, which, I fear, chiefly interested me as being the original model on which the White City at Shepherd's Bush was built. On the way back we stopped at the Victoria Park where free food and clothing were being distributed to the poor of Lucknow in commemoration of

David's visit. They all collected round and we had quite a struggle to get out before being 'gassed'.

We next visited one of the places in India which I have always longed to see for its glorious connection with all that is best in our history: The Residency. As we drove up, the first thing I caught a glimpse of was the Union Jack flying from the battered old Residency tower, reminding me of Tennyson's beautiful lines, 'And ever o'er the topmost roof our Banner of England flew.'[1] Now I do not pretend to know much history but of late I have been studying the history of the Mutiny fairly carefully, paying especial attention to that of Lucknow and Delhi, so that I really did know something about what I was seeing.

The Redan battery faces one as one drives up, but we walked first to the cemetery. I was struck by the number of 'family' tombstones, frequently bearing the name of father, mother and children, all having perished in 'The Garrison of Lucknow', as the wording has it. The most interesting one to see though, was that of Sir Henry Lawrence, the first Commander during the siege, which bears the epitaph dictated by himself, 'Here lies Henry Lawrence, who tried to do his duty, may God have mercy on his soul'. In ghastly contrast to this I was shocked to see the efforts of some filthy Non-Co-operator on the wall of the room near the Residency in which Sir Henry was killed by a cannon ball. There were written these words in an illiterate pencil scrawl: 'Here Henry Lawrence died (The Mutiny 1857)' and below this: 'May God send him straight to Hell'.

We visited the Tykhana, a small building off the Residency in which an excellent model has been built showing the British stronghold and the positions held by the enemy, in places only thirty yards away. This was a God Send, as it really did show one everything. We went to the downstair room, which used to be used for coolness in the hot weather. In this place some 220 women and children were collected and lived. All the windows near the ceiling had been sandbagged, so that there was scarcely any light or air. Deaths and even births were of frequent occurrence, and half the unfortunate occupants are known to have been suffering from dysentry and diarrhoea.

There they stayed for nearly five months until the second relief. I was shown, by the old guide, the place in which Jennie Brown had her

---

[1] Or, more accurately, 'And ever upon the topmost roof our banner of England blew.' From 'The Defence of Lucknow'.

famous 'dream' in which she saw Havelock's Highlanders marching to the relief two days before they actually won through.

After dinner, and singing many songs, we departed by train.

MONDAY, 12 DECEMBER   Allahabad was the first private arrival, and the occasion was celebrated by making lounge suits the rig of the day. The suggestion put forward that we should each have a cigar in our mouth to further emphasise the informal nature of the arrival was squashed on the grounds that it was too early after breakfast (9.30). I was one of the lucky ones who drove straight to Government House. In the meanwhile David was doing a slight stunt at the university, which turned out to be somewhat of a frost owing to the absence of the bulk of the students. Likewise, the streets were, for the first time, almost deserted and both may be put down to the same cause. Only a short while ago the ring leaders of the Non-Co-operation movement in Allahabad were arrested and hurled into jail, which ought really to have been done months ago, as I was informed by one of the leading native citizens of the place.[1] This appears to have rankled the people somewhat and those who remained at large succeeded in keeping them away from David.

The pipers of the 1st Battalion, Black Watch, played at dinner, and afterwards we returned to the train and left for Benares.

TUESDAY, 13 DECEMBER   The arrival at Benares struck me as being quite humorous. Most of the Staff were wearing frock coats, the two senior members had on grey tail coats while David himself appeared in a lounge suit and soft collar. What is more, he was so quick in jumping out of the train and saying his official 'How do you dos' that, by the time the equerry-in-waiting arrived from his compartment at the other end of the train, David had already left, with me, as the A.D.C.-in-waiting, on the box of the car.

We drove straight to Nandesar House, which I think is where the Agent to the Governor lives. It has a tablet on the outside which states that it was the residence of Mr Davies, when he was Magistrate of Benares in 1799. It further goes on to say that he defended it single-handed, armed only with a spear, against 200 armed men led by the rebel Nawab Wazir Ali.

---

[1] Among those arrested was Motilal Nehru, father of India's future Prime Minister. It was shortly after the visit to Allahabad that the Prince of Wales wrote to King George V to say that he was deeply depressed by what he felt to be the total failure of the tour.

I received the Maharaja of Benares, when he came to pay his official call, and was present at the ceremony when David gave him itr and pan. I also received the fat old Maharaja Kumar when he was sent with a deputation to fetch David for the return visit. We drove out seven miles through absolutely deserted streets, though of course practically the whole way led through country. We had to cross the Ganges by a pontoon bridge to get to Ramnagar Palace. Here the usual return visit ceremony was gone through. I had forgotten to bring a handkerchief and the P.M.O. very kindly passed me his for me to have my itr put on. I was sorry for him as the itr was particularly strong.

We now crossed the Ganges in a motor boat, the steps of the Palace Ghat being lined by queer old irregular State Troops and two of the gorgeous state barges being moored up near by.

At the other side the Maharaja had a silver barouche waiting and landaus for the Staff, in which we drove to the Benares Hindu University. Here David and His Highness the Chancellor (the Maharaja of Mysore) exchanged addresses. David's was excellent, consisting mostly of sound advice to the undergraduates, which was almost entirely wasted since those rude young cubs had not troubled to turn up. Although the term was in full swing only just over 100 out of the odd 1500 turned up.

The official lunch took place on return. The Maharaja, who is too orthodox to eat European food, sat by and watched, exchanging speeches with David at the conclusion. We now once more embarked in the motor boat and processed down the river.

Benares is too picturesque for words from the river, especially the countless ghats or waterfront steps, which were crowded with people who waved a welcome to David. In two places we saw fires at which bodies were actually being cremated in the crudest possible way, while further dead bodies lay waiting their turn, covered only with flowers. Temples were everywhere.

When we got back I changed into a lounge suit, and went into the tent where exhibits of local craft were being shown. I had always heard of the wonders of Benares brocades and handwoven stuffs in gold and silver, and bought half a dozen people Christmas presents of these attractive stuffs. I also attended a parade of pensioners with David before leaving by train at 7.30 p.m.

WEDNESDAY, 14 DECEMBER We arrived at the small terminal station of Bhikna Thori at 10.00 a.m. and were met by the Prime Minister of

Nepal, H.H. Maharaja Sir Chandra Shumsher Jung Bahadur Rana. Jung Bahadur is a fine old man with a genial smile and a good flow of English at his command. On the platform there were at least eight or more men who looked very alike, these proved to be sons, grandsons, sons-in-law, nephews, etc. of the old man. We embarked in our good old Crossley cars and drove about a quarter of a mile up to a point where a white signpost said 'Nepal Frontier' and beyond which a triumphal arch had been erected. On either side were drawn up Guards of Honour, one from a very smart Nepalese Regiment, the other from the escort of the British Envoy to the Court of Nepal. The former are men of the same type as our Gurkhas, that is to say Mongolians, but coming more from the centre of Asia they are much taller. They were dressed in smart red kourtas (shirt-like coats) and had an excellent European brass band; the latter are native Indian troops.

After David had inspected the Guards we drove on to the Camp which had been pitched about another half mile on. We are now no longer in British territory, for Nepal owes us no allegiance and though a faithful and loyal ally it is a foreign country, and a most exclusive one at that for no foreigner may pass the borders without the Prime Minister's permission on pain of being shot.

A road has been constructed through the jungle and a great space has been cleared and turfed on which our camp has been pitched. All round a strong zareeba of stout branches with pointed ends has been built to keep out the various wild animals which abound in the jungle round about, such as tigers, bears, rhinoceroses and wild elephants. As a matter of fact the zareeba will not keep out wild elephants and as they are sacred and may not be shot the only alternative has been to build a kind of platform about 30 or 40 feet from the ground, or machan as it is more correctly called. This is roughly built of branches and is scaled by rickety steps made of branches bound round with grass. Two herds of these wild elephants are known to be in the district, one of them even came up to the camp only a short while ago. They have also laid huge bonfires to frighten them and other wild beasts away, and of course dozens of sentries are on duty all round so we ought to be safe enough amidst these wild surroundings.

The camp is bounded on one side by the steep and precipitous bank of a river, which is dried up except for a small trickle. The view is simply magnificent. I can't help thinking of Kipling's jungle books and fitting Mowgli and all the animals into this jungle.

About 11.00 a.m. our party split up, some going about twenty miles out after a tiger which had been tracked from its kill that morning, while David's party in which I was included went to a place only four or five miles from camp. Here we left the cars and selected pad elephants, which knelt down to let us mount. I got a most delightful little fellow, with a funny fast walk. The pad is made of leather and is usually quite plain, with handles in front and behind to hold on to. One sits immediately behind the mahout, who sits astride the creature's neck, one leg behind each ear. The mahout usually holds a thin stick with which he thumps the elephant hard on the head every now and then, the latter taking about as much notice of this as though he were being tickled with a straw.

However, the mahout also has an ankus as an alternative, which is a nasty-looking instrument consisting of a large iron spike and a hook mounted on a short and thick wooden shaft or else a steel shaft. It is only used when the elephants become unmanageable, as when near a tiger, the pointed end being used to prod the beast on behind the ears, the hook to hook into its ears and pull it round or back. The queerest instrument of the lot however is a wooden mallet, like a nine pin, which ordinarily hangs by a piece of string from the back of the pad. When it is desired that the elephant should hasten its pace much more than usual, the mahout's boy, who stands behind holding on to two lines from the girth, turns round and picking up the mallet proceeds to belabour the root of the elephant's tail, with that side of the mallet which is studded with nails. If only a slight increase of speed is desired the other or plain side of the mallet can be used, but as a rule with only little effect.

We set off on these pad elephants, I carrying my two rifles with me. Presently we came to a spot where there were a number of other elephants, some with howdahs, some with tables and chairs and food for luncheon, and some with photographers, etc. We waited here till word came that the tiger had been successfully ringed and then we transferred to the howdah elephants. I, being modest, waited till the last and so got the worst howdah. The ordinary shooting howdah is made of basketwork and wood, with sides sloping up till it is high enough in front for one to stand, without fear of being thrown out, to shoot. My howdah was a highly modern contraption, with sides no higher than my knees, so that it was out of the question to stand up and I had to shoot sitting down. The sides were made of metal and padded on the inside. The seat was only raised one inch off the floor, which was covered with rubber matting like in a motor car. The front of the howdah had little shelves and cupboards and cartridge racks, and on the right there were positions for a double barrel and a single barrel rifle. My elephant being slightly smaller than the three preceding ones and the howdah so much lower I was not troubled by overhanging boughs much, those that seemed at all likely to be in the way were promptly cut off by the mahout with his kukri, which all gurkhas carry.

After half an hour's ride we came upon a huge line of elephants which we joined, thus entering the ring of elephants encircling the tiger. All the guns were put together at one place, three each side of David. We advanced slowly towards the centre of the circle, whose diameter must have been quite half a mile. Presently we halted and some specially trained elephants were put into the centre to drive the tiger towards us. Presently there was a rustle in the undergrowth and much yelling on the part of the men and something streaked by, which I could not properly see. I was afraid that this was our tiger, but it turned out only to be a sambhur, a kind of large deer. Another advance, halt and false alarm, as a barking deer leapt out quite near me.

The circle was much smaller now, not more than two or three hundred yards in diameter, and the elephants in the centre were busy nosing about, when suddenly some of them started trumpeting loudly and all the mahouts yelled furiously and in the distance I could see the long grass and undergrowth rustle. I was duly thrilled to learn that this time the rustle had been caused by a tiger.

After a further wait we distinctly heard the tiger growl. Then there was a rush along the line and more trumpeting and yelling. I was feeling thoroughly excited now and peered anxiously ahead for a glimpse of the tiger. Presently I was rewarded, for I saw the grass parting and as I got my rifle up a light brown body flashed past an opening in the undergrowth and was gone.

Another wait. The elephants beat down towards us again and this time the tiger came out on my left, but so perfectly has nature camouflaged his coat that he was very hard to see, the more so as he was decidedly not standing still. David fired, two more shots rang out, and then I fired although the tiger had passed a good way to my left. He appeared to be all right, for a little later an incautious mahout approached too near and with a roar the tiger charged and got the elephant in the leg just as it was escaping. Finally they succeeded in driving him down again and this time I saw him so distinctly that I took careful aim and fired together with several others. We waited to see results. After a while, as nothing happened, our side advanced cautiously to find the tiger stretched out full length, dead, a bullet having passed through its neck. This shot is attributed to Col. Worgan's[1] last shot, and another shot in the hindquarters to David's first one, and according to the custom which gives a tiger to the first shot it was called David's.

The tiger was a fine one measuring 9 ft 3 ins in length up to the tip of his tail. We had lunch near by and returned to the cars by pad elephants, reaching there about 4 o'clock.

THURSDAY, 15 DECEMBER   We arrived at the place at which our elephants were about 11.45 and at once transferred to them. We went out a mile or so on pad elephants and then transferred to the howdahs. This time I took care to get a first-class howdah, mounted on a really big and intelligent-looking creature. Hardly had we got settled before further news came to say that the tiger had broken the ring and got away. We proceeded however and joined in the line of elephants that were sweeping out, endeavouring to ring the tiger afresh. In this we proved unsuccessful and as it was by now half past one we stopped and had lunch. I was deeply grieved to find that they actually expected the royal party to eat off the ground like mere mortals out shooting, as they had not brought any tables and chairs on elephants!

I saw several perfectly pathetic looking calves tied to pegs at various places, waiting to be killed by some tiger. I think that is the most unpleasant aspect of the whole affair.

On our way back to the cars one of the Prime Minister's sons, the one who is running this camp and shoot, came up to me and said, 'And why should not the noble lord shoot a rhinoceros?' I looked round but as there seemed to be a dearth of noble lords in the immediate neighbourhood I came to the conclusion that he must really be addressing me and answered, 'Why indeed not?'

He then promised to take me out himself after one in a day or two and went on to talk about Papa, saying that he was still remembered in Nepal and how Jung Bahadur, himself, took him into his howdah to shoot his tiger. At first I wondered if he knew who I was and who my father was but when he went on to speak of the debt of gratitude everyone, including Nepal, owed him for his order to the fleet to stand

---

[1] Colonel R. B. Worgan, attached to the Prince's Staff to supervise transport and other such arrangements.

fast in 1914[1] I began to realise that this man knew a lot. He is General Kaiser Shumsher Jung Bahadur Rana, son of the Prime Minister and son-in-law of the King, a general by birth and a very nice and intelligent man.

We took him back in our car and I have rarely been so entertained by a flow of witty and intelligent conversation. He knows all the family, since he was in London in 1908 and also studies all the newspapers assiduously. He knows all our old and new names, who my brother is, whom he married and when. About me he knew less since he asked, 'Are you a married man?' The reply being in the negative he proceeded, 'Please write to me when you are, so that I may share your joy.'

FRIDAY, 16 DECEMBER   New of a tiger came about 9 o'clock this morning. There were two kills which they were endeavouring to ring and we waited in camp until the news should come that this had been accomplished. It was not until shortly after noon that the news came and we started out.

We motored to a place called Baghai about 13 miles from Bhikna Thori and there mounted our elephants, some going on pads, others, including myself, in howdahs. The tiger was inside a patch of high reeds and pampas grass, surrounded on two sides by trees. Those trees that were in the way were quickly cleared by elephants, who can push over fairly large trees with their heads and pull branches off with their trunks. On my side there were no trees, and the shikar elephants started beating from my corner. After about five minutes two shots rang out in rapid succession, followed shortly afterwards by a third shot. These proved to have been fired by David and Joey. The latter fired the first two at a range of about twenty yards and thought that he had hit the tiger in the head. David loosed off at the tiger as he passed him at high speed and did not think he hit him.

For the next twenty minutes or so the tiger gave no sign of his existence, although the shikar elephants were moving about.

I felt sure that Joey had killed him and sat down in my howdah. Hardly had I done so than there was a roar, unmistakably the voice of the tiger, and I leapt to my feet. In a minute he appeared out of the tall grass in front of me some twenty yards away. I fired at his shoulder and he leapt back into cover, as he did so I fired the second barrel of my express rifle and then Armstrong handed me my shot gun, which

---

[1] A deed for which posterity too often gives the credit to Winston Churchill, though in fact he did no more than endorse the First Sea Lord's decision.

was loaded with contractile bullet cartridges, and I blazed away both barrels at where I could still see the grass moving. Armstrong thought I hit him three times, but the mahout was wiser and said to him in Hindustani, 'No, the Sahib hit the tiger in the foreleg once only.' As the tiger had come out with his left side facing me this meant that I had hit the near foreleg, and on subsequent inspection of the body this proved to be the case.

Another five or ten minutes passed during which the wounded tiger lay low, and as the shikar elephants were having no success our side of the ring was ordered forward. I advanced with them, but slightly in advance so as to give a better radius of fire. Presently there was a roar and the tiger charged out at an elephant to my left. I swung round but there were two elephants in the line of fire and I could only fire as the tiger was returning to cover.

Another three minutes passed and this time I advanced well in front of the line so that if he charged again I should get a clear shot. Sure enough there was a snarl and the tiger came out straight in front of me not ten yards away. This time I was ready and, aiming, as I had been taught, between the eyes, I fired.

The result was amazing, for he simply crumpled up and fell in his tracks. He proved to be a very fine tiger measuring 9 ft 7 ins between two pegs placed at the tip of the tail and the nose. The Nepalese usually measure round the curve of the back, which would bring this one's length up to nearly 10 ft. Its weight was estimated at 450 lbs. Its coat was in good condition and was well marked. There were three holes visible; the one in the leg, which was the one my mahout saw me get, the one in the forehead where I had finally killed him, and another in the back of the head.

This I at first attributed to Joey and I said to him, 'If this is your shot, as you fired first it is your tiger.' He replied, 'I thought I hit him but am not certain, so it may be your tiger.' Colonel Worgan decided that the whole question must be settled by Mr Ellison, the taxidermist attached to the camp, after the beast had been skinned. To this we all agreed. Mr Ellison when he saw the skull at once decided that both holes in the head had been made by one bullet, passing in at the front and out at the back, which could only have been my final and fatal shot. In other words the tiger had only been hit twice and on each occasion by me, so that it was my tiger. Naturally I was frightfully pleased but I am afraid that I talked a good deal too much about the whole question and as to the possibility of it being mine or Joey's tiger, which was silly of me and I am sure could not have added to my popularity with the others.[1]

SUNDAY, 18 DECEMBER   In obedience to H.I.M.'s wishes there was no shooting, much to the disgust of the Nepalese, who do not understand our Sunday. They were also disappointed that David did not go out after big game yesterday, as he merely shot jungle fowl and snipe in the afternoon, but I am afraid that David very definitely does not care for this ring tiger shooting. It is not very sporting, as the tiger has practically no chance of escape, and whenever David goes he feels that he is stopping other people from shooting until he has shot first, although he has issued orders that no one is to wait for him to shoot. In fact he is too keen about his riding and polo to care much about anything else and he goes down every morning to knock a polo ball about.

I went down to the skinning camp and saw my skin. It was interesting but I could have done with some itr.

MONDAY, 19 DECEMBER   Another blank day for me and at the same place, Kasra. I have now motored 120 miles after rhino without seeing even a sign of one. Two rhinos were supposed to have been marked for us by trackers, but one got away too far before we arrived. We were hot on the trail for the other one, expecting to see it any minute, when suddenly my elephant shot forward, nearly throwing me out of the howdah. I naturally thought that we had come across the rhino and it had charged.

It afterwards was explained to me that the big tusker I was on had suddenly gone 'must'.[2] This is exceedingly dangerous as it is the only time when an elephant will not obey his mahout and generally sees red. This one first went for the cow elephant ahead of me and rammed his tusks into her. The mahout hit him an awful thump on the head and away we went. The elephant banged the howdah up against trees and branches so that we had to cower down in the bottom and hope for the best. I have rarely been so buffeted about, and it was ten times worse than a P boat in a gale. The old bull elephant careered over the roughest ground and was eventually brought up by the mahout, who

---

[1] 'I have been having slight troubles with the Staff – partly my own fault and partly not –' Mountbatten told his mother two days later, 'but everything is all right again.'
[2] Or musth, a state of frenetic sexual excitement which periodically afflicts male elephants.

had drawn his kukri and was slashing away with the blade at the brute's forehead, cutting it to ribbons before he got the elephant at all under control.

WEDNESDAY, 21 DECEMBER This was our last day in Nepal. Personally I was sorry, as life in camp amid all the wild jungle surroundings has had a great fascination for me. For David's sake I am glad that we are going back to places where he can play polo, as he has been caring less and less for this shooting. In fact he has spent three out of the seven shooting days after small game. On Saturday he went out after birds, and both yesterday and today he waited in till after 2.00 p.m. for news of cover near by and when this did not come he went out walking up game with a shot gun. Today, as well as jungle fowl, pea hens and green parrots, he shot a large snake nearly ten foot long, of a species which has not yet been identified but which is believed to be poisonous.

There are no telephones or telegraphs in Nepal, neither are there trains. The road into Katmandu, the capital, is so arranged that the last stages of it can only be accomplished on an elephant and the few cars that are used in the city have had to be conveyed there in pieces by elephants.

The Maharaja has presented all of us with a very fine kukri and a set of Nepalese coins each. Mine has a sheath covered with silver, the arms of Nepal being worked in in gold. Besides this General Kaiser has given me some ordinary kukris and is sending me his photo.

It is reputed that this shoot has cost Nepal 46 lakhs or about £300,000. Anyway it is safe to say that the total is at least a quarter of a million sterling. About 30 head of big game have been obtained, all told, and so each animal may be considered worth £10,000. I believe that there are only between three and four hundred elephants here and not seven hundred as I was told before.

Another feature I have so far omitted to mention is the magnificent view one gets from the camp of the Himalayas. The peaks are about 150 miles distant. They make the Alps appear like valleys, as the Red Queen would have put it. Incidentally the name is pronounced here 'Hm*ah*lyers'.

THURSDAY, 22 DECEMBER Patna was reached at 10.00 a.m. The metre gauge train only took us as far as Paleza Ghat where the S.S.

Benares awaited us. In this we proceeded down the Ganges, landing at Commissioner's Ghat on the opposite side.

At Commissioner's Ghat our landaus, etc. were awaiting us. Then followed a long drive to Government House. There were more people than expected in the streets, but local people state that but for intimidation by the police many more people would have turned up.

FRIDAY, 23 DECEMBER   David, Fruity, Lord Cromer and I went down to the polo ground before breakfast to knock a polo ball about. I have come to the conclusion that in my present state this is of greater benefit to me than actually playing in games, so I knock about whenever I can.

The landed 'magnates' gave a garden party in Hardinge Park, which we all attended. An incident occurred here which, while demonstrating the zealous loyalty of the whites, is typical of that short-sighted policy of intimidation which is doing so much to keep the crowds away. A car, flying a large red flag, manned by some of those gallant volunteers, the Bihar Light Horse, joined into the middle of our procession, with rifles and it is reported even Lewis guns held up conspicuously. David was very angry.

The garden party itself started with the super pomp of native India and finished with a truly democratic crowd of every conceivable caste, creed and odour. In fact it resolved itself into a football scrum, with David as the ball, like it used to be in Australia and New Zealand.

After dinner we left by train for Calcutta.

SATURDAY, 24 DECEMBER   Punctually at 10.24 we drew in at Calcutta Station. Everything was beautifully arranged, a red carpet led from the spot they expected David to step out on to, to the barouche, while on each side Officers in cloth full dress were drawn up, with H.E.[1] and notables in the centre. On either side of this strip of carpet, just behind the Officers, a thick jungle of palms and ferns had been erected.

There was only one miscalculation; they had forgotten to allow for our second engine and it proved impossible to draw David's carriage up opposite the red carpet, as the first engine was hard up against the buffers. Consequently David had to struggle through the 'jungle' and got into the middle of the ranks.

However the whole arrival and procession otherwise went off very

[1] The Governor of Bengal, the Earl of Ronaldshay, later to become Marquess of Zetland and Secretary of State for India.

well. He received a better reception than anybody expected, but not so good as it might have been some years ago.

David lunched with the Stewards of the Calcutta Turf Club and afterwards attended the races. I was feeling rather seedy, so turned in and had a sleep. I then felt well enough to attend the dinner party and small dance held afterwards, which was quite good fun. It finished quite early.

SUNDAY, 25 DECEMBER   It seems incredible that today should be Christmas. The naval members of the Staff actually wore whites for church, and it certainly was hot enough. All our Indian retinue have been profuse in showering Christmas wishes upon us, even the Postmaster sent me an official missive of good wishes. As for all these Nepalese Generals and Maharajas we have met, and even some we did not meet, they have simply snowed us under with cards of generous dimensions. In some cases the same exalted personage has sent two cards, or a wire in addition to a card. All this will keep me busy for a long time answering them.

I gave Hiscock a kukri and a tip and Kanickum some backsheesh, which later caused the latter to complain of fever or what we would call 'a head'.

MONDAY, 26 DECEMBER   David lunched with the Governor of Assam[1] onboard the *Sonamookhi* and made a speech there. This he tried to repeat to me on return as he considered it so very good, but I wasn't having any. The remainder of the Staff lunched here at Government House and afterwards left for the races in motors, while the unfortunate David was drawn in semi-state round the course.

The races were quite amusing, though it is hard to raise enthusiasm over horses one has never heard of before belonging to unknown owners and ridden by strange jockeys. I only had one bet on the Viceroy's Cup and that was on 'Goodhealth' as I knew the owner – Hari Singh of Kashmir – who is attached to the Staff here.

TUESDAY, 27 DECEMBER   My bearer called me at 6.45 a.m. and mumbled something in my ear which I did not quite catch. After the barber had finished shaving me (one is always shaved in bed out here, even in the train) I fell asleep and only just woke up in time to get

---

[1] Sir W. Marris.

above: A group at Viceroy's House. H.R.H. is flanked by Lord and Lady Reading. Mountbatten is one from the end on the right of the back row.

below: H.R.H. with the Maharaja of Patiala and Captain 'Fruity' Metcalfe.

The wistful figure of H.R.H. in the uniform of Jacob's Horse (35th/36th Cavalry).

dressed by 7.30 when we were due to leave. I sent for my bearer who explained that he had fever. On going further into the matter it turned out that he was feeling the effects of Christmas and my tip.

Anyway I went off with David and about half the Staff for the paperchase. As there is no hunting out here the local enthusiasts have invented the next best thing, paperchasing. A trail is laid, over a different course every time, which has to be followed. It usually contains some twenty jumps, mostly mud walls, and some perilous tracks through the jungle where it is only by the greatest luck that one avoids emulating Absalom.[1]

There were nearly two hundred riders at the meet, but luckily it had been arranged that they should start in two main heats. I had originally wanted to go paperchasing but as none of our horses seemed to be up to what was required of them and the supply of other horses was limited I had given up hope and had made no effort to try any jumps or even look at the course. The night before the C.O. of the Viceroy's Body-guard, which has been lent to David in Calcutta, offered some Body-guard horses to us and I for one accepted the offer.

The horse they lent me was a charming creature called Lobster. Their best jumper they lent to our best rider, Aubrey Metcalfe.[2] David had a very special (and as it turned out much too special) mount lent him.

The first heat now lined up before the first jump, a typical mud wall, specially built, and not nearly wide enough to accommodate even the first heat. From where we were these walls looked enormous, but I suppose that they were really quite small. Presently we got the word to go and everyone went hard for the wall. Poor Aubrey and his prize jumper, who were next to me, took the most ghastly toss, which did not encourage me too much, especially as I had a job to avoid them on the ground. Aubrey got slight concussion and is now in bed.

As soon as we had left the second heat started and then anyone else who wanted to, including numerous ladies. The P.M.O. who was watching the first jump counted fifteen falls at this wall alone, yet really it is nothing so very formidable to look back upon.

A second wall followed immediately and the trail started jinking about, turning sharply to the right and left, over jumps, up and down banks, through jungle tracks, where one had to ride in single file and

---

[1] Who was suspended by his hair from a tree (2 Samuel XVIII).
[2] Not to be confused with 'Fruity' Metcalfe. H. A. F. Metcalfe was seconded for the trip from the Indian Civil Service.

over all sorts of different country. The whole course was between 4 and 5 miles long, and is just about as fair a test of a horse as can be desired. David had quite set his heart on coming in first and was soon leading the field. He paid dearly for this mistake as the trail is not easy for a novice to follow and he overshot the mark several times when it turned very suddenly. I had been told that my mount was safe but not fast and so hung back a little and to my amazement came in 7 or 8 places before David at the finish, which is about 12th or so in the whole field I think, and not too bad for a humble rider like myself.

In the afternoon there was a large Indian entertainment on the Maidan, to which poor David had to drive in semi-state, while the rest of us motored. It opened by David being blessed in every creed by various priests, which was interesting, though hardly improved by the band, which drowned some of the chanting by playing a foxtrot.

First a musical pageant went by. This consisted of the following English notes: C, D, E, F, G, A, B. Each note was sounded on a trumpet and then a carriage was drawn past containing the note's deity and attendants, music being considered of divine origin.

The next procession consisted of six principal Ragas of the Hindus A Raga or Rag appears to be a sort of God representing a season of the year possessing a tune also called a Rag, which was sung by attendants before each carriage containing the God.

Two dances followed this, the first being the Tibetan Lama Dance, a religious rite being performed before us by priests dressed in weird clothes with fearsome and huge masks of various animals and monsters. The other was the Manipuri Dance, done by young girls, not unlike a Nautch. The Nowroz Procession, similar to those held a century back, closed the show.

WEDNESDAY, 28 DECEMBER   At 10.45 a.m. we had to get into our blue full dress again and drive in state to the Victoria Memorial, which David opened. It is a magnificent building of white marble, and was designed as long ago as 1901. We had to process very pompously up a long strip of red carpet and, to everyone's consternation but to David's secret joy, a sweet young thing ran out into the middle of this to present him with a black cat mascot.

Inside the building a museum of relics of the Victorian era has been arranged, which we inspected. There are also wall paintings on the inside of the great dome depicting the principal events in great grand-mama's life.

THURSDAY, 29 DECEMBER   David and some of the Staff went by river in the S.S. *Empress Mary* to Barrackpore to present Colours to the 2nd Battn of one of his regiments, the Royal Scots Fusiliers, but as the new Colours had not arrived from Bombay he had to content himself with inspecting them. He lunched with the officers and returned so late that there was not time to change for the garden party at G.H.

I lunched with the remainder and changed into a grey tail coat and top hat for the garden party. The mixture was comic, as David appeared in a glengarry, some of the Staff in uniform and some in top hats. The garden party was of a thoroughly democratic character as regards the tail end of the list of guests.

There was a dinner party followed by a dance. I danced a couple of dances with Lady Ronaldshay, as usual. She is a good dancer and a most charming person. I am afraid that she does not care for India too much, which is a pity as people are apt to notice this and run her down.

FRIDAY, 30 DECEMBER   We left shortly after 7.00 a.m. for another paperchase. I had arranged to ride the same horse, Lobster, and had privately determined to be in the first ten or even the first six, now that I knew something of the game and my horse.

Accordingly when we lined up I took care to secure a good place, and the end of the first two jumps found me lying about sixth in the whole field. For five glorious minutes Lobster and I sailed over mud walls and small ridges and held our own in the throng; I even passed David.

Then it happened: there was so much dust about that neither Fruity Metcalfe, who was on my left, nor I saw the open ditch we came to round a corner. In fact hardly anybody saw it and it was just luck if one's horse took it in its stride or went in. Mine went in and so did Fruity's. I think Lobster must have turned a somersault, anyway I landed on my face and left side on the hard and dusty ground. I was a bit dazed, but I had had my chin strap down and my heavy topee had taken a good bit of the shock.

Behind me thundered the rest of the field, an odd hundred or so, so I got up to run out of the way. No sooner had I got to my feet than I was knocked endways by a kick on the head from a horse which someone had ridden into me. Luckily my topee once more took the shock, but before I got finally clear I had two more horses over me, one of which stepped on my left foot and another on the inside of my right elbow joint.

By this time Fruity had also got clear, having escaped with only a hurt shoulder. We stood and watched the remainder of the hard riders go past and then trudged along the paper trail.

Fruity was very silent on the whole, considering that he had been mounted on one of the most famous hunters in India and himself was no mean horseman. He did just let forth one stream of invective in which he traced the ancestry of the man who had laid the paper over that hidden ditch and even treated me to a short dissertation on the manufacture of the paper which had led us to our undoing, but I forget exactly what he said and I expect he does too.

When we got back the P.M.O. had a look at me, and put me on the sick list as my foot had swollen up considerably and my elbow was cut and bruised, so I couldn't take my day on, which I was supposed to have today. Considering that there were three concussions and one broken collar bone Fruity and I got off light.

After lunch we all left for Outram Ghat where we embarked in the despatch vessel, *Pansy*, a converted sloop. The pontoon was crowded with people who cheered tremendously as we shoved off. We proceeded about forty miles down the Hooghly to Jellingham Anchorage, where we transferred to the *Dufferin*.

After dinner onboard the *Dufferin* weighed and proceeded to sea.

SATURDAY, 31 DECEMBER I felt somewhat stiff and my foot was swollen so I spent the forenoon turned in. David has given up the idea of lunch aboard the *Dufferin*, but I did not forgo this meal. Afterwards David and I practised knocking a polo ball about in the pit they have constructed in the waist of canvas, according to the suggestions I put forward when I came onboard on the Thursday morning. The 'pony' has had a head and neck built on to carry the bridle, which makes it resemble a camel.

We are all messing in the Ward Room, except a few of the press men, for whom there was not room and who, to their own discontent, are messing in another saloon. It being a 'Saturday Night At Sea', David, as usual proposed the time-honoured toast of 'Sweethearts and Wives', followed by a 'New Year's Toast'.

I turned in fairly early after dinner and read some correspondence, so that I was awake when David struck 16 bells at the end of the middle.[1] I also had the doubtful pleasure of hearing the C-in-C's band, which he had lent for the trip, having a fight over 'Auld Lang Syne' and 'For he's a jolly good fellow' with all the rest of the party who were endeavouring to sing it.

I think we are all sorry to leave Calcutta, where we have had a good time on the whole. The reception David received from the natives was a hundred times better than that accorded to Uncle Arthur[2] this time last year, but not so good as the King Emperor's.

Anyway there was no rioting, though the 'Civil Guard' enrolled from the Europeans and the fire engines which careered through the streets with clanging bells may have had not a little to do with this.

SUNDAY, 1 JANUARY 1922 This ship is an old trooper and as such ideal for taking a large party of officers and retinue, like ours. I have quite a comfortable cabin next to David's, though I must say it is unpleasantly hot. She is run by the Royal Indian Marine, a sort of Naval Service, wearing R.N.R. stripes though a different badge.

The Nawab of Palanpur, who was attached to our Staff in Bombay, has sent a few of us including me New Year gifts. Mine is rather a magnificent old silver bowl on a black stand, with quaint old figures worked on it in relief. It appears that we have to either (1) return it (2) hand it to the Toshakana or treasury or (3) give a gift of equal value in return. All three courses are unpleasant but I anyhow have determined to hold on to my bowl so I suppose I shall have to comply with (3).

MONDAY, 2 JANUARY *Dufferin* secured alongside Lewis Street Jetty, Rangoon, at 8.30, and after the Governor, Sir Reginald Craddock,[3] had paid his official call, we all landed officially.

After inspecting the naval and military Guards and receiving an address from the municipality, David entered the Governor's landau for the official drive, the rest of us following in motor cars, as we had brought no carriages to Burma. The route to Government House was some three miles long and at all parts thickly lined with people, who

---

[1] At midnight on New Year's Eve the eight bells that mark the end of a watch are struck twice. This is not 'at the end of the middle', however, but at the end of the first or beginning of the middle watch.

[2] The Duke of Connaught, who had visited India the previous year and opened the new Legislative Assembly.

[3] In fact Lieutenant Governor. His successor, Sir Harcourt Butler, was the first Governor.

gave David as good a reception as he had had anywhere since Bombay. It was noticeable that there were remarkably few actual Burmans out, but there are two feasible explanations. Firstly, they have been intimidated, and this is apparently an easier thing to do to a Burman than the rest of the inhabitants. Secondly, less than one half of the population of Rangoon is Burmese.

Government House is a fine building, in which we have settled down comfortably in spite of the oppressive heat. Lady Craddock is well-meaning but old and is handicapped by a perpetual nodding of the head; her married daughter who is here is like her in some respects.

The rest of the forenoon was free, so David dashed off to knock a polo ball about. As they are still continuing to put fomentations on my arm I was not able to do very much.

Just before four we went to the University where David received an address and poem in the vernacular from the students. They had all sorts of weird jazz bands of the local variety on show and we also saw four undergraduates playing the national game of basketball. The ball itself, as the name implies, is made of basket wicker, about twice the size of a cricket ball. The game consists in keeping the ball in the air by 'heading' it or kicking it with the knee or foot and it is most entertaining to watch. A good player will let the ball drop close behind him and then kicking up backwards send it back over his head.

On the way to the University we passed a large number of men of the 1/96 Berar Infantry who had gathered without any white officers to cheer David. They collected all round and hanging on to the car ran, cheering, with us for at least half a mile.

We next motored to Dalhousie Park to an ex-service men's gathering. The park is lovely, with a winding stretch of water in the centre, the grass and trees being as green as in Regent's Park. Here again David received a wonderful ovation, especially on leaving, as they all collected round the car so that David had to stand up, like in Australia, to be seen better.

In the evening there was a dinner party followed by a reception of some 700 people, in which they had private and public entrées, just like at levées.

A good day, comparable to any in Australia or New Zealand.

TUESDAY, 3 JANUARY We left at the early though cool hour of 7.45 for the racecourse for the Proclamation Parade, celebrating the anniversary of 1876 when the Queen was proclaimed Empress. The Admiral and myself were all on top line to ride with David but owing to a scarcity of horse, none of our own having been brought over, only the three military officers rode. Those who were dismounted were hustled about all over the place before we eventually picked up our billet at the saluting base. Various salutes were fired and given, including a *feu de joie*, after which David rode down the lines. The show ended up with quite a good march past.

On return I played tennis with David for four sets, singles but using doubles court. I played badly and it was blazing hot, yet when I refused to go on David took the Admiral on at singles. I've never seen anybody take so much exercise on so little food, as he only eats biscuits for lunch. After lunch, at 2.25 to be precise, off we went to the polo ground and knocked about for 1½ hours in the blazing sun. Nevertheless I must admit to having loved this. The ponies out here are only 12½ to 13½ hands and the polo sticks are nearly six inches shorter so that it really is much easier for a beginner like me to hit the ball. They carry up to 12 stone without a murmur and are very fast and handy. I got one ball from behind one goal through the other in four shots!

A garden party took place immediately on our return, at which a display of basket ball and native juggling was given, as well as some native pwe dances being danced by Burmese girls.

WEDNESDAY, 4 JANUARY   David and I left at 9.15 and motored to the Native Infantry Lines, where the men of the 96th were drawn up. David inspected them, asking several of them questions in Hindustani, which they seemingly understood as they all replied volubly. Whether David understood their replies is another, and altogether unimportant matter. On departure they again gathered round the car and ran with it cheering.

After an informal dinner we left by train for Mandalay.

THURSDAY, 5 JANUARY   We spent up to tea time in the train as Mandalay is some 400 miles up country and the line is too rocky to permit of speedy travelling.

The train is a non-corridor one, which is a great nuisance, though it is possible to get from David's coach to the dining car through a middle car, which the Admiral and I have taken over. Our coach is enormous, the size of a pullman with two hard bunks which the Admiral and I are using. There are dozens of lights, but only one switch so that I had to go to sleep in a great glare, while the Admiral was studying his mail.

We stopped at a number of stations during the day at each of which there were sufficient crowds collected for David to get out, which made life rather difficult for him in the heat, and rest impossible. In several places the headman and a number of others would be kneeling in a prostrate position on a little carpet. In one case, during the breakfast halt, they remained like this to my knowledge for half an hour and possibly more.

The arrival at Mandalay was official with the usual attendant stunts, including 8 umbrellas, 4 open and 4 closed, under which David and the Governor could walk, but no one else.

The route was moderately well filled with crowds in places, and of course nearly entirely Burmans, which was satisfactory. They kept absolute silence, according to their ancient traditions of behaviour in the presence of Royalty, though the school children cheered loudly. The police have orders from Delhi to have their men facing the crowds to keep an eye on them. So literally do they interpret this order, that in places devoid of people the police still stand with their backs to David.

FRIDAY, 6 JANUARY   We left at 7.45 a.m. for another parade, similar to the one at Rangoon, but omitting the 'Proclamation' part. The rest of the forenoon we spent in selecting polo ponies for the afternoon's tournament. Just before lunch we went, in uniform, to the ex-service men and pensioners' camp, where the usual stunt took place. Afterwards we motored to the Palace of the old Kings of Burma, which is situated in the centre of Fort Dufferin, the fort being a large area now devoted to Cantonments, surrounded by a large moat. The top of the pagoda-like pinnacle of the palace is indeed held to be the Centre of the Universe by the uneducated Burmese. We were shown round by a Frenchman, and it was a most interesting place. It consists of a series of high wooden bungalows, somewhat crudely finished off. The wooden pillars are mostly gilt, the only other decoration being small bits of looking glass let in here and there.

There are a great number of throne rooms called after different animals or flowers. I actually saw the following throne rooms: lion, duck, bee and lily. Each throne room consists of an audience chamber of generous dimensions, usually with open sides, where the Princes and chief officers of state assembled, and a much smaller back room immediately behind the throne in which the women folk were permitted to wait. The throne itself was reached by steps leading up from the back room and was set in the middle of the partition wall. The King's private chambers were the only ones built of stone.

In another room they had preserved in glass cases the state robes of the King, Queen and other notables, including that of a military officer which had the weirdest shaped helmet and regalia attached to it. The whole place had such an air of antiquity about it that I was flabbergasted to learn that the last King held his last levée there in 1885.

There is a great fascination about the whole of Burma and no one could really mistake it for India. The natives look more Mongolian and the men wear a sort of silk skirt called longis, the grander form of which with a complete fold of silk hanging down in front is a paso. Some of the men, including soldiers, have long hair, some of the women have bobbed hair. It is a most confusing country. In the evening's entertainment we came across a tribe whose women, to be beautiful, have to be the possessors of giraffe-like necks. This effect is achieved by coiling heavy brass tubing round the neck till they can neither bend it nor turn it, and when I had a close look it made me feel rather sick.

After dinner we visited the Shan Camp and saw various tribes perform.

SATURDAY, 7 JANUARY   We started out at 8.00 and having driven five miles in cars came to a light railway line, where we transferred to trolleys. These were pushed at the most amazing speed by men, two to each trolley, running along the rails which could not have been above an inch thick. David went off in one party, Cromer and I in another after snipe. It meant wading through deep mud and water in places in the paddy fields. Twice I got into mud as far as my knees and had to be pulled out by my two natives. Once I all but stepped on a small snake about 18 inches long, which happily wriggled away. There were not so many birds where we were. I got my usual four while Cromer got seven couple. However as we were out for nearly four hours it was good exercise.

At 4.30 there was a vast garden party at G.H. on the lawn next to the moat. There was also canoe racing going on on the moat, which was fascinating to watch. Some of the tribes row standing up using their legs. They curl the outboard one round the paddle and, supporting the handle with their hand, put great force into the stroke. There were thousands of Burmese on the opposite bank and arrangements had been made for David to show himself to these people. Accordingly he entered the state barge, which was made in the form of a large fabulous monster resembling in some respects an eagle and bearing on its back a domed papier-mâché pagoda. In the centre of this a large chair had been placed for David. The whole contraption looked as though it might fall to pieces at any moment though luckily this was not noticeable at a little distance off. Two racing canoes towed it, but its progress was slow and I was not sorry that there had not been sufficient room for me to go too.

On return there was another group of native jugglers to see, who played a form of basketball with glass globes and another endless pwe dance. These pwe dances, though of undoubted interest, are incredibly monotonous as the pwe girls hardly move at all and usually just strike attitudes while chanting their unmusical song. Their dress consists of a tight skirt about six inches longer than their legs and a little jacket with two sickle-shaped projections at the back of the bottom of the jacket. Their hair is wound in a tight coil round the tops of their heads, leaving just a fringe hanging down.

After the garden party we went into a room in G.H. where native wares from the Shan Camp had been laid out. I bought several things, little crude lacquer bowls and part of a woman's head-dress, which will make a wonderful cushion. I also got 3 dhars or native swords of varying lengths. One was about nine feet long, another three inches long and the third was made in the shape of a blunderbus with a concealed blade in the stock. We left by train at 9.30.

SUNDAY, 8 JANUARY   The journey down to Rangoon was very similar to the journey up, only hotter and more aggravating for David, who was in very bad shape.

We reached Rangoon at 5.00 p.m. and immediately drove to G.H. as the arrival was unofficial, nevertheless a very good crowd filled the station platform and lined the first half mile of the route. They had also relaxed the police restrictions and allowed the crowd to stand within a few feet of David's car, as it passed. The normal arrangement, as ordered by Delhi, is to keep them a clear 15 yards off and further at corners, which is all very well but hardly an inducement to come and see David. The police too, have always to stand with their backs to David, and if there are people they not infrequently hit those within reach over the head as a slight compensation for the trouble they have taken to come and see David. In fairness I must add that the police force are composed of fine men, who would willingly lay down their lives to protect David, and see in every spectator a potential assassin.

At 3.15 we set out for the Royal Lakes in Dalhousie Park, where a native entertainment had been organized by the citizens of Rangoon. It entailed another trip in a state barge, I being included this time. After this we witnessed some native fighting. They call it boxing, but I cannot really follow why, for one of the chief objects of the game appears to be to kick your opponent and below the belt too. There is a certain amount of hitting, usually with the open palm at the other fellow's face, but then they also catch hold of each other round the neck as in wrestling. In fact the only rules appear to be that you must not bite or pull the other fellow's hair, which is usually long. After we had seen several fights one fellow had a few teeth knocked down his throat and was led up for our inspection, his bleeding and disfigured mouth being an obvious source of satisfaction to the victim.

TUESDAY, 10 JANUARY   We left Government House at 10.15 a.m. and stopped at the Guard House to inspect the Inner and Outer Cordon Guards. The whole route to Lewis Street Jetty, where the *Dufferin* was lying, was lined with crowds, thin at first but gradually thickening to nine and ten deep near the ship. In places too the police had allowed the crowd to get near but in another part of the town they were back to their 15 yards on either side. The crowd was wonderfully enthusiastic, even the demure little high-caste Burmese ladies cheered. Towards the end all barriers were broken down and we advanced in the usual scrimmage amidst deafening cheers. It really did one good to see David get a good reception again. Burma may have its troubles but it is many times more loyal than India, anyway at the moment.

We said our farewells on the jetty to save time. The foreshore and jetties all down the Irrawaddy were lined with people, and many boats and tugs accompanied us. One tug was towing a couple of barges on which a stage had been rigged up, and where to the accompaniments of a native band, some Burmese girls were dancing a pwe.

We soon settled down to ship life. In the afternoon I got out a pogo stick, which I forgot to mention I had brought ashore at Rangoon where it was used, and those of the Staff who were new to it tried their hand at pogoing. We also practised knocking a polo ball about in the canvas pit, which has been rigged up again.

After dinner we sang songs, including 'On the Road to Mandalay'.

WEDNESDAY, 11 JANUARY   An uneventful day, though moderately cool thanks to a pleasant breeze. David, attended by the Naval Staff, inspected the ship's company, who are mostly Lascars, at Divisions, and walked round the upper decks.

THURSDAY, 12 JANUARY   Another cool day, though I found it hot enough in the Engine Rooms and Stokeholds when I accompanied David down there.

I never described a pagoda while in Burma, and this is a serious omission since the whole place bristles with them, even in quite deserted parts of the country. A pagoda is a kind of temple, which it is the ambition of every good Burman to build. It may vary in height from a few feet to the size of the Shwe Dagon Pagoda in Rangoon, which can be seen for miles round. The shape is that of a hand-bell, where the base of the handle is as wide as the top of the bell.

Shwe Dagon, the glory of all the pagodas, besides being enormous and built on an artificial mound, is covered with thin but solid plates of pure gold, which shine quite wonderfully in the sunlight. Unfortunately the Burmese priests or Pugis have started a strife, more political than religious, about the removal of footgear by Europeans, which has never been a custom in Burma, so we could not go and see it.

FRIDAY, 13 JANUARY   At 8.30 we arrived at Madras and secured alongside West Quay. While I was having breakfast in the Ward Room I heard a to-do and much noise upon bugles, or as Shakespeare would put it, 'Alarums and Excursions without'. Judging (correctly) that the Governor[1] had arrived I felt that it was time for me to put in an appearance. Accordingly I walked along the disengaged side and by taking the party in the rear managed to mingle with them in such a way as not to arouse suspicions.

Her Excellency Lady Willingdon had proposed coming onboard when His Ex. paid his official call, and although anxious signals were went by W/T last night she turned up on the quay, but did not come onboard. Had she really intended to come onboard nothing short of

---

[1] Lord Willingdon, a future Viceroy and Governor-General of Canada, had been George V's favourite partner at tennis. His wife was notorious for her addiction to the colour mauve and drove the architect Sir Edwin Lutyens to distraction by the 'improvements' she made to his Viceroy's House in New Delhi. He described her as a '*mauvais sujet*'.

a file of marines would have stopped her for even in our short acquaintance of her we have all, I think, fully realized what a very determined lady she is.

Anyway, on disembarking from the old *Dufferin*, where we have all been comfortable and contented, the usual parlour tricks occurred, including a couple of guards and a couple of addresses with replies, suitably varied, finishing up with presentations, a state drive and more guards at the other end. The route was uncommonly well lined with natives, which must have been quite a blow to our friends the Non-Co-operators who had expected their boycott to be a complete success. As in Bombay, so here, on finding that their Non-Violence system produced no results they resorted to Violence. Shortly after we arrived at Government House a number of known bad characters collected outside a little cinema belonging to a loyal old native. His crime appeared to be that he had had the temerity to decorate the front of his theatre with patriotic flags and mottoes and had announced a special programme in honour of David's visit. Anyway they went for that place and smashed it to pieces, even burning the 'special programme' of films. The proprietor, realizing he was up against it, produced some old firearm and killed one man and wounded two. All this occurred almost within view of my bedroom window and although I did not see the commotion I heard it. Another lot of rioters overturned a tram and threw stones at all Europeans driving cars; I, myself saw the broken wind-screens and damaged parts of the town. Three armoured cars, who had been held in readiness for just such a contingency, leapt down the trail and opened fire with their machine guns, accounting for several more rioters.

A taxi, driven by a white man, and engaged by Government House, was driving along, empty, when the chauffeur saw a man standing about a hundred yards ahead in the road with a large brick in his hand ready to throw. The driver pressed down the accelerator and the car jumped ahead at nearly 50 miles an hour. The man just had time to throw his brick, which, though it smashed the wind-screen, missed the driver, before the car went over him with both wheels, leaving him a somewhat shapeless mass in the road.

SATURDAY, 14 JANUARY After attending a small luncheon party at Government House we all drove out to Guindy in motors, David transferring at the racecourse to the barouche for the official drive to the grand stand, while we motored direct.

The races were quite good but did not thrill me. The combined Staffs of David, H.E. The Governor and H.E. The Naval C-in-C numbered about thirty and as they were all dressed alike in grey tail coat and grey top hat (a rig which hardly anyone else was wearing) they reminded me for all the world of the male chorus of the Gaiety at some stage race meeting. Before the arrival of the Willingdons two years ago, the course was practically non-existent, and the Madras Race Club owes its prosperous position chiefly to the efforts of Lord Willingdon. There was a primitive course in existence nearly fifty years ago to which Papa went.

SUNDAY, 15 JANUARY There was the usual small lunch party at Government House. I had ordered a motor for the afternoon, and finding three waiting got into the nice little yellow 19.6 Crossley and drove off. It later transpired that I had taken the car the Admiral had ordered and so he had to take mine, and as my driver did not know the way to the place the Admiral was going, the Admiral was both late in arriving and unjustly incensed with me.

Anyway I drove out along the Marina, a glorious, straight, broad, tarmac-ed road that runs along the beach. The little car did 57 m.p.h. without a murmur and in ten minutes I was in Adyar, an outlying district of Madras. I had no difficulty in finding the buildings of the Theosophical Society, which contain several buildings named after prominent Theosophists. In Leadbeater's Chambers I found the rooms occupied by Louise's little Russian protégée, the Baroness de Kuster, with whom I had tea. She is a nice little person full of enthusiasm for Louise, David, England, India, Adyar and above all theosophy, which latter religion formed the basis of a very interesting conversation. The rooms reminded me of rooms at the Varsity. Food was produced from the usual cupboard, likewise the crockery. The 'bedder' it is true was black and called an *Ayah* but that did not entirely dispel the illusion that I was in some College.

The surroundings are lovely, as the building faces that most attractive of rivers, the Adyar, and only half a mile from its mouth. A belt of fir trees and coconut palms separate the house from the sandy beach, which can be seen across the river. Lovely flowers were out in the little garden and a cool sea breeze swept the verandah. No wonder the little baroness is happy out here, though I fear she may not like the place quite so much when the hot weather comes.

She spoke so enthusiastically of David that I wondered if she had ever met him and questioned her on the subject. She replied, 'No, not here, but I have often met him on the astral plane.' I was too astounded to laugh, and too interested to stop at that and we were soon deep in a religious discussion. Only the little baroness's obvious fervour presented my smiling occasionally at some of the things she asked me to believe. More than once I found a flaw in some of her statements, which she was unable to explain away. Unfortunately there is always this answer ready, 'There are many things we believe that we do not yet understand and they have not even been revealed fully to "The Masters".' She also informed me in confidence (though she gave me permission to tell my family) that it had but lately been revealed to Mrs Besant (whom I have seen both here and in Benares) that David's last incarnation had been in the body of Akbar, the great Moghul Emperor of India, a contemporary of our Queen Elizabeth. David was not over-pleased at the idea of having been a 'black man', so I did not inform him that his soul had previously been shared by a group of horses. In fact before the horses it had had to work up from lesser animals and tracing his soul backwards it appears that it had passed through a vegetable and a mineral stage, and before that through three elemental stages. Elemental I, in the first chain, is really rather a pretty idea. It is merely the 'thought' of God. The transition period between this and slime I don't like so much. The idea appears to be that this 'thought' gradually takes shape like a cloud or a puff of air and having materialized more and more in stages II and III the soul passes into mud. This part of their religion takes away a lot of its beauty, it seems to be descending from the sublime to the ridiculous.

Each soul, by the way, has the name of some constellation given it whereby it may be recognized through its different human bodies, even as Irving, the actor, retains the name of Irving whether he be playing Macbeth, Shylock or Henry VIII. One weakness of the scheme, which I had not the heart to point out, is that all souls occupying the bodies of Theosophists last came from some King or famous man. None has ever appeared under the humble name of Smith or Jones.

I was interested to learn that Vajra, whose last habitation had been the body of Madame Blavatsky, the founder of the movement with Col. Olcott (and a proved fraud more than once), has just appeared on earth again, this time in a man or rather boy just born, near the Himalayas. One of the 'masters', so it was revealed but a short while ago, has been detailed for duty with David during his tour of India, and will look after him.

MONDAY, 16 JANUARY   David started stunting at 8.30 a.m. doing boy scouts, girl guides and school children, etc. Later on, after he had had a game of squash, he had a police parade and a review of ex-service men followed by an inspection of his regiment, the Leinsters, at the fort, where he also lunched. They are all heartily sick at this Irish Free State business for it means the disbandment of all the fine Irish Regiments, except the Irish Guards, and none of the Leinsters appears to wish to join up under the Irish Free State.

I took the yellow car about 11 o'clock and drove to the Victoria Institute, where one can buy wonderful native wares. I got rather a nice Dutch chest, inlaid and bound with brass, which I am sending home to Audrey as a wedding present.[1] Her fiancé, Dudley Coats, having only left Rangoon the day before we got there I presumed that he would have bought her all she wanted in Burma and so had not got her anything there. I also got a set of a dozen little brass insects and a brass fish with jointed scales, not to mention a delightful fibre mat.

After tea I brought Baroness de Kuster, whom I had had invited, up to David for five minutes' conversation.

TUESDAY, 17 JANUARY   After lunch we split up, some of the party going on ahead to the races, others remaining behind altogether, while David, Her Ex. and some of us motored to the Victoria Institute, which was my undoing as I continued shopping where I had had to leave off yesterday. This time I got two rather attractive but very roughly made figures of a native snake charmer and a basket maker. I also got three attractive wooden toys, a top, a set of little boxes, one within another, and a box of small cups etc. I also got myself a silk muffler for only 8 rupees!

We have just heard by letter that that snake which David shot in Nepal, and which everyone poo-pooed as a harmless snake, was a Hamadryad or King Cobra, the most dangerous snake in India!

From the Victoria Hall we went to the Aquarium, where we saw some quite wonderful fishes being fed. I tried hard to get an 'electric shock' off the torpedo fish, but I reckon his battery had run down. There were also 'sea horses' which I had not seen since Venice, the Lido Aquarium, I think.

---

[1] Audrey James, former girl-friend of Mountbatten's. She preferred a scion of the great cotton family of Coats, thus, as some wit put it, abandoning a coat of arms in favour of the arms of Coats.

Finally we went on to the races at Guindy. Having a day on I stuck to David and so foiled Her Ex. in her attempt to use me as an extra A.D.C. again. David dined at the Madras Club in the evening, but I dined at G.H. We all joined up again at the Island, where we witnessed the best fireworks of the tour. At the departure from the station at 10.20 p.m. Burt and I had great trouble in getting the police to allow the crowd through, as usual.

WEDNESDAY, 18 JANUARY   We arrived at Bangalore at 8.30 a.m. and were faced at once with the prospect of an official drive in full dress without having had breakfast. The drive, nevertheless, went off well and the route was well lined by natives. The native police have had their truncheons removed, presumably to stop their hitting innocent members of the crowd. If this was the reason it did not have the desired effect for, no sooner had the royal barouche passed than the policemen removed their leather belts and dealt a number of skilful blows with the buckle end, so that some at least of the loyal people of Bangalore will have something to remember David's visit by.

On arrival at the Residency, for Bangalore, though a British Army centre, is in the native state of Mysore, we breakfasted. I then had a forenoon off, and as Kanickum is a native of Bangalore I gave him the day off to spend with his family. Contrary to my fears he returned sober and almost up to time. David had a parade, police review and pensioner stunt before lunch. He sat through lunch with Lord Ruthven, who commands the Bangalore area. I say 'sat through' advisedly as David has not eaten more than a few biscuits for lunch for some considerable time. Afterwards they saw a snake charmer at work.

There was a small dinner party at the Residency followed by a dance. We left by train at 11.45 p.m. for Mysore.

THURSDAY, 19 JANUARY   We travelled by narrow gauge, though not in our usual train. The Maharaja of Mysore had built a special car for David, very cosily fitted up, but with no corridor connection, so I had a camp bed in his sitting room and was very comfortable.

The arrival was in every way similar to that at Bangalore, save that we used the Maharaja's barouche and five of his landaus. There were exceptionally good crowds lining the entire route. It is noticeable how contented the people look here and how scrupulously clean all the streets and buildings are. Some 60 pikemen ran alongside the barouche the entire way.

FRIDAY, 20 JANUARY   David and most of the party motored out with the Maharaja to visit the Cauvery Dam, of which H.H. is very proud, and also to see Seringapatam which we captured from Tipu in 1799.

After a small dinner party at G.H., which I organized and at which I incidentally got myself into trouble in doing so by putting the lady David wanted to talk to next to him instead of the lady who should have sat next to him owing to her great age and seniority, we drove to the Maharaja's palace. The whole building was gorgeously illuminated and many thousands of people had been allowed to throng into the courtyard. After watching a display of club-swinging with torches we heard different forms of native instruments and also an organ recital and small concert.

The palace, both from without and within, more than fulfilled my expectations of Eastern splendour. Vast halls and courtyards connected by galleries and marble staircases seemed to form the lower storeys of the palace. In places I noted solid silver massive doors, and each room had curtains hung at one end, with crescent slits cut in them. At each slit one could just see a pair of eyes. If one came too near there was a rustle and the eyes would disappear again as the ladies of the harem withdrew. Being bored with the music I spent most of my time wandering about and exploring the wonders of the building. In the armoury was every conceivable type of weapon, including the most fearsome knuckle-dusters and a set of steel claws which could be worn on the inside of the fingers by rings and with which one of the old rulers of the state slit the face of the Moghul Ambassador while simulating an affectionate embrace. There was also a spear with two pistols fitted just below the head. On applying pressure to the point of the spear the two pistols were automatically discharged. Another room, known as the Doll's Room, contained every conceivable type of costly doll's palace with many dolls magnificently dressed.

I should have mentioned a most interesting interview which several of us, including David, had with a famous Indian thought reader, Professor S. Coomaraswamy. He said I could think two questions, one after the other, and he would write down the gist of my thought and the answer to the question. I first sat and thought, 'Will I ever be any good at polo?', then when he told me he had read that thought, I thought, 'Will Audrey's marriage turn out a success?' Next he told me to think of a number under 10. He then scribbled for a moment on a piece of paper which I put away, folded, in my pocket. He now asked me to tell him what my thoughts had been, which I did. Next he made me tell him the number I had thought of and multiply it by 200. Finally he gave me permission to look at the paper in my pocket on which was written: 'Polo – yes. Friend – yes. 3.' 3 was actually the number I had thought of. We were alone at the time and I am convinced that there was no trickery.[1]

He now offered to read one past event in my life if I gave him the date and thought of that event. I gave him September 1921 and thought of Papa. I may add that it was not until nearly the end of the interview that I told him my name. He went through the same performance and this time on the paper was written, 'Death of dear Member'.

He then asked me if I were engaged and on receiving a reply in the negative said that it was decreed that I should marry young and that my marriage would be the happiest event of my life. He also wrote down on a piece of paper the initial of my future wife, which he handed to me to see if it would not come true. He said that my mother would live to see my eldest son's eighth birthday at the very least.[2] He said that I would live till 71 at the least. He told me that I had started my naval career at the age of 16, which is when I went to sea.

He prophesied another great war between America and Japan in about four or five years' time which would be of comparatively short duration as we would intervene and bring about peace.

David only saw him for ten minutes and he read his one thought correctly.

SUNDAY, 22 JANUARY   The Maharaja has arranged a shooting camp out here, at Karapur, some 43 miles from Mysore city. As he brings all very important guests, such as Viceroys and Royalty, out here, he has built one or two permanent bungalows, and in one of these David, Lord Cromer and I are living. Some of the fishing enthusiasts who had been out for the last two days went out at daybreak again but with no success, though yesterday Joey got a 60-pounder and the Admiral a

---

[1] He was right about the polo but wrong about Audrey James's marriage, which did not last long.
[2] Mountbatten never had a son, but his mother easily saw her grand-daughters through their eighth birthdays.

69-pounder. The mahseer fishing here is considered about the finest in the world, the record being 119 pounds.

Towards noon the party assembled and we motored another five miles on to witness Keddah operations. Every two or three years these operations are carried out with a view to catching a fresh supply of wild elephants and breaking them in. The Maharaja can then keep such elephants as he may require for personal or state purposes, selling the others for at least 4000 rupees each.

Although in Nepal elephants are never bred in captivity there are other places where this is done, but on the whole the system of catching wild elephants and training them is preferred owing to the difficulty of breeding, and as elephants once caught will often be of use for as much as 80 or 100 years.

We disembarked at the roping stockade, into which it was intended to drive the wild elephants by means of tame ones. This stockade is built of the stoutest timber, driven well into the ground with cross bars lashed to the uprights at regular intervals. The openings along the bottom are of sufficient size to enable a man to get in and out. Along the top a covered-in platform had been built, a sort of 'dress circle' from which to watch roping operations, one side being screened off for the ladies who are in purdah.

The diameter of the stockade could only have been about 15 yards, so I failed to see how it was going to contain 25 wild elephants as well as a large number of tame ones at the same time. Nevertheless I was assured that they could just get in and that the tighter the elephants were packed the less fight could the wild ones show while being roped. The entrance to the roping stockade was about 8 feet wide and could be closed by a gate made of roped timber. The inside of the stockade, including the mouth and the actual ground, was camouflaged with fresh branches and plenty of green leaves, for the Hathi is a wily animal, and will face fire and steel rather than what he suspects to be a trap. It was also known that one or two cows among the herd had been in a keddah before and would be extremely suspicious.

For at least a month before our arrival men had been busy driving in wild elephants from all the country within 60 miles of Karapur and had succeeded in collecting a total of 25. In the meanwhile a 'keddah' had been constructed. This is done by digging a ditch at least 10 feet wide and 10 feet deep and about 1 mile in length from one side of the roping stockade round in a big circle to the other side. Once constructed such a keddah can of course be used for future operations if desired and in our case the keddah was not new. One part of the trench is either not dug to begin with or, in the case of an old keddah, is filled in to allow the elephants to be driven into the otherwise enclosed area. The particular herd that were at present within the keddah had been driven in across the river, with 'fire' coracles moored in two lines across it to prevent their escaping up or down stream. As soon as the last elephant had entered the area, which practically adjoined the river, the remainder of the ditch was quickly dug, while the diggers were protected by a line of fires in front of them. The elephant herd now had quite a large space in which to roam about and feed, but escape they could not owing to the ditch, as elephants cannot, of course, jump.

In the centre of the keddah a machan of generous dimensions, and consisting of two storeys had been constructed, and thither we were conveyed by means of pad elephants. As soon as we were all in position the signal to commence was given and some two dozen koomkies or tame elephants were sent round to the far side to start the final drive into the roping stockade. Each koomkie carried three men on his back, the mahout, a man with a long thin bamboo spear, and another man with a shot gun, bugle or split bamboo to make a noise.

Presently the wild herd began to move towards us and we were able to see an exceptionally fine tusker amongst them, at once christened 'Harry',[1] followed by 'Willie', a slightly smaller tusker. Actually the tuskers came last, for the cows led the herd and with the cows we could see one or two butchas or babies, one of them no higher than his mother's knee joint.

Now as the keddah is more or less circular in shape it would be well nigh impossible to drive the herd through an 8-foot entrance without building a 'V'-shaped stockade with the entrance at the apex.

This had been done, but one arm of the 'V' stuck out into the centre of the keddah, so that if the elephants went to the left they would be driven to the mouth of the stockade but if they went to the right they merely ran into a cul de sac.

What occurred, owing to poor staff work on the part of the man in charge, was that the herd was driven no less than three times into the cul de sac, and, on being driven out of it again, was twice allowed to break back to the left. After two hours of this they had organized a sufficient force of koomkies to drive all the herd except perhaps half a dozen who broke away at the start, into the 'V'.

[1] Presumably a tribute to the future Duke of Gloucester, though the inspiration for Willie is more obscure. The Kaiser?

As soon as the remaining 19 or 20 elephants were within the 'V', fires were lighted to prevent their breaking back and the koomkies advanced with much rattling and blowing of bugles. One cow and 'Harry' got as far as putting their heads inside the stockade when it is presumed that the cow, with her previous knowledge, scented the trap and made a desperate charge back. In spite of being stuck with the bamboo spears and having shot guns discharged at them the entire herd stampeded right through the koomkies and fires and made for the back of the keddah. Four smaller elephants were however successfully turned back.

Realizing that they would not get the rest of the herd in for a long while the Maharaja gave orders to carry on getting the four in, while we proceeded back to the stockade.

To start with the four wild hathis were pushed and buffeted about by the koomkies, and when they were least expecting it men ran in under the roping stockade and handed over big, soft hawsers to the mahouts who slipped the nooses over the wild elephants' heads. These ropes were then hauled taut and secured round 'bollards' outside the stockade. As soon as they felt the rope the elephants went mad with rage, trumpeting and squealing and straining every muscle to break the rope or the stockade. Now the old tame elephants started work. They started by gently pushing the obstreperous ones about, but finding this was not enough in one or two cases they took a run and fairly knocked the wild ones endways. One little wild tusker was knocked down three times in quick succession, the third knock winding him so that he lay still for several seconds. The mahouts seemed rather unnecessarily cruel with their spears and ankuses but they were certainly brave men, and at least one of them only escaped being pulled off and trampled underfoot by leaping off on the other side.

MONDAY, 23 JANUARY   David, the Admiral and I went at 7.30 a.m. to a pool just beyond the keddah. David caught no less than four mahseer in the first hour. The Admiral had one splendid run out; his reel fairly shrieked but the fish got under a snag and so away.

I remained the other side of the river, which is rather full of snags. However I enjoyed myself very much and my line ran out a good way twice before the fish passed under a snag, and so away. Mahseer fishing is really rather simple: one has a huge hook which one buries in some sort of brown dough bait as big as one's fist. A native then hurls this bait out into mid-stream, while one sits and waits for a bite. All the same, once a good fighting fish is on the line he gives you plenty of fun. The Admiral took 23 minutes to land his 69-pounder on Saturday.

We had 'brunch' on return and motored in to Mysore City, the Admiral driving David and I driving the second car. After dinner at G.H. we departed by narrow gauge train for Hyderabad.

TUESDAY, 24 JANUARY   Of all the Staff I must say that I like Fruity best so I was highly delighted when David fixed up yesterday to take him on to Japan as extra A.D.C. and then home in the *Renown* for the leave which has been owing to him since before the war.

WEDNESDAY, 25 JANUARY   We arrived at Hyderabad at 8.30 a.m. There followed the longest drive on record, some 6 miles or so through the city and narrow streets of the bazaar up to Falaknuma Castle, one of the Nizam's five palaces, which is built on the top of a hill overlooking the town. The route was well lined, the more so taking into consideration that this is the principal Mohammedan State, and that the Mohammedans are so bitter about our treatment of the Turks.[1] Perhaps it is owing to their strong dislike of their own ruler, His Exalted Highness the Nizam, 'Faithful Ally of the British Government'. The Nizam, although he and his state played up splendidly in the war, is not of prepossessing appearance, nor does he enjoy very good health, and all the people out here tell one that he scarcely ever goes out for fear of an attempt upon his life. Nevertheless in point of rank he is the premier Mohammedan ruler in India, ruling over a state the size of France.

The castle we are living in is delightfully situated and I very grandly have the entire left wing to myself, with a private telephone, and two yellow liveried chaprassies, who take watch and watch outside my door all day.

In the evening there was a state banquet at the Chowmahalla Palace, where the Nizam is living. There were some 250 people sitting in a long room. I was at one end of the centre of the three tables according to the plan and sat down in a place without a name card corresponding to my seat in the plan, and I ate my soup. Presently one of the Resident's staff came and fetched me and told me that I was sitting at the wrong end of the table, so I had to wander hundreds of places up and had a second helping of soup on arrival. Godfrey was

[1] Lloyd George was bent on the destruction of the Turkish Empire, and was adopting a strongly pro-Greek line, to the indignation of Muslims the world over.

not so lucky; first he couldn't find his partner, then when he had found her he wished he hadn't. Finally there were no seats for him or his partner, they were put in somewhere but although Godfrey was given a gilded chair one of its legs was missing so that he had a great job balancing it throughout the meal.

SATURDAY, 28 JANUARY After tea we motored to Secunderabad for the military sports. The best stunt was put up by an armoured car company, who disguised cars as the *Renown* and also a weird animal.

We left by train from Secunderabad for Nagpur at 6.00 p.m.

SUNDAY, 29 JANUARY The extraordinary part about the route we are following on this tour is that having left Poona over two months ago and travelled several thousand miles right across India in the north, to Burma, to the south of India and then north again we today reached a station called Dhond, about breakfast time, which is only about 40 miles or so from Poona!

It was pretty hot in the train, and if one opened one's window without lowering the gauze screen, a plague of flies ensued.

The country round about Hyderabad City is strewn with big boulders, frequently placed one on top of the other, as though deliberately by some ancient giant. Towards the afternoon the plain we were running through suddenly became broken in places by small hills with absolutely flat tops to them.

In the evening and after dinner we all sat down and composed limericks about each other and various people, such as the Nizam, which, although exceedingly humorous, are not fit for publication.

MONDAY, 30 JANUARY We arrived at Nagpur, the capital of the Central Provinces, at 10.00 a.m. and drove to G.H. The route was not remarkably well lined but there was certainly no complete absence of crowds as at Allahabad. All the roads are covered with small flakes of mica which glisten prettily in the sun and give one's servants a lot of trouble in brushing them off one's clothes.

A small Durbar was held under a shamiana in front of G.H. All the principle Feudatory Chiefs paid homage as well as a host of other notables. There is of course no shaking of hands as David has to sit on the silver throne we always carry round with us, and the chiefs afterwards get itr and pan.

There was a dinner party at G.H. followed by an evening garden party given by the Feudatory Chiefs. It resembled nothing so much as the keddah, especially as we all managed to eventually break away without being 'roped'.

TUESDAY, 31 JANUARY   We left Government House, Nagpur, feeling both cold and hungry, at 8.15 a.m. There was quite a good crowd on the platform to see the train off.

I spent the forenoon explaining the guts of a motor car to David: 4-stroke engine and differential drive. Thence we wandered on and discussed astronomy, asdics and Einstein. A most intellectual morning!

Griffiths, the I.C. Police,[1] recounted to me some of the murder cases he has had charge of. Most of them were far more interesting than fiction. He tells me that when the white police are baffled they give the natives a free hand, except that no actual cruelty is permitted. The natives have a sort of 'third degree' method of their own, which rarely fails. In consequence of this no confession made to a police officer is accepted as evidence in a court of law, as actual proof is also necessary.

After dinner we transferred to the narrow gauge train. The transfer was completed in half an hour. I watched the operation and was amazed at the perfect organization. Many hundreds of pieces of private luggage not counting bedding, food, office gear, etc. had to be tran-shipped from certain compartments to the corresponding ones. And the same thing had just been done for the supplementary train!

WEDNESDAY, 1 FEBRUARY   We arrived at Indore at 8.30 a.m. with the usual pomp. The Palace of Maharaja Holkar (the ruler of Indore) which we visited has some magnificent marble in it. This palace is called Lalbagh; we are living in a smaller one called Manikbagh.

THURSDAY, 2 FEBRUARY   The first thing on the programme was a Durbar at Daly's College. The college, like the one at Ajmer, is for chiefs' sons, but they were mostly crowded out of the way today and only performers were allowed in the body of the big hall. Poor old Fruity had to be there at 9.00 a.m. to receive the 18 Ruling Princes. Each came at 5-minute intervals, juniors first. Each got a separate salute from a guard of honour and his correct gun salute as well,

---

[1] Possibly Francis Griffith, the Commissioner of Police for the Bombay District.

though wherever two or more were entitled to the same number of guns they shared the salute.

Each chief brought from two to twelve sardars, making about 140 in all. The show started by an I.C.S. man making a bow and saying, 'Have I Your Royal Highness's permission to open the Durbar?' The poker enthusiasts had suggested that David might reply, 'You may open it for a couple of lakhs', but luckily he merely nodded his head. After each prince had made his bow separately, David read a speech and then gave them itr and pan. Then six of the Staff got busy, and as the result of a dress rehearsal yesterday, itr-ed and pan-ed all the 140 sardars in 12 minutes, thus creating the itr and pan record!

FRIDAY, 3 FEBRUARY   David left at 11.00 for Mhow for the parade to be held there. Personally I thought it rather a good show, though the soldiers pooh-poohed it afterwards. The 'sixtieth' did an excellent march past and the 7th Hussars did a very good gallop past. There were also two native regiments and a brigade of gunners.

The Maharaja of Dhar has been on duty here and one of his cavalry regiments was also on parade this morning, led by one of his small daughters in the regimental uniform, who gave the order 'eyes right' in a very clear little voice.

After lunch we changed for polo. There were eight chukkers. The first three was our Staff team against a local team, the fourth was a scratch chukker in which I played, the next three were another match and the eighth was another scratch one in which I played. I played Basra, and he has never played better. I myself played far far better than usual or anyway I think I did and I certainly enjoyed the game quite enormously.[1]

After tea we drove to the station and entrained.

SATURDAY, 4 FEBRUARY   We arrived at Bhopal at 8.30 a.m. and as the morning was bitterly cold we all absolutely froze. We are staying at one of the Begum's palaces, Lal Kothi, and as usual there is a camp pitched in the grounds as well. Her Highness the Begum met us at the station in her veil. She is a very small person and held in great awe in her state.

Hamidullah, who is on the staff and also the youngest and favourite son of the Begum, lent us some of his ponies so that we were able to

---

[1] 'I have really for the first time in my life become keen about a game,' Mountbatten wrote to his mother that evening. 'I'd sooner be good at polo than anything.'

play polo this afternoon, our own ponies not having come on from Mhow yet. I played in four of the chukkers and David played for nine! As both my ponies were strange and took a lot of riding I did not play as well as yesterday, which means to say that I played pretty badly. In the last chukker I got a back-hander full on the fingers of my right hand so that I could scarcely hold the stick for the rest of the game. All the same I enjoyed my game immensely.

At tea time the Begum asked that I should be introduced to her, as she had known Papa. She speaks English rather well in a soft, quiet sort of voice. An oval slit is cut in her veil level with her eyes, and covered only with gauze, which produces rather a weird effect, as one can just see her eyes but nothing else.

SUNDAY, 5 FEBRUARY   This being a Mohammedan state there was no church or ham for breakfast. David and I slept till after eleven. About noon a number of ex-service men paraded whom David saw.

David and six of us departed for a so-called shooting camp at Kachnaria. It turned out to be a magnificent summer palace which had just been completed by the Nawab, the Begum's eldest son. He is a delightful old man (nearly 60), very shy and 'jungly' in appearance. Unfortunately the Begum dislikes him and stints him in consequence in any way she can. We dined quietly and afterwards hopped[1] round the place like lunatics, before turning in.

MONDAY, 6 FEBRUARY   I was called at 5.45 a.m. and after a short breakfast our party left by motor about 6.30. It was quite inconceivably cold as the sun had not yet risen. Personally I have not been so cold for quite two years. Then, as the sun got up it soon was so hot that we had to take our coats off. At the 50-mile post we disembarked and crept as noiselessly as we could to our machans, Cromer taking the right-hand one and I the left.

Presently on the utter stillness of the jungle there rose the faint and monotonous cry of the beaters as they came towards us. Here and there one could hear a native drum or gong being sounded but otherwise all was still.

In a short while one could feel that the jungle was on the move. I don't quite know what it was that gave me the impression first as I don't recollect hearing anything for several minutes after the beaters

[1] On pogo sticks, presumably.

had started. The first noise I heard was faint but distinct, a sort of crackling of twigs which gradually grew louder until three nilghai broke out of the jungle on the opposite bank. They never stopped to look but lumbered straight ahead, almost as clumsy as a domestic cow. When they came to my side they all three fell into a deep pool and had to swim. I could have shot them easily, but the beat was for tiger and we had orders to shoot at nothing less.

The next noise was far fainter and it heralded the coming of sambhur. The leading doe peeped out cautiously from the undergrowth and then stepped out followed by two more and later by a stag. They walked across in a leisurely manner, the stag even came to within forty yards of my machan and stopped there for a moment, then he must have winded us for he bolted with his wives.

The next party consisted of three worried otters who plunged straight into the pool near me. Peacocks and various other birds also flew out, but I never saw a sign of a tiger, though presently I heard some shots ring out, which proved to have been fired by Cromer. He got two small tigers with them, though the second one having hidden himself in an island of grass took a lot of finishing off.

We had brought a khidmatgar with us who now laid out lunch. While we were having this meal a party of women arrived and started singing. On enquiry it turned out that they were rejoicing at the death of two tigers at the hand of the mighty Cromer Sahib.

WEDNESDAY, 8 FEBRUARY We arrived at Gwalior at 8.30 a.m. and got into state howdahs on magnificent elephants. David and the Maharaja went ahead on the old Royal Elephant while the remainder of us followed, two in each howdah. Blue full dress is not the most ideal of kits to go for a ride on an elephant, before breakfast, in, but it certainly was very interesting and picturesque.

About tea time David performed the opening ceremony for the new King George Park, which has been constructed near the palace, by unlocking a huge gold lock. We then motored round the park and watched native sports, such as wrestling, juggling, weight-lifting, etc. The most fascinating thing to watch, however, was a thing called a 'chakri'. It consists of a wooden spool on which about 60 ft of string is wound, a native swings this round and round, the chakri rising to about 50 or 60 ft as the string unwinds and then coiling up till only 3 ft of string shows as it passes the ground.

In the evening the state banquet took place, which was brightened by the presence of a miniature silver electric train, which ran round the table on rails, carrying port, cigars and chocolate.

THURSDAY, 9 FEBRUARY   I joined Godfrey and Aubrey about 11.30, where the special baby train of the Gwalior Light Railway was awaiting us. The gauge of the rail is only 2 ft and the show was started as Scindia's toy, but now it is a working (though miniature) concern. We were joined by some local people and then set off. It took an hour to go the 11 miles to the Maharaja's bungalow in his black buck preserve, where we had lunch.

After lunch we split up into three parties. Godfrey had a bullock cart and I had another, in which we put our kit, walking behind so as to avoid disturbing buck, ourselves. I touched my near bullock amidships with my finger and he at once whisked it away with his tail. This rather amused me, so I called out to Godfrey, 'Come and touch this bullock and something very funny will happen to you.' So Godfrey, very trustingly, put his finger on the spot indicated, whereupon the old bullock let fly with his hind leg and caught him on the upper part of his leg. The look of pained surprise that crossed Godfrey's face as he staggered back kept me in fits of laughter the whole afternoon, I regret to say.[1]

I never have any luck with tame animals, first my elephant went must in Nepal and then this wretched bullock took fright as soon as I fired my first shot. Both bullocks bolted and ran into a tree, when Godfrey's friend started trying to get into the cart.

SATURDAY, 11 FEBRUARY   I had a lot to do before leaving the main party to go ahead in the advance party to Delhi. I had an early lunch, during which Hiscock went down to prepare the way for my coming. When I arrived I was met by the station master and ticket collector, who conducted me to a chair which they had placed in the middle of the platform. This seemed rather too public a place to sit down so I walked about till the Bombay–Delhi mail ran in. I was given a reserved first-class compartment, which was large enough to take even the trunk I was bringing with me. The ticket collector mounted guard and turned away other passengers who tried to get in, so I offered him some 'backsheesh' which, however, he proudly waved away, saying that he knew Uncle Arthur and could not accept money from me. He did

---

[1] 'Godfrey I quite like but don't altogether trust,' Mountbatten told Edwina. The mistrust might fairly have been reciprocated.

however want a 'certificate', so I told him to write to me. What I can say on it beyond the fact that he shut the door of the compartment without slamming it after seeing me into it, I can't think, but it seems to be a custom out here.

We arrived about 7.30 at Delhi.

SUNDAY, 12 FEBRUARY I spent the morning getting through as much of the 'business' as I could. The Readings[1] have asked a number of guests to stay for David's visit and among them is Edwina, whom I met just before lunch, as she had only arrived in the early hours of the morning by the 'English Mail' train.

I saw quite a lot of her in the afternoon and heard all the latest news from home, not three weeks old yet. She is looking awfully well and fit, I think.

There was a slight dinner party in the evening, nothing serious, but still it necessitated our wearing mess dress, which one apparently always does do at Viceregal Lodge. There certainly is at least twice as much pomp here as in other places, but I suppose it is necessary. Lady Reading seems a charming old lady. She has taken an immense amount of trouble over the building and decorating of the bungalow they have specially built for David. Usually everyone except a very few live in tents, as Viceregal Lodge is so small, and the new one in New Delhi is of course not ready.[2]

We played happy families after dinner, and then Edwina instructed me in all the new steps that have crept into London dancing since we left, in Mrs Greville's sitting room.[3]

MONDAY, 13 FEBRUARY The whole of Delhi is just one mass of camps, as I was able to see on my ride this morning. There are several British and Native Cavalry and Infantry Regiments here, as well as Horse and Field Gunners, and they are all under canvas. The house party at Viceregal Lodge is going to be at least sixty in number by tomorrow night, so that the viceregal camp is fairly large too.

---

[1] Rufus Isaacs, 1st Earl (later 1st Marquess) of Reading, was former Ambassador to the United States and Lord Chief Justice. He was the first Viceroy of other than aristocratic, or at least upper-class, origin.

[2] Edwin Lutyens had begun to design New Delhi in 1913 but the war slowed things down and work did not finish until 1930. It became Mountbatten's official residence in 1947.

[3] Mrs Ronnie Greville, a rich old lady and socialite, who was a fellow guest of the Viceroy.

TUESDAY, 14 FEBRUARY The afternoon was entirely cut up by preparations for David's arrival. It was the first time I had seen these preparations and I was much struck with the excitement which prevailed, in such contrast to our 'routine' and dull public arrivals. People got the wind up quite early in the day and some appeared in full dress literally hours before anything was due to happen, again a marked contrast to our party who are frequently caught slipping into their tunics as the train begins to slow up at a station. Even so I believe that there was less excitement here than anywhere as the Viceroy himself always travels about in such state. It was interesting to watch both the Viceroy's and later David's processions arriving, with all their cavalry and artillery escorts.

After dinner there was a small dance. I danced 1 and 2 with Edwina; she had 3 and 4 with David and the 5th dance we sat out in her sitting room, when I asked her if she would marry me, and she said she would.

WEDNESDAY, 15 FEBRUARY I hope that no one will imagine from the bald statement which appears at the end of yesterday's page that I do not realize that it is probably the most momentous statement that I am ever likely to make. I do realize. I also realize how very lucky I am; I am also happy beyond my wildest dreams, but in this diary it is not my intention to set forth all my feelings on this subject. We told only David, who was wonderfully delighted.

After breakfast we motored to an open space opposite the fort where the All India Memorial to Uncle Bertie[1] has been erected. The Staff 'crocodile' that preceded David and His Ex. consisted of 50, quite a record. After David had unveiled it we had to stand and wait while a salute of 101 guns was fired.

In the evening there was a gigantic state banquet for which we had to wear full dress. As soon as we had changed into mess dress I took Edwina and two others to the dance at Flagstaff House. After the dance we visited the fair David had just been to, and danced some more there. Then we motored out to King Humayun's enormous tomb, which we saw at 3.00 a.m. by moonlight. Very wonderful and romantic.

[1] King Edward VII. The term 'uncle' in Mountbatten's usage covered a multitude of relationships – though in this case it was near the mark, the King being his great-uncle.

THURSDAY, 16 FEBRUARY   We once more struggled into full dress after lunch and did a State drive to the fort for the big Durbar. The Durbar was perhaps the most gorgeous and brilliant we have seen. Unlike the others no homage was paid, but various speeches were read. By a delightful stroke of luck my seat was facing Edwina's seat in the audience and only a few feet away.[1]

After the Durbar there was a garden party given by the Chief. Edwina and Mrs Ronnie in a fit of false modesty disdained the Pavilion for the Viceregal house party, where we all were, and disappeared to the other end of the grounds.

FRIDAY, 17 FEBRUARY   David suggested our cabling home for permission to announce the engagement, but we decided to sleep on this idea and had a further discussion today. We also consulted Lord Cromer, who was most kind and sympathetic, but counselled writing instead of cabling.[2]

In the forenoon we motored out to New Delhi where David laid the foundation stone of the Kitchener College for educating the sons of Indian Officers. It was interesting seeing representatives of every single regiment of the Indian Army, who afterwards marched past David.

After lunch we motored with Mrs Ronnie to Schwaiger's art establishment, where Edwina chose an old Indian ring, which I gave her until I could get a proper engagement ring. On return we went to the so-called Royal Pavilion where we had tea with David in his rooms.

SATURDAY, 18 FEBRUARY   After lunch, or 'tiffin' as they call it out here, we both went down to the Pavilion, where David lent us his room. To prevent anyone bursting in unexpectedly upon us he has locked the door to the hall and given me the key, so that the only approach is through his bedroom. It is really much safer to use David's room than Mrs Ronnie's as people are continually coming in expecting to see her and are covered with confusion on finding us there instead. Then they go away and announce to the world in general that they

---

[1] Edwina's presence presumably distracted Mountbatten from the Prince of Wales's speech, which was one of his happiest efforts.

[2] Cromer had been consistently kind to Mountbatten, telling him 'that Papa had always been so good to him, that he wished to try and repay some of the kindness by helping me'. But Mountbatten told Edwina that he was 'loquacious but not very sagacious'.

Mountbatten and Edwina Ashley watching the Police Parade in Delhi – an illicit snapshot which the photographer promised not to publish since the couple were not yet officially engaged (20 February 1922).

above: General Sir George Barrow indicates points of interest to H.R.H. at the Khyber Pass (5 March 1922).

below: H.R.H. netting (or, more probably, missing) duck in the Hima Palace gardens (17 April 1922).

have seen us together, which merely aggravates the hopeless amount of gossip which already exists.

Edwina and I decided to send one very guarded wire to my family, so they would not be overcome with surprise and could guess what we meant without giving the show away in the cable.

SUNDAY, 19 FEBRUARY   Both Bikaner and Hiru had asked me to lunch today so I accepted and went. They had also asked Mrs Ronnie, who had stayed with them at Christmas time, and she had asked if she might bring Edwina. Edwina sat next to some high official from Kashmir at lunch and as usual without any apparent fishing obtained an invitation to visit Kashmir. As far as I can make out whenever she sits next to a stranger at a meal she receives an invitation to visit his part of the country. This is a useful gift and one that I am looking forward to making use of!

MONDAY, 20 FEBRUARY   We felt that it was only fair to tell Their Exs. about what had happened, since they were looking after Edwina out here. We decided this yesterday but first told Mrs Ronnie, since she had been our constant chaperone, when we had one at all, since we have been here. Then this morning Edwina told Lady Reading, who was very nice about it and told the Viceroy.[1]

David inspected a police parade on the lawn and Edwina and I went out and watched it with a crowd of others. The photographer took a snap of us, but has promised not to publish it.

TUESDAY, 21 FEBRUARY   Edwina and I went out for a ride by ourselves this morning to the site of the 1911 Durbar and a little beyond. On our way back we passed David and the Viceroy going out for a ride, but they did not see us as we took shelter behind a battery of artillery moving along the road.

After breakfast I ordered the little yellow Crossley and drove Edwina to Kingsway station, where our two trains were drawn up ready for tonight's departure, and I showed her over our train. We then drove out to New Delhi to look at all the new buildings, which are growing up there, which was very interesting!

On return Lady Reading wanted to see me; she was very nice. I sat next to Edwina for nearly the first time at lunch at Viceregal Lodge,

[1] Lady Reading wrote apologetically to Edwina's father, Colonel Ashley, 'I hoped she would care for someone older, with more of a career before him.'

and afterwards we went down to the Pavilion, where we spent a very happy afternoon.

I took Edwina in to dinner tonight and danced with her and sat out with her till it was time to go (10.50). She came to the station and saw us off. I hated leaving. I hated it very much.

WEDNESDAY, 22 FEBRUARY We arrived at Patiala at 8.30 a.m. and did the usual full dress drive before breakfast.

We are living in Motibagh Palace guarded by Sikh sentries in beautiful claret-coloured uniforms with cream facings and white spats. Lord Cromer's bathroom, which normally is used by the Maharaja, is quite wonderful, having one dozen different sanitary appliances distributed about it, and the wardrobe room next door is a reproduction of the tailoring department in any large stores, even including counters! In his room he also has a dentist's chair, a stuffed black buck and the most immoral statuettes conceivable, but no writing table. All the same we are very comfortable and the Maharaja has considerately washed out all the visits, etc. and has put on his state parade so that David was able to get that over in the forenoon.

There was only a small dinner at which the Maharaja and two or three of his staff were present in evening tail coats with pugarees, his staff having yellow facings on theirs. After this there was a dance in the palace. The Maharaja has invited about 100 guests, mostly girls we have met before in Delhi, for David's visit and these all turned up for the dance. I looked in with the others, but when the music started I felt I just could not dance and so faded away again. There had been talk of Edwina coming here too, but the Viceroy didn't want her to go.

FRIDAY, 24 FEBRUARY We were all supposed to be going out for a shoot but David has become so keen on pig-sticking that we did that instead, while the remainder of the party did the shoot. On the way out I saw a fakir, with his face painted white, tied up to a tree in such a way that only his big toe touched the ground, and swaying to and fro gently, all the time.

The party in the general shoot had good fun, though as a matter of fact two panther, which they secured, had been taken from the zoo; doped and laid out under suitable bushes! They had originally laid out a rare and valuable black panther as well but when they heard that David was not shooting they returned it to the zoo and revived it.

SATURDAY, 25 FEBRUARY   After the state banquet last night we departed by train and arrived at Jullundur at 9.30 a.m. Here about half the Staff, including myself, accompanied David 'ashore'. First David laid the foundation stone of the King George Military College, which is for the sons of Indian Officers, like the Kitchener College.

After this over 800 pensioned Indian Officers walked past him, while he shook hands with many and talked to them. Then he walked among the ranks of the 4000-odd pensioners and a similar number of regular troops. These pensioners had been brought in from miles around and are all fine, loyal old men. It is really rather pathetic to think that there had to be an armed guard at the station to prevent Ghandiists from molesting these old men. The show lasted till noon, when we returned to the train for lunch, while it proceeded to Lahore.

We had to get into full dress once more for the arrival and state drive in Lahore. The place is quite near Amritsar, of evil reputation, and as there has been trouble here too, we got ready for bombs. There was nothing of the sort, however, and really he had quite a good reception here.

SUNDAY, 26 FEBRUARY   This is a very pleasant place; the atmosphere is cooler and the grass and plants are greener than we have seen elsewhere in India. It was here that Kipling started his career with the scissors and paste in the office of the *Civil and Military Gazette*, an imposing looking building which we saw in yesterday's drive.

The Nawab of Bahawalpur, who is only 17 but looks considerably more, as indeed all these young natives do, is on duty with the Staff here. He is a nice boy, though they say that he has gone off considerably since he started his harem last year. We discussed, among other things, the irrigation project which he, Government and Bikaner are taking on, to water their territories from the Sutlej.

MONDAY, 27 FEBRUARY   In the morning David visited the North Western Railway workshops, where our train was built. He had a great reception from the workmen and was presented with an exact model of his own coach, correct in every detail even down to the roll-top desk, which worked.

We saw today the Nawab of Mamdot. When he was 21 he weighed 21 stone. The top of his polo boots would make an excellent corset for any lady. It is almost cruelty to animals to let him mount a polo pony, but he himself is quite nice to talk to.

WEDNESDAY, 1 MARCH   I had a day on today and accordingly went to the parade held at the Cantonment. There were representatives from all units serving in the Lahore district as well as two or three thousand pensioners. The condition of most of the pensioners one sees out here is really terrible. The relations, instead of helping a man incapacitated in the war, look upon him as a fool to have gone, and try and sponge on him for the entirely inadequate pension which the Government of India allows him. When the pensioners are told that it is the native members of council who refuse to sanction an increase of pension, they answer, 'But it is the Sahibs that rule out here, so why do they allow these natives to stop our pension?' And as the word 'Montague' conveys nothing to them one cannot give them an answer to that.[1] The native legislators of course realize that our last real hold on India is through the army and that if they can spread disaffection in its ranks they are giving the death-stroke to the British Raj in India.

The trouble is that these reforms please neither the natives nor the British and the only tangible result is an enormous loss of British prestige, which grows worse with each succeeding day.

The departure at 11.00 p.m. drew wonderful crowds, we also saw a Khattack fire dance near the station.

THURSDAY, 2 MARCH   At 9.30 we stopped at a wayside halt outside Jammu, the city itself being out of bounds as it has the plague, and were met by the Maharaja of Jammu and Kashmir and his adopted son and heir Hari Singh, who is on our Staff. We drove in the usual carriages to Satwari Camp, where we are staying.

The last Mizaj Pursi and exchange of visits took place here. The Shamiana in which we received the Maharaja was covered inside with the most beautiful and priceless Kashmir shawls. In the distance we could see the 'eternal snows of Kashmir', but later clouds hid the mountains completely.

FRIDAY, 3 MARCH   David attended a parade of the Kashmir State Troops and then visited the exhibition of local wares, to which I

---

[1] 'Montague' might have conveyed more, since presumably Mountbatten had Edwin Montagu in mind, co-author of the Montagu-Chelmsford Report and on the point of resignation as Secretary of State for India.

had preceded him. There were many wonderful things, mostly very expensive, all the decent Kashmir shawls running into thousands of rupees. I bought 2 small 'shawl' table covers, 2 papier-mâché candle-sticks and a small carved wooden box. Hari Singh managed to secure for Godfrey and me two of the masks which the Lamas used in last night's dance. I got a hideous great thing with three eyes, known as 'Gonpo', the God of Death and King of Ogres.

We departed by train at noon and reached Serai Alamgir, near Jhelum, at 5.00 p.m. First David laid the foundation stone of King George's Royal Indian Military School, which is for the sons of Indian Officers, as at Jullundur. Then he inspected troops and finally did the usual pensioner stunt. The natives have a child-like but touching belief in David's power to instantly right all wrongs and are bitterly disappointed when they find that however sympathetic he may be he frequently can't help them. One man, holding up the stump of his arm, loudly declared that he had lost it fighting for us and if we couldn't help him he wished we'd put another bullet through him. We left in the train at 7.00

SATURDAY, 4 MARCH   There was the usual public arrival at Peshawar before breakfast this morning. The first reminder that one had reached the 'danger zone' of the frontier was to find most of the Government House chaprassis wearing revolvers and bandoliers over their scarlet coats and soon our own retinue appeared armed likewise.

There was a garden party at Government House given by our host, Sir John Maffey, the Chief Commissioner of the North West Frontier Province. I saw two extra devout mussulmen bring out their carpets just before sunset, and there in front of all the guests deliver the evening prayer to Allah.

SUNDAY, 5 MARCH   Some nine or ten miles of good road brought us to a little frontier fort, built of stout mud walls, with loop holes, and in general resembling those toy forts one gets at Hamley's to put tin soldiers in. The place was surrounded by barbed wire entanglements and sentries and all the troops were paraded for David to inspect. What other people there were were all armed, though for the time being friendly. The fort is called Jamrud Fort.

Another two or three miles brought us to the entrance of the Khyber Pass, the only satisfactory gateway into India so long as we keep command of the seas. I think in a way I was more keen to see the Khyber than anything else in the whole tour, as it is a place full of historical happenings from the time of the ancient Greeks onwards and it is also considered to be the most picturesque pass in the world. Long before we actually entered I noticed the 'Telfer Span' overhead railway, which has of late been put up to bring food and supplies to the garrison all along the pass and to the army which was operating in Afghanistan. It consists of metal 'frame-work' towers with pulleys on each side carrying an endless wire, which pulls up the loaded bogeys and returns the empty ones at a slow but steady pace. Throughout the trip up the pass this Overhead Railway was a source of constant interest to me; the way in which a bogey would pass a ridge only three feet off the ground and then swing off into space with a clear hundred foot drop was fascinating to watch. But even this scheme is incapable of keeping an army fighting in Afghanistan properly supplied, and of course no re-inforcements can be sent by it, they are therefore undertaking the vast project of running a broad gauge railway line through the pass under the peaceful guise of opening up trade with Kabul, Bokhara and the interior. As it is they have two complete and separate roads right the way through, as it is too risky to have traffic passing on a narrow road with certain death waiting on one side for the unwary driver, and besides the road is full of hairpin bends of the worst description.

The road climbs steadily from the time it enters between two mountains until it eventually attains a height of 3000 feet at Landi Kotal, where the main Infantry Brigade is quartered. The gorge itself beggars description. Looking from the eighth car to the first car on another bend of the road it reminded me of a fly crawling along the side of a house, so completely do these giant mountains dwarf all that comes near them.

The troops were paraded at each camp and outpost and at frequent intervals one could see the Kassadars, the local native irregular police and the true Guardians of the pass from their own marauding brothers, with their quaint rifle and bandolier and khaki and green pugaree, their only badge of office. They are well paid by us unless there is trouble in their section when we fine them. The Afridis, of whom we saw plenty at Landi Kotal, think nothing of sniping people in the pass when the pickets aren't out, and they are only out on Tuesdays and Fridays when the pass is open.

We drove on to Landi Khana whence we obtained a wonderful view of Afghanistan, beyond which is Russia.

MONDAY, 6 MARCH   We were originally billed to do a full dress drive into the city to receive an address, but David somehow managed to wriggle out of full dress, which was very pleasant, and then it was changed to motor cars which was better still. The night before, without any previous indication, a hartal was declared and today all the shops were shut and the reports sent up showed that there was bad work afoot. Most of the political people tried to dissuade Maffey from carrying out the city drive, but he said that, although he would lose his job if anything went wrong, he felt he could not altogether haul down the flag in the face of the Ghandiists. So far so good – a man after David's own heart – not to be cowed by the agitators, although it is far more dangerous on the frontier here than anywhere else. Unfortunately he gave way this much in that he decided that after receiving the address he would hurry David back by a short cut instead of returning by the advertised route, where all the soldiers were lining the street. Had he consulted David all would have been well, as the latter would have insisted on returning by the advertised route, but he didn't and thereby incurred David's everlasting wrath. During the reading of both address and reply men in black pugarees went round shouting out the Ghandiists' cry 'Mahatma Ghandi Ki Jai'. David felt that people, especially the soldiers lining the route, would feel he had funked the drive back, and as nothing was further from his mind he reached Government House in the blackest rage I ever hope to see him in and has rowed everyone well. Personally I do not think one soul will think David funked it.[1]

TUESDAY, 7 MARCH   Peshawar is situated more or less in the centre of Peshawar Vale, and looking from the city one can see an unbroken line of mountains for more than three quarters of the horizon, as it is almost entirely enclosed by the Himalayas.

The unfortunate battalion of British Infantry (the Warwicks) who are stationed in the Khyber Pass are not really required there, we are told. In the event of real trouble on a big scale they could be hurried up from Peshawar together with the other battalion in the city, but they have to be kept there to impress on the native legislators the necessity of British troops.

We left by train at 11.00 p.m.

[1] 'H.R.H. is most acutely hurt at having been sent out by what he calls the back door,' Sir John Maffey told the Viceroy's Secretary. 'Nobody but himself has this feeling.'

WEDNESDAY, 8 MARCH   We reached Mardan at 9.30 a.m., got into the waiting motors and drove the twenty-odd miles to Dargai, where there is a fort, as at Jamrud, at the foot of the hills.

From here the road commenced to ascend and follow the hills in a similar way to the entrance of the Khyber. After about three miles, when we had ascended about 900 feet, we reached a new 'valley' surrounded by hills called the 'Swat' Valley after the tribe which owns it. Here, as in the Khyber, only the road is British, the country all round being 'independent'. Presently we reached the furthest northern outpost of the Indian Empire – Fort Chakdara. There are two neighbouring hill tribes here, who are quarrelling over a fertile stretch of valley just in front of Chakdara. These tribes 'Swat' and 'Dir' declared war last November and have been fighting ever since with an average casualty list of 8 a side every day. The opposing armies can muster between 30 and 40 thousand rifles, but at present only one tenth of each army is fighting. Each man comes up for a week with his own week's provisions and at the end of a week he is relieved by his brother, etc. The two lines are entrenched and are only 60 yds apart, though we could not actually distinguish them.

At 7.00 we moved on in the train.

THURSDAY, 9 MARCH   The train passed Attock, a most picturesque old walled city on the River Indus. The view both up and down stream from the railway bridge is really magnificent.

Taxila was reached about lunch time, and here we left the train and had lunch with Sir E. Marshall, the Director of Archaeology, who showed us over his interesting museum afterwards. We also motored out a little distance to where an old Buddhist monastery of the fifth century stood, parts of it being in excellent repair. We also saw the foundations of the ancient city of Sirkap.

Fruity and I got Col. Worgan's permission to go on ahead in a car to Rawal Pindi. When we got to the signallers waiting for David's car I made the 'wash out' signal so they shouldn't signal our arrival. Nevertheless when the saluting battery saw us they started off and got through seven guns before we could stop them, so we got a 7-gun salute. All along the route natives salaamed to us, men took off their hats and women waved.

FRIDAY, 10 MARCH   This morning I was down in 'Staff Instructions' to ride to the parade with David and the soldiers on duty, accordingly

I donned my blue breeches, black butcher boots and brass spurs, and was the envy of all who saw me. I rode Robert and he went very well and didn't let the Navy on horseback down in the eyes of all the soldiers. The parade was one of the best, though certainly the dustiest I have ever seen. We then cantered back along a dusty road and by the time we reached the Circuit House my monkey jacket and breeches might have been khaki for all one could see of the blue.

There was polo in the afternoon on the slipperiest ground I think I have ever played on. I only had two chukkers, but Basra nearly came down twice and once in each chukker another player came down altogether. I played worse than ever before, which was an especial pity since this was our last game in India. I wept on Basra's nose at the conclusion of the game as he is going home to Jodhpur now. He is the first horse or pony I have ever really become fond of and I shall miss him very much indeed. He is a small but very sturdy arab chestnut, with lovely white marking down his nose. I think he got to know me too, as very few of the others ever played him.

SATURDAY, 11 MARCH   We rode down to a delightful natural amphi-theatre, surrounded by small wooded hillocks, leaving just the grass lawn in the centre. Here three guards of honour were fallen in. On arrival we dismounted and took up our posts near the Flagstaff, while David inspected the Guards, which were then marched off and replaced by representative units of all troops in Pindi. The ceremony of the presentation of the Colours now took place, followed by an investiture. One very gallant sepoy received the V.C. for great gallantry on the frontier about a year ago in the Waziristan War. Another man, an army doctor, who already possessed the V.C., D.S.O. and M.C., got a bar to his M.C.

Before departing at 11.00 p.m. we attended the sergeants' ball.

SUNDAY, 12 MARCH   We arrived at Kapurthala at noon. The Ma-haraja has quite a nice daughter; she has more go than her brothers and only induced them to take up polo by playing herself. His daughter-in-law, the Tika Rani, hails from Kashmir and was educated in Paris; one can scarcely believe she is Indian. Describing the tired-out appearance of the Staff, she said we all looked 'pulled', a good word!

After the state banquet there was a conjuring performance, but I left before this show and went to the station, where I went on in our supplementary train to Jullundur Cant. where I got out and waited for the Delhi Mail.

MONDAY, 13 MARCH   The mail train ran into Delhi Main at 9.00 a.m. Although I had had a compartment to myself I had been very uncomfortable, chiefly due to the filth and dust everywhere and to my having become spoilt through travelling in the royal train. I had obtained three days' leave to go and see Edwina before we left the country. The remainder of the party have gone on to Dehra Dun today.

I spent the morning with Edwina and we had plenty to tell each other. By the English Mail that arrived yesterday I had had some very nice letters from home I was able to tell her about. The papers at home have been the limit as they have published photos of us and say that the announcement is expected shortly.

At lunch I sat between Her Ex. and an American friend of hers, who is staying here, a Mrs Crozier. I had been warned what to expect but it was all I could do to keep a straight face when my neighbour quite seriously addressed the Vicereine as 'Queen Alice', thinking she was being respectful!

We all had dinner on the verandah and afterwards Edwina and I went for a walk by moonlight.

TUESDAY, 14 MARCH   We drove out to Humayun's tomb, which we had last visited almost exactly one month previously, and saw it this time by daylight. Edwina having just lately been to Agra and seen the Taj Mahal was full of scorn for this poor little tomb, although it was the size of a large church. All the same it was very nice going back there and we both enjoyed seeing it again.

WEDNESDAY, 15 MARCH   I ought to have mentioned that I received a most charming wire from Cousin George yesterday, giving his consent to the engagement.[1]

The royal train is due to leave Gajraula at 7.00 p.m. passing through Delhi about 9 o'clock. Edwina got permission for us to have a small dinner in her sitting room, a little earlier than the big dinner. While we were having it most of the house party and staff came in to say 'good-bye' to me. They obviously know by now that we are

---

[1] King George V. His consent to the marriage under the Royal Marriages Act was technically required, though something of a formality.

engaged. We then drove down to the station and arrived so early that the supplementary train had not yet left, so that Edwina to her great joy was able to say good-bye to Fruity.

We walked about on the red carpet till the royal train came in and then I took Edwina in to David's sitting room, where David joined us for a little as he wanted to see Edwina.

THURSDAY, 16 MARCH   I woke up with my mouth caked with dust. I closed my mouth, the dust gritted against my teeth. I sat up and looked round, everything in sight was a uniform khaki colour. We were in the Sind desert.

For sheer heat, filth and discomfort the journey across this desert takes a lot of beating.

After lunch I went round and privately told each member of the staff of my engagement. They were all very nice about it, and none of them showed the least surprise. Col. O'Kinealy[1] went so far as to say that our ages were medically just right, which was good news!

As I work under Captain North arranging dinners etc. I had suggested having all the Staff on board for a final dinner on Friday night, but this proved impracticable, so I suggested getting the fellows from the supplementary train in to ours and making tonight's dinner the final one. This was done and after a very cheery dinner with much champagne de Montmorency made a speech, referring to each one of us by name and also referred to my engagement. David had given Worgan a large silver cup which was filled with champagne. Seventeen of us drunk half and various people were asked to finish it off but refused. They then said I must and I did.

FRIDAY, 17 MARCH   I felt very ill all today as a result of drinking half a challenge cup full of champagne, and it is the last time I shall ever do anything of the sort.

We reached Karachi at 9.30 a.m. We drove to Frere Hall, in the grounds of which David presented colours to the 126th Baluchis, subsequently unveiling the Baluch War Memorial. This was a badly run show, the climax being reached when David pulled the cord and it came away in his hand without even shaking the flags covering the memorial. We then drove on to Government House, where the

---

[1] Lieutenant-Colonel F. O'Kinealy, a member of the Prince's staff seconded from the Indian Medical Service.

Commissioner in Sind lives, though as a matter of fact the Governor, Sir George Lloyd, has come up from Bombay. There was a native garden party in the afternoon to which I went and on return we drove for the last time in the carriages to the docks, where we bade farewell to the Indian staff and went aboard *Comus* who was alongside. *Comus* then proceeded to the end of breakwater and anchored. We transferred to *Renown* by tug, and proceeded to sea at once.

SATURDAY, 18 MARCH   Sad as I am at leaving India with all our good friends there it is nice to be back onboard the old ship and to be at sea once more. I found a very nice telegram from Edwina just after we had sailed on my desk and sent her a wireless. It is already stiflingly hot, especially in my cabin.

TUESDAY, 21 MARCH   *Renown* arrived at Colombo at 6.00 a.m. At 7.00 a.m. an officer from the shore came and informed me that he had come to fetch our luggage. I told him, very politely, to go away and come back at a more Christian hour, 10.00 a.m. to be precise. This he did, for he was an obliging man, but his orders were to always fetch our luggage at this unearthly hour, whenever we made a move in Ceylon.

On the jetty were the usual Naval and Military Guards of Honour and collection of notables. The Chief Headsmen of the Cingalese wore an entirely original costume, consisting of yards of material wrapped round their legs like a skirt, with a huge bundle of the stuff tucked in in front of their stomachs. They wear a short-sleeved, puffed at the shoulders, gold-embroidered coat and an embroidered square cushion footstool affair, with a tassel, on their heads. An alternative rig some had on might quite well be worn by a Swiss Admiral. They all seemed short and fairly stout.

A seven-mile official drive followed. The streets were wonderfully crowded and David received a remarkable ovation, which was a pleasant change from the usual Non-Co-operation in India.

WEDNESDAY, 22 MARCH   Today I asked David is he would be my best man at the wedding, and he said he would.[1]

---

[1] Mountbatten originally asked his brother Georgie to fill this role, 'as I believe married men are allowed to be, and I want no one else.' Georgie replied suggesting that the Prince would be more appropriate.

THURSDAY, 23 MARCH   This is the first move by train, which I ran as regards retinue and luggage. I had orders typed out last night about it and turned out at 7.30 a.m. to see those orders carried out. David and the whole party, except the Admiral and myself who motored, went by special train at 9.00 a.m. to Kandy. We have brought on two small Crossleys, and it was in one of these cars that we drove up, doing the 70-odd miles in just over three hours, the Admiral driving.

When within five miles of our goal we came to a level crossing, both gates of which were shut and padlocked, with two important looking Cingalese railway officials leaning against them. I happened to know that the royal train was not due for at least another half hour and therefore got out and politely requested the nearest official to open the gates, pointing to the Feathers on the car and to our pass, and explaining that this was the car that had to fetch David at the station at Kandy. I had to get the chauffeur of another waiting car to interpret as the man only spoke Cingalese, nevertheless, in spite of threats to report him, the railway man was adamant and refused to open the gates.

It was now that I observed a suspicious bulge in the neighbourhood of his inside coat pocket. I seized both his hands and held them with my left, while with my right I undid his uniform coat, searched his pocket and produced the keys, unlocked the gates, let the stream of waiting cars through and returned the keys to the infuriated and jabbering man.

A little further on we were met by a despatch rider who led us through the various police and military cordons up to the King's Pavilion, which is the Governor's residence in Kandy. It is rather a hopeless house, for although it contains many large and airy reception rooms, there is an entirely inadequate supply of sleeping apartments.[1] Nearly all the staff, including myself, are living outside the house. Eight of our party are sharing an eight-sided erection, made entirely of some sort of dried rushes. Even the external walls and roof are of this, so if it rains we shall be in for a nice time. Each room is wedge-shaped, as they have in all eight plaited screens joining in the centre. It is also very hot within, although Kandy is considerably higher up than Colombo.

After a small dinner party we motored to the audience hall of the old Kings of Kandy, where Ceylon was originally ceded to the British and where David now held a Durbar of the Chiefs. Next we walked

---

[1] This deficiency did not stop him taking up residence in the King's Pavilion during his time as Supreme Allied Commander in South-East Asia in 1944.

to the Temple of the Tooth, and saw the sacred tooth of Buddha. This was followed by a procession of elephants.

FRIDAY, 24 MARCH   The servants had to pack up and leave half an hour before us and they succeeded in packing David's tie, consequently he appeared without one. I immediately jumped into a car and with the electric klaxon permanently switched on we careered through the streets like a fire engine to the station, where I had his suitcase opened, the errant neck-gear extracted, and returned within 9 minutes. However by this time Joey had lent David his tie and was wearing a coloured handkerchief instead.

We motored to the Peradeniya Gardens,[1] where David planted a tree. As soon as he got back into his car the crowd rushed forward to cheer him, and I should imagine successfully ended the life of the little tree, after being in the ground only one minute.[2] The gardens are very lovely and having had a drive round we went to the station.

SATURDAY, 25 MARCH   We left Government, or rather 'Queen's' House, at 10.30 a.m. amd motored to the jetty. There was a sad moment here when we had to say good-bye to Lord Cromer, who has been our Chief of Staff since we left London. He has been kindness itself to everyone and was especially sympathetic and helpful to me at Delhi. The Admiral now becomes Chief of Staff, as on the last tour, and Brigadier-General Woodroffe has joined the staff as Military Secretary. He is our expert on Japan.

---

[1] Where Mountbatten was to establish the headquarters of his Command in 1944.
[2] The tree was certainly no longer in evidence in 1944. Mountbatten planted one instead.

The Journey to Japan

TUESDAY, 28 MARCH   We steamed down the straits of Malacca this morning. At 1.30 p.m. we anchored at Deepwater Point, some 2½ miles from Port Swettenham, which would have been a far better site for the port than the present one. The High Commissioner of the Federated Malay States Sir L. Guillemard paid his official call at 3.45 p.m. He is a nice old man but I gather that there is no love lost between him and the Chief Secretary to the Government, who is also a nice man, Maxwell by name. It seems a pity that the two highest in the land cannot get on. Maxwell refused to come off in the same boat as H.E. to pay his official call and signs were not wanting elsewhere of this feud. Maxwell is indeed reputed to have started a movement to abolish the post of High Commissioner altogether.[1]

We landed officially in the barge at 4.15 p.m. and were met ashore by the usual notables, including the four sultans of the Federated Malay States: Perak, Selangor, Negri-Sembilan and Pahang, who wore solid gold lace trousers and Yankee brogues made of the same material. Perak, who was educated at Oxford and is quite a nice little fellow, drove with David, when we did the 30-odd miles to Kuala Lumpur by motor car. We drove along a crowded route in the city and finished up at Government House.

THURSDAY, 30 MARCH   In the forenoon David and some of us motored to a rubber plantation. The road ran through miles of forest, consisting of systematically planted rubber trees; the view became distinctly monotonous after a few miles. On arrival we first went into the plantation and watched coolies making fresh cuts in the bark of the tree. The cuts are usually 'V' shaped and a channel is cut leading to a little spout, from which an ordinary china cup is hung. Presently the milky white sap runs along the cut and channel into the cup, which

---

[1] Mr W. G. Maxwell, recently promoted from being Resident in Perak. Maxwell lost the battle, and had left by the end of the year.

it will fill up to half-way once every day, taking from 30 to 45 minutes to do so.

I dipped my finger into a cup and rubbed them together and presently the juice had all dried up and formed into a strong white piece of india rubber. We next visited the factory itself. Here the coolies bring in the juice in buckets and pour it into a large tank, which is divided up by wooden slabs. Dilute acetic acid is now poured into the tank, which causes the sap to coagulate and by the morning when the slabs are removed a thick sheet of pure white rubber is found between each. This stuff is so soft that I found it would retain my finger marks.

The sheets of this rubber are now run between roller machines not unlike ordinary mangles, which squeeze them out and compress them. They next run over a roller which ribs them. After this they are hung up in a smoking room and are dried and smoked. Very simple!

We returned to G.H. and then drove back to the station and went by special train to Port Swettenham, where we sailed for Singapore.

FRIDAY, 31 MARCH   We anchored in the ample harbour of Singapore, though a fair distance out, about 8.00 a.m.

The seats of all the cars were so hot that we all jumped up with a yell of pain and had to crouch above them trying to look unconcerned. An address at Raffles Statue, and an unveiling of the war memorial, punctuated by short drives in the crowded streets finishing up at Government House completed the morning's programme. 260 head hunters from Borneo or rather Sarawak lined the route near Government House and let out a fearsome war cry as we passed.

SATURDAY, 1 APRIL   Captain North, Godfrey and I went to the Malay-Borneo Exhibition again and had a real look round. What interested me most was to see a number of Chinese women walking about as awkwardly as if they were on stilts. On closer inspection it turned out that they had artificially deformed feet, which are so much admired by the Chinese, and were wearing shoes only about three or four inches in length. It rather revolted me.

We also visited the collection of indigenous animals which are being presented to the London Zoo, through David. The long-nosed monkey interested me most. The nose projects two or three inches beyond the usual limit and makes the monkey look hideous, though unfortunately more human. An attractive sort of monkey is the wah-

wah, from Borneo and besides this there were also diminutive baby orang-outangs, which clutched at one's fingers. I saw a python 27 ft long and a number of very small mouse deer.

I bought a genuine old Malay kris from Perak, a small war gong from Brunei and some delightful toys from Brunei. Raja Brooke has brought over two of his tribes from Sarawak, which we saw lining the route yesterday. They have built themselves crude huts which rest on poles about ten feet off the ground and we got hold of one of the men in charge who offered to show us over the huts. He was informed by one of the head hunters that they had been disturbed by bad dreams (probably the result of taking too much of their dearly beloved gin) and had some ceremonies to perform to appease the bad spirits before they would let anyone in.

At dinner I sat next to an officer in a strange uniform, he had no royal badge or cypher or crown on any part of his uniform but wore some strange 'arms' as badges. I was so interested that I enquired and found out that he was the Private Secretary to the Governor of North Borneo. North Borneo is not British except in as much as it is owned by a British Company called the North Borneo Chartered Company. He was not wearing the King's uniform, therefore, but the Company's uniform. The Board of Directors, in London, appoint the Governor (with the sanction of the Colonial Office) and pay him as well as all their police and district officers. Like Sarawak, which lies near it, it does not really owe allegiance to the Crown, though both are British Protectorates.

After dinner I had a most interesting talk with Vyner Brooke, the third Raja of Sarawak. His wife (H.H. The Ranee) is Lord Esher's daughter and he himself is of course pure English. His grandfather was an old sea captain and by organizing and commanding one party in the civil war which was raging in Sarawak he easily defeated the other side. The victors asked him to be their Raja, and he consented. Since then Sarawak has been ruled over by the Brookes, who have been successful autocrats.

His two tribes, the Dyaks and the Kians, came up after dinner and performed head hunting dances. Three Chiefs stripped themselves bare and laid their regalia at David's feet at the end. There was a ball at the town hall and a Chinese torchlight procession. About midnight we returned aboard *Renown*.

SUNDAY, 2 APRIL   We weighed at 6.00 a.m. and proceeded to sea.

THURSDAY, 6 APRIL   The fog was so thick in the morning that we had to anchor outside Hong Kong and send the *Durban* ahead to find the entrance. After about an hour's delay we went ahead and finally anchored a little after 9 o'clock. David got into a 'Chinese chair' and was carried through the streets to a specially built reception pavilion. His 'chair' was a very grand affair, being carried by eight liveried Chinese coolies. A 'chair', as its name implies, is an ordinary light armchair lashed to two long poles, by which the coolies carry it. The ordinary chair one hires in the street is only carried by two coolies. The three which carried the senior members of our Staff away from the reception pavilion were carried by four coolies. The grander one is the more coolies appears to be the rule.

David received four addresses at the pavilion, one in Chinese which it was interesting to listen to. We had walked behind David's chair as far as the pavilion, but now we drove slowly behind it in cars. Hong Kong is such a hilly place that rickshaws can only be used in that part of the town which lies near the water and is fairly level. For the climb as far as Government House chairs or motor cars have to be used.

Captain North and I share a little bungalow in the grounds of Government House, which was only completed yesterday and smells vilely of paint and varnish. The A.D.C. is a marine called Neville.[1]

FRIDAY, 7 APRIL   We paid an official call onboard *Kiso*, the Japanese Flagship. The entire squadron had manned ship and fired a salute on arrival and departure. I was struck with the great similarity between this ship and any of our own. This was most noticeable when one went below, except that everything was much smaller, especially the chairs and tables. They have our system of wiring, section boxes, etc., also our navy phones, ventilation shafts and hatches.

After I had changed into household clothes in the evening I hired a 'Chinese chair' for 20 cents to carry me about, so that I could see what it was like. I think it is as comfortable a way of moving about, if you are not in a hurry, as I have tried, though I couldn't quite get over being carried by human beings.

At 8.00 p.m. we drove to the 'Tai Ping' Theatre. We had dinner in the auditorium, while a play was acted in Chinese on the stage. The menu consisted of 10 Chinese courses, such as, Bird's Nest Soup, Fried

---

[1] Later General Sir Robert Neville, and one of Mountbatten's oldest and closest friends.

Garoupa, Shark's Fin, Fairies' Delight! Only chopsticks and a small china ladle were provided. I got on very well with them. The Wan Tau Lok Company gave an old Chinese musical drama.

SATURDAY, 8 APRIL   The ship sailed at 9.00 a.m. escorted by *Durban* and 3rd Japanese Cruiser Squadron.

Japan

Japan was singularly instable at the time of the Prince of Wales's visit (a statement which seems to apply to almost all the countries he toured). The Prime Minister had been assassinated in November 1921 and a series of patched-up administrations had failed to establish themselves. It was not till the tour was over that Admiral Baron Tomosaburo Kato became Prime Minister and reasserted the authority of government.

The situation was made no easier by the condition of the Mikado. In theory the Japanese Emperor, though a constitutional monarch, enjoyed enormous personal power. However, the Emperor Yoshito had become progressively more unfit to rule and was now reputed to be insane and secluded somewhere in the royal palace. Certainly he was never in evidence during the Prince's visit. His son, the Crown Prince Hirohito (still on the throne today), had been appointed Regent in November 1921, but in a society in which age was revered, a substitute monarch who was only twenty-one could not be expected to wield great power.

WEDNESDAY, 12 APRIL   On looking out of the bathroom scuttle at 6.45 a.m. I was able to catch my first glimpse of the famous Fujiyama. Somehow, having seen so many pictures of this famous mountain and heard so much about it, I felt that I might be disappointed when I saw the real thing. I was not, however, and I don't think I shall ever forget how glorious Fuji looked in the morning sun. The foreshore was all hidden by mists and the symmetrical snow-capped peak was the one outstanding feature on the mainland.

I came on deck in time to see the Japanese First Fleet fire their

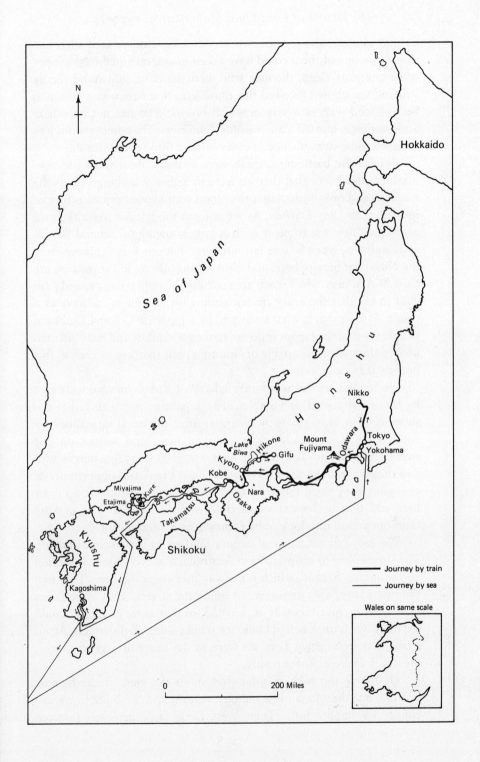

N

Hokkaido

Sea of Japan

H o n s h u

Nikko

Mount
Fujiyama

Odawara

Tokyo

Yokohama

Lake
Biwa

Hikone

Gifu

Kyoto

Kobe

Nara

Miyajima

Kure

Etajima

Osaka

Takamatsu

Shikoku

K y u s h u

Kagoshima

Journey by train

Journey by sea

0   200 Miles

Wales on same scale

21-gun salute. Next to our own service I have never seen such fine ships; any one of them could have taken us on, on equal terms. They were spotlessly clean, the men who were manning ship stood rigidly still and somehow I received the impression that here was a power to be reckoned with in a way in which no one who has not been here and seen for himself can possibly conceive. That impression was destined to be strengthened at every minute throughout this day.

Besides the battleships, there were cruisers, destroyers and sub-marines, and I was glad that we were in as fine a looking ship as the *Renown* and only wished that the *Hood* could have been escorting us instead of the tiny *Durban*. As we entered the breakwater a flight of aeroplanes flew out to meet us. It is largely owing to General Wood-roffe's efforts, when he was last out here, that our R.A.F. are teaching the Naval Air Service here, and most of our officers in the mission are ex-R.N.A.S. men. The French are teaching the military wing, and I am glad to say that the army are not getting on so well as the navy as a result. At least that is what I was told by a Japanese Colonel. Our own people say that the Japanese do not make good pilots and have hitherto proved themselves incapable of 'stunting', but they are as keen in this branch as in every other.

On landing at the 'temporary wharf' at Yokohama we were met by the usual crowd of notables. The Japanese are so tiny that the shortest of us look giants by contrast. After the usual formalities we entered the 'court train', as it is called here, and started on our twenty-mile trip to Tokyo. The lines are narrow gauge, but so well laid that the train hardly rocked at all. David took this opportunity of changing from naval full dress to Welsh Guards' uniform and I must here add that he looked wonderfully well in his bearskin, making everyone round him look quite common and insignificant.

We drove in magnificent lacquer landaus to the Imperial Palace. The streets were as crowded as in Australia, and everyone was smiling and shouting 'Banzai', which is the way they cheer out here. They had the best part of two divisions out lining the streets. They were fallen in, four deep, on either side of the road, so that as far as the eye could see there was a thick belt of khaki stretching along all the streets. Again I had that feeling that here we were in the heart of a great power, greater than we at home realize.

Of course the soldiers somewhat spoilt the view of the humble civilian, but then Japan is a military nation, and the humble civilian counts for mighty little. There were fairly large gaps left between regiments, however, and here the policemen squatted down, as well as the first six rows of the crowd, to let those behind have a better view. This is an excellent idea, though I am afraid I can hardly picture a London crowd doing the same.

The Imperial Palace is a real old Japanese bungalow, with endless corridors filled with bowing officials and small Japanese dressed like the frog footman in *Alice in Wonderland*. Personally I think it quite pathetic to see these little men, who look so fine in their native clothes, struggling to look dignified in our European clothes, which never seem to fit them. We were led along these endless passages to a large room, where we waited. Presently yet more officials arrived who bowed even lower than before and conducted us to a little ante-room, where we again waited.

Then each of us in turn stepped to the door of an inner room and made a low bow, advanced to where David was standing with an insignificant looking little lady, in European clothes, who turned out to be the Empress, and made another low bow. We then shook hands with Her Imperial Majesty, made another bow, turned towards the Prince Regent and bowed again. David also presented us to the Prince Regent and after this we bowed again, walked out backwards and bowed at the entrance before joining the others. I shall have a very supple neck by the time we leave Tokyo.

We now drove on to the Akasaka Palace, where we are living. It resembles Buckingham Palace from the front, though it is considerably smaller. It is built entirely on European lines and its interior decoration reminds one of a cocktail, as a little bit of every European style has been taken and mixed up. We are very comfortable, though it is sad to think that we should have travelled thousands and thousands of miles to be put up in a building which isn't even faintly reminiscent of Japan. It was built some fifteen years ago for Prince Hirohito to live in when he started his own household but he has stuck to the old Japanese palace and I admire him for it, consequently this magnificent palace has stood empty since it was built and we are its first occupants.

David drove round Tokyo shedding visiting cards on about a dozen different members of the Imperial Family. He got back just in time to have members of the diplomatic corps and other high officials presented to him at the palace. I have not seen David in such good shape since Australia. He stopped and chatted with almost everyone and said just the right thing, so that everyone was enchanted. I was especially interested to see old Admiral Togo, the hero of the Russo-Japanese War, who is still alive, though getting on in years.

We all had to struggle into full dress once more for dinner, David wearing naval uniform. All meals are at an unusually early hour out here and we had to leave for the State Banquet at the Imperial Palace at 6.40. I don't know when I have seen so much gold lace in one room. Everyone bows to everyone else several times. The courtiers go about with hanging heads, which give them a quite unnaturally obsequious air. To be really humble one rubs one's knees as one bows and remains in that position while addressed by royalty without daring to look up. When dismissed one backs away and draws in one's breath through one's teeth as one stands erect again.

The meal seemed to me to be endless, though the people and the room itself were fascinating to study. The Imperial Family sat at the head of the table and I was sorry to see that even the ladies wore European clothes, though a few of the ladies of the court were wearing the picturesque old Japanese court dress. Besides the Empress, there were, I think, 7 princesses present and they all wore the 'Order of the Crown', which has a broad ribbon over the right shoulder, and is for ladies only, like Russia, if I remember right.

About this time an earthquake is known to have taken place; I regret to say that neither David nor I noticed it, though they say that the whole palace shook for a minute. We watched two old and lengthy Japanese classical dances after this known as 'Bugaku' dances; they were called 'Shundeikwa' and 'Nasori'. We then processed back along endless corridors and spent an hour at supper. We then returned to the main room and only left at 12.

THURSDAY, 13 APRIL At 10.00 a.m. David received addresses from the House of Peers and the House of Representatives, not to mention numerous other bodies in the palace. After this was over we drove to the Tokyo Imperial University, where David had an address read to him in Japanese. He handed over his own reply and proceeded to make a good speech, extempore, to the three or four thousand students, in English, which most of them must have understood, as it is the language of the educated man out here. This is the first time David has made a little speech on his own for months; altogether he is doing too marvellously and seems to be quite his old self again, in spite of trying conditions.

In the evening we were invited to dinner at a native tea house, called the 'Maple Club', by some of the Japanese Suite. Our hosts wore Japanese clothes and looked twice as fine as in European clothes. I was interested to see the different little designs worked into their outer kimono, which they told me was their family crest and is always worn by all high-class men and women.

The 'Maple Club', I am glad to say, was pure Japanese. On arrival we had to take our shoes off, which weren't needed on the delightfully clean mats in the house. The ceiling was only about 7 ft above the floor and the walls were sliding partitions, while the windows were of paper. We sat down on the floor of one room and warmed ourselves at little earthenware braziers, in wooden boxes, while we smoked and drank Japanese tea.

Presently we all moved into the next room and there were 10 flat cushions with 10 baby tables in front of them laid out for us. We sat down cross-legged, though the Japanese way is to sit on your legs, and presently in tripped 10 delightful little geisha girls. Each took on one of us and brought in food of many quaint varieties, which they set before us and which we had to eat with chopsticks. While we were eating they sat exactly opposite us about 2 ft away, watching every movement and giggling at our efforts to use chopsticks. They also poured out 'sake', the native drink, for us. It is served warm and is quite good. The girls expect to be offered a turn at the cup occasionally.

After the meal was over, the partitions were opened and some of the geishas went out in front and danced, while the rest came and sat by our side. I had rather a nice little one called Sakeyu. We left at 10.00 p.m. with many promises to return.

FRIDAY, 14 APRIL As it was Good Friday today we had to attend church officially. David unveiled a couple of memorial tablets for British Language Officers and residents from Tokyo who were killed in the war. About 20 Japanese Officers were present, mostly friends of the fallen men. I thought it very tactless of the padre to read the prayer for heretics and infidels in their presence.

The Prince Regent is giving each of us a complete Japanese costume; the magnificence of this gift will be appreciated when I add that each costume costs at least 500 yen (9 yen 34 sen to £1 is the present exchange). The costume consists of three separate kimonos, the really attractive ones being the inner ones, which no one sees. We spent a good part of the afternoon choosing our stuffs and being measured for the costume, which are being supplied by the leading firm in Japan

– Mitsukoshi. I am quite enchanted with my stuffs and I can conceive of no more comfortable or attractively unostentatious costume to go to a fancy dress ball in. The family crest is always worked into the outer garment and they are going to copy mine in.

SATURDAY, 15 APRIL Today the announcement of our engagement was made in the Japanese press, as a result of press cables on the subject from London.

At 9.45 a.m. David, disguised as a Japanese General but looking far more like an American Captain, accompanied by most of us, drove to Yoyogi Parade Ground, where the Guards Division were drawn up on parade. This division consists of over 10,000 men. All the little men are the same height, look the same and in fact have had their individuality submerged to a degree hitherto only attained by Germany. When at the 'slope' they hold their arms in the same way as the Germans do and when they marched past the picture was completed by their performing a fairly creditable imitation of the 'goose step'. Nevertheless they were very smart and took themselves very seriously. The Cavalry went past very well though one would hardly accuse the Japanese of being a nation of horsemen.

David and some of us lunched with Prince Tokugawa, who is the adopted son of the line of Shoguns. The Shoguns were for some two or three hundred years virtually dictators in Japan, and the influence of the Tokugawa family is still immense. At the conclusion of lunch we witnessed some remarkable native wrestling in front of the house.

The champion wrestler was one of the biggest men I have ever seen and for a Japanese he was a veritable giant. He weighed 330 lbs, we were informed, and was wonderfully strong in spite of a double chin and over-hanging tummy. He delivered one of his opponents such a hefty smite on the jaw that the unfortunate victim turned a complete somersault and landed some three feet outside the ring. They fight in a real 'ring', that is to say a circle of about twelve foot diameter is marked out with a raised edge and he who gets any part of his opponent's body to touch the ground outside the ring or gets his opponent's knee and hand on the ground anywhere is the winner. There were a good many contests, which always ended quickly though the ceremony of starting may take any length of time as the umpire only gives the signal when the spirit has moved both men at the same time with a desire to fight.

SUNDAY, 16 APRIL   Today was Easter Sunday and so all of us once more trickled off to church and all that sort of thing. On return David saw some 90 leading newspapermen and read them a speech. These delightful people had organized a boycott of news relating to David's visit as they said that our Embassy and the Japanese court officials had left them out of several important functions. As usual it was left to David himself to extricate the blunderers from their muddle, which he did as successfully as ever.

At 2.50 the entire party set out for Shinjiku Palace for the Imperial Cherry Garden Party. There are two of these held every year, one at 'cherry blossom' time and the other in the autumn for the 'chrysan-themum'. Unfortunately the cherry blossom came unusually early this year so we missed the first blossom, but some trees bloom twice and there were a number of that sort here, which made the whole place look too lovely. We walked miles through rows of guests, of which there were 6000, and then had tea in a specially erected pavilion.

MONDAY, 17 APRIL   I came to the conclusion that my Japanese costume was so nice that I would like to get Edwina one too and accordingly enlisted the help of Col. Tsunoda.[1] He promised to take me to the big stores, who were making our costumes, so that I could do my shopping there and said we would have to start at 8.30 a.m. I enquired why we couldn't start later and he replied, 'Because we must be back by twelve o'clock.' I said, 'Surely it will not take over three hours to get a lady's kimono?' but he persisted and so we started at 8.30 a.m. and what is more we did not get back till twelve.

On arrival at 'Mitsukoshi' (the Harrods or Selfridges of Japan) we were met by the manager and an assistant, who conducted us to a private room at the top of the building. Here we were given armchairs and offered cigarettes. Presently a little geisha girl came in with Japanese tea, which she set before us. After another ten minutes' wait the manager returned with the sales manager and several heads of departments to whom I was introduced with much bowing on both sides. We then discussed the weather. As we had by now been at least quarter of an hour in the shop without getting on with the shopping I asked whether they would let me see some ladies' kimonos. This was a blunder and a very tactless one. I could see that they were pained that I should have introduced such a sordid subject into our delightful

---

[1] Lieutenant Colonel Masanosake Tsunoda, one of the Prince of Wales's Japanese staff officers.

little breakfast party. They shrugged their shoulders and called for the little serving girl who now brought in some European tea, which I politely drank. I again ventured to remind them of the reason of my visit. This time the girl was sent for cakes, which we all ate with chopsticks.

Presently one of the managers went out and returned some five minutes later with two assistants carrying a box. 'Good,' thought I, 'the kimonos at last.' Of course I was mistaken. It was a large camera and a tripod, which they unpacked and proceeded to erect. I had begun to realize that the best thing I could do was not to refer to the painful subject of the kimonos again but take an interest in whatever else they brought.

Well, they took a photo of Tsunoda and me sitting at the breakfast table. Then the two managers-in-chief came and stood behind us and another group was taken. After this two enormous albums were brought for my inspection. I was shown Arthur's signature in three places, also that of poor Charles who is staying ashore with the Belgian Ambassador. Finally I was asked to sign.

After this two male and two female assistants, dressed in Japanese costume, entered the room and bowed. I looked at the clock, and the hands pointed at twenty-five minutes to ten before I even saw a sign of the first kimono.

When the kimonos did start arriving it was a case of 'thick and fast, they came at last'. I was bewildered. I was completely swamped. At least three or four were invariably held up simultaneously for inspection. The simple-looking ones cost fortunes, others that looked complicated would be one quarter the price of the simple ones. Ninety-nine per cent had obviously been made to suit a dark-haired girl, and by the time I had picked out the one I really thought would suit Edwina another hour had passed.

Then came the choice of the 'obi' or sash, which is 1 yard wide by 4½ yards long and is considered of far greater importance than the kimono. The highest priced obi I was told was five thousand yens! Besides this I had to choose the silk socks with the separate big toe and the sandals, not to mention the string that fastens round the obi with a fancy fastening, the silk scarf that holds the obi up behind and the inner collar. Finally the choice of lining was simplified by fashion, which decrees that it shall be a bright scarlet. So Tsunoda was more than right in making me start at 8.30.

We motored out to the Hama Palace for lunch with the Prince

Regent and after lunch we indulged in that sport of sports, the catching of duck in butterfly nets! Candidly I was a trifle disappointed. I had had visions of running over fields, wearing horn-rimmed spectacles, with a poison-bottle at my side, pursuing the wily duck with my butterfly net. Actually the net is a sort of glorified 'landing net' with a long bamboo handle, being some 7 or 8 feet in length in all, while the costume is an ordinary lounge suit, except in the case of Sir Herbert Russell, who chased the duck in top hat and frock coat! The event is officially described as a 'duck hunt'.

First we were taken to a dummy canal, where we assiduously practised netting unfortunate trapped pigeons, tennis balls and each other's head-gear. The first lesson having been learnt, and pages 1 to 3 of the pamphlet of instructions being engraven in our memory, we were allowed to mingle with the more experienced 'nets' of our party and walked to the first 'cover'. As we neared the canal our guides all said 'Shish' so loudly that I thought it would frighten the ducks. Following their motions we approached on tip-toe, our nets lowered.

There are ten nets allowed to a canal, five a side. From the beautiful lacquer Imperial Duck Hunt Plan of Positions I noted that I had drawn No. 1 'net' on the left. I accordingly was presented with a red badge with 1 on it. Those on the left have to hold their right hand above the left in catching hold of the net, the people on the right bank vice versa. A gentleman who rejoices in the title of 'Master of the Hunt', but is in reality a 'keeper', now approaches a wooden door let into a large earth mound and peeps through a narrow slit in the door to see if the decoy ducks have succeeded in bringing in some wild ones.

I should really have described a 'canal' before. The 'canal' is led off from the central lake and is about 4 foot wide. The depth from the top of the banks on either side of the canal to the water is quite 5 or 6 feet, which distance the duck have to fly, of course, before you can attempt to start netting them. The banks are built up some 2 or 3 feet higher than the ground so as to afford cover to the 'nets', while they are creeping into position, and they terminate in the aforementioned mound, which acts as a screen behind which to marshal the 'nets' before they take up their positions for the 'hunt'.

The Master of the Hunt having given the signal to advance, the 'nets' move forward cautiously with lowered nets, and when in position he claps his hands and the wild ducks fly up, in most cases almost straight into the waiting nets. I caught one.

This performance was repeated at another canal further along and

I caught another duck. I then turned my net over to someone else and watched the netting at three more canals.

I took one more turn at netting and caught a third duck, so I got three in all, which must have been about top score, as others never had a duck anywhere near them. Watching was almost as good fun and certainly the most interesting part was when they let one duck escape and got it with a hawk or falcon. In fact this was done three times, and it was the first time I had ever seen 'hawking'. In one case the duck was given a twenty-yard start but the hawk was on it in thirty. They keep a ball of string attached to their wrist with one end secured to the falcon's leg, and the string just whistles out as the bird flies.

Really the most wonderful part about this system of duck-netting is the training of the decoy ducks, which are taught to swim out into the lake and collect wild ducks by 'quacking'. They then lead these wild ducks to a canal for netting and when the wild ones fly up and are caught these remain down. The captured duck have their wings tied together over their heads and are put into bottle-shaped baskets.

TUESDAY, 18 APRIL Today we spent the morning at the peace exhibition, which was interesting but very wearying and from there went on to the farewell luncheon party given by the Empress and Prince Regent at the Imperial Palace. It is the custom in Japan, when any important personage is giving an official meal to hand round with the dessert beautiful silver boxes, usually marked with the crest of the person giving them, which contain little sweets and which one is expected to keep. A very pleasing custom. The one I got today is already my fifth.

After lunch we took our official farewell of the Empress. We walked through the 'forbidden' grounds of the palace, which very few Japanese and as a rule no Europeans are ever allowed to see. They are lovely, but it is a ghastly thought to be practically shut up in them, as the Emperors used to be.

WEDNESDAY, 19 APRIL In the forenoon David played golf with Hirohito.[1] After lunch we drove along an exceptionally crowded route to Uyeno Station, whence we departed for Nikko. The train only stopped at one station and here all the notables of the district were

[1] Only when the Prince Regent failed to hit the ball at his first five attempts did the Prince of Wales suspect that he was something of a novice.

drawn up in frock coat and top hat. Everyone had a frock coat no matter how badly it fitted, and in fact no one is anyone in Japan unless they possess a frock coat. So I fear that I am a very definite no one, unless a uniform frock coat counts. I think it does as there were an equal number of military officers drawn up on the platform.

We reached Nikko after a pleasant run of about 3¾ hours.

THURSDAY, 20 APRIL   At 9.00 a.m. I went with the P.M.O. to visit the two famous Shinto temples, Toshogu and Taiyubyo, and was well rewarded as they are quite lovely. The former is about 300 years old and the latter about 270. They were built by the Shoguns and have the Tokugawa family crest worked into them at every conceivable place, without in any way spoiling the general effect.

The part that interested me most was to see the old lacquer work, which has stood wind, rain and sun for 300 years and still looks better than the modern lacquer. This lacquer work is said to be a lost art in Japan, but I have heard the theory put forward that the race have lost the patience to go on and on and perhaps spend a life-time on one small job, and that it is this patience which was the secret.

FRIDAY, 21 APRIL   I spent most of the morning at the diary, while the others went out and shopped. At 12.30 we drove to a more distant station along a wonderful avenue of tall evergreen trees, with some unpronounceable names. Here we entrained once more and had lunch shortly afterwards.

On return to the Akasaka Palace at Tokyo we found that our Japanese costumes had arrived and hastily tried them on. They are quite difficult garments to put on correctly and I took a number of lessons. Besides a lovely under-kimono there are two outer-kimonos, skirt-like trousers and a haori with our own crests on it.

We dined with Baron Mitsui, whose wealth is said to be beyond the means of counting. He certainly gave us a most excellent dinner and a very lovely silver box for sweets as well.

SATURDAY, 22 APRIL   We left by train at 8.55 a.m. from Tokyo for Yokohama, arriving about 10.00 a.m.

The latest Japanese warship (the largest afloat, being of some 34,000 tons displacement), the *Mutsu*, is here. She was the ship so much fuss was made about at the Washington Conference,[1] and

[1] The international conference which, *inter alia*, imposed limits on numbers and maximum size of warships.

Rear-Admiral Yamanashi, who was there, tells me that rather than give her up they were prepared to let us build two more capital ships. Her officers were the only ones that did not call on the British ships, presumably to avoid having our N.O.s paying a return call and coming onboard to have a look over. She was sent away from the fleet, I hear, after our arrival until just lately, when she returned for David to inspect her. Our naval attaché has never been allowed onboard even. My luck therefore is all the more inexplicable in getting the Minister of Marine's permission to pay a two-hour visit to the ship before David's arrival.

I think that they rather regretted having given me permission as I was informed that the boat would only be sent in one hour before David's instead of two as originally promised. I managed after panting round a bit to get it sent in two hours before after all. As I was visiting a foreign man-of-war I was piped over the side; this being the first time I have ever been piped I was duly thrilled.

The Commander who was to have shown me round and presumably have kept his eye on me was called on board the Flagship by signal very shortly after my arrival and the W/T Officer showed me round. He was very polite and let me see all over a 16″ turret as far as the shell room, a submerged flat and above water tubes as well as a number of other interesting things. We mutually drew the line at examining her fire control or W/T gear. The *Mutsu* is a wonderful ship. I take my hat off to the Japs for her!

I watched David's arrival and followed him round the ship, but now each one of the N.O.s of the party was closely watched including, funnily enough, myself, so that we could not have broken away from the main party if we had wanted to, and in consequence saw nothing of unusual interest.

SUNDAY, 23 APRIL   They wouldn't let us off church although it meant a great rush for the train which we caught at 11.10 a.m. for Odawara. We reached Odawara Station at 12.25 p.m. and motored to Prince Kan-in's new villa, where he entertained us and the Prince Regent to luncheon.

About three o'clock we drove on to Umoto, where David and I are staying at Baron Iwasaki's villa. The Umoto party went to tea with Mr Imamura at the villa next door. There we saw a native potter at work. I tried my hand at the wheel and made a wine cup of indifferent concentricity and thickness. We also painted various prepared trays and jars, which were then glazed and baked, while we watched. The

left: H.R.H. poised for a round of golf with the Prince Regent, later the Emperor Hirohito. The Prince Regent's deficiencies as a golfer were about to be embarrassingly displayed (19 April 1922).

below: H.R.H. acts as rickshaw coolie for the Admiral, with disastrous results for the rickshaw.

above: The royal party try on the Japanese costumes presented by the Prince Regent (14 April 1922). From left to right: Captain North, Admiral Halsey, H.R.H., General Woodroffe, Surgeon Commander Newport, Hon. Piers Legh; and in the back row, Mountbatten, Hon. Bruce Ogilvy, Sir Godfrey Thomas, Captain Metcalfe.

right: H.R.H. with King Fouad – the barking monarch – in Cairo (11 June 1922).

head potter had an irritating habit, peculiar to most Japanese of the lower orders, of sucking in his breath through his teeth at the end of each remark to a superior. When anyone spoke to him he went into fits of humble and respectful giggles, which so got on my nerves that I just itched to crack all his pottery over his humble head!

MONDAY, 24 APRIL   One of the delights of this place are the baths, which are kept constantly supplied with very hot water from natural springs. The one I always use is a deep round one, with a stone seat at one side. The hot water flows in at the bottom all the time, and the bath overflows into a tiled space which has waste pipes in it. There is a cold water tap at the top, which supplies icy cold water at will; most necessary, since the bath is too hot to get into straight away. However dirty one makes the water it is always beautifully clear by the time one has dried oneself. For the hot water tap at the basin there is a little electric pump, which one has to switch on when one wants water.

TUESDAY, 25 APRIL   It rained only intermittently today, but the view of Mount Fuji, which we were all so anxious to see, was still obscured. Owing to the bad weather our trip to Shoji over the mountains was abandoned and we decided to stay on here an extra two days.

We heard the sad news of Leo's[1] death last Saturday, today. The Japanese Court are also going into mourning for him.

WEDNESDAY, 26 APRIL   Today we heard Fujiyama could be seen, so we hopped into cars and left at about 10.00 a.m. for the hotel. We did not notice anything unusual on the way up, though of course we were jolted about a good deal on the rough road. When we arrived we found all the hotel party in a state of great excitement as they had been inside the hotel about five minutes previously when the worst earthquake Japan has had since 1894 occurred. Of course people imagined that the whole place was coming down, as it rocked and quivered terrifically. When we arrived the hanging lamps had scarcely ceased swinging. People differed in their opinion as to the duration of the worst shock, from five to thirty seconds. The cables that came later

---

[1] Leo was Lord Leopold Mountbatten, son of the first Marquess of Carisbrooke. Edwina, on her journey home, saw a wireless message reporting the death of 'Lord L. Mountbatten'. It was twenty-four hours before she could establish which Lord L. Mountbatten it concerned.

from the seismograph people in Tokyo showed that it actually lasted for just over ten seconds.

Of course we experienced the earthquake on the way, but must have thought it a specially bad piece of road. Telegrams came later to say that people had been killed and injured in Yokohama, and houses had collapsed. The damage throughout the country has been roughly assessed at a million yen. Both *Renown* and *Durban*, who had just got under way, felt such a violent shock, although in no way connected with the shore, that they thought they had hit a rock or submerged wreck. Of course we were very disappointed not to have known what we were experiencing. This is the third earthquake I have been through without noticing anything unusual.

After everyone had recovered we got into cars and drove up the Nagao Pass. As we emerged from the tunnel at the top of the pass one of the most magnificent sights it has ever been my luck to behold met our gaze; right before us rose the sacred mountain of Japan, Fujiyama.

Looking at this wonderful mountain one can easily realize how in days of old people fell down and worshipped it. It has such a strong attraction that the more one sees of it the longer one wants to look. We ourselves were standing 2000 feet up and the valley dropped before us only to rise again, at first gradually, then more steeply, in perfect even lines to the flat summit of old Fuji, which is 12,365 feet high.

I had seen so many pictures of the mountain that I knew what to expect, but the real one is so infinitely more wonderful than any pictures will ever make one realize that it quite took my breath away. I think one of the great secrets is the fact that it stands quite by itself and also the snow round its summit brings the top into very clear silhouette. At sunrise and sunset this is tinted a delicate pink.

THURSDAY, 27 APRIL The train arrived at Kyoto at 9.30 a.m. and we drove to the Omiya Palace, where David, the Admiral, General and Godfrey are staying. The rest of us then drove on to the Kyoto Hotel. I had almost entirely unpacked when a message came to say that they were putting me up at the palace as well, so I packed again and moved.

There was no room ready, but I took over the smoking room, next door to David, and shifted some suitable furniture in. The delightful part about this house, which is unadulterated Japanese, is that one can make the whole place practically one room by sliding partitions aside, or many small rooms. One can walk from the garden one side to the courtyard the other side by just pushing the partitions aside as one goes straight through.

Before lunch, David, the General and I went for a motor drive to see the city, which, in contrast to Tokyo, is attractively Japanese and as yet fairly unspoilt by European influence.

Lunch was at the palace and afterwards we got into uniform and drove out to the Imperial Mausoleum, where David placed wreaths at the foot of the tombs of Their Late Majesties. These tombs consist of plain but impressive piles of stones.

FRIDAY, 28 APRIL   Today was very wearying. We set out at 10.30 a.m. and were away for about fifteen hours. First we drove to Otsu, a small town on the shores of Lake Biwa, which is about the largest lake in Japan. Here we embarked onboard a large steamboat specially built for us and proceeded for a trip round the lake.

During the trip David put a lot of carp overboard, which had been brought out for the purpose of re-stocking the lake. We were also shown specimens of the various fish found in the lake, including some terrapin or 'snapping turtles' and some large oyster shells, in one of which we found a diminutive pearl. We had lunch onboard and afterwards sailed round two pretty small islands.

At 4.10 p.m. we went alongside Hikone Pier and walked to the cars. We drove a short while and then got out and walked up to the picturesque old remains of Hikone Castle, whence we obtained an excellent view of the lake and surrounding country.

We now motored on to the station, where we picked up our train and went on in it to Gifu, to see the famous cormorant fishing. Here we embarked onboard several barges, which were lying in the river Nagara. Six coolies towed each boat by separate lines made fast to a towing stanchion. They had hard work as there is a fast running current, which in three places actually becomes a 'rapid'.

On the way dinner was served; we stopped at a cooking boat half way up to pick up a couple of hot courses. We reached our final destination, the Imperial Fishing Place, about 8.30 p.m., by which time it was quite dark, and moored up.

In the distance, upstream, we could distinguish ten flaring lights which gradually approached us. These came from braziers, slung on poles over the bow of each fishing boat, lighting up the water all round so that one could see the bottom, as the water was so beautifully clear.

These boats descended upon us, the occupants making a great din to encourage the cormorants. In the bows of each stood the chief fisherman, dressed in old-fashioned costume, holding about a dozen lines in one hand, which he kept cleared with the other, while the cormorants, who were attached to the other end of each line, dived in and out amongst each other in their efforts to chase the fish.

At the same time this wonderful man would tend the brazier and pull in those birds that had swallowed as many fish as their crops would hold. He would then make them disgorge their captives.

A ring round the bottom of the cormorant's neck prevents it from completely swallowing the fish and is also used for attaching the line to. Amidships stood the assistant fisherman, who only manipulates four birds, though even this calls for skill in no small degree.

It was the most fascinating thing to watch these birds chasing fish under water and catching them and swallowing them; big ones they would throw in the air and catch so as to swallow them head first. Frequently the birds would fight amongst each other for the possession of a particularly big fish, and the victor would proudly swim about with a quite ridiculous bulge in his throat till hauled aboard and forced to disgorge into the basket. The light seemed to stupefy the fish, who swam about near it without making any efforts to escape.

These birds have to be continually trained, but are highly intelligent and inordinately proud of their capabilities. At the conclusion of the fishing we were shown the birds placed in a row on the gunwale. There is a distinct order of precedence according to skill, which we were informed the cormorants were well aware of, and indeed if this is violated there is a great squabble among the wronged birds.

We caught the royal train at 10.20 p.m. and reached the palace about 1.15 a.m. Even at that hour there were a number of people waiting in the streets to give David a 'Banzai'.

SATURDAY, 29 APRIL We motored out to see the Imperial and Nijo palaces. The former is where the Emperor is always crowned and here we also saw some ancient courtiers in the old dress playing a sort of 'basketball' game with a football of sorts, called Shukiku. The other palace belonged to the Shoguns, and both contain some of the finest old mural paintings and wood carvings of old Japan.

After this we dined with the Governor of the Prefecture at Baron Fujita's house. It was an official meal, but Japanese, and so we sat on the floor without shoes, and were served by geishas. Afterwards we danced and sang with them and played the usual childish games. People at home have quite the wrong idea about geisha parties. They are the most innocent things.

SUNDAY, 30 APRIL   We motored up to the picturesque Shugakuin Palace, where we had a so-called picnic lunch and admired the view and grounds. Later in the afternoon the General took me out for a walk up 'teapot hill', as I was searching for a teapot for Mama. We must have seen some forty or fifty shops where they sell teapots, but in none of them could I see quite what I had promised to get for Mama. Eventually I bought the two most like what I wanted and also some 'birds' made to sing by rubbing squeaky bits of wood together.

MONDAY, 1 MAY   At 11.30 a.m. we visited the East and West Hongwanji Temples. These are the principal Buddhist temples of the district. They were deliberately separated by the Shoguns, so that neither party should become too strong and thus too great a menace. I was very interested at seeing these temples, so different from the Shinto ones at Nikko. They are less decorative and have fewer but infinitely larger buildings and shrines.

I was especially interested to see some 36 fathom 13″ cable laid hawsers of an unusual material. This material turned out to be human hair supplied by the self-sacrificing women of the Hongwanji, when specially strong ropes were needed in 1880 to lift timbers for rebuilding part of the temple which had been destroyed by fire. Indeed 52 of these ropes were made in all.

Another interesting thing to see was the fire extinguishing arrangements: iron pipes run up the inside of each wooden building and in case of necessity 150 plugs will open and let out powerful jets of water. We were given a demonstration of this. West Hongwanji has never been burnt and is therefore nearly three hundred years old.

TUESDAY, 2 MAY   Sayonji gave a Japanese dinner to some of us. I am getting quite skilled with chopsticks and know my way about the various queer dishes we get a little better. By now we also know most of the better class geishas, which makes it more amusing. The nicest one is quite a pretty little person called Shidzu-yacco, which I believe means Quiet-fellow. We also know a dance called Isodushi which is very simple and which we usually join in. I tried my hand at the Samisen, which is a sort of three-stringed guitar they always play. Then there are various games, such as musical chairs with cushions and 'meeting' on the lines of the mats, which always produces howls of glee from the geishas. They are like overgrown children, though it is true the 'half-geishas' are frequently only 13, which may be between 11 and 12 by our reckoning, as they count 1 the day they are born and 2 the following new year's day!

THURSDAY, 4 MAY   We left Kyoto by train about 9.00 a.m. and arrived about 10.30 at Nara, motoring direct to the Nara Hotel, which has been entirely taken over for our party.

After lunch we motored 9 miles out to see Horyuji Temple, which having been established in the year 607 A.D. is believed to be the oldest wooden temple in the world. The Central Gate (chu-mon), the corridor, the Principal Sanctuary (kondo) and the famous five-storied pagoda are original workmanship, unspoiled and untouched, but buildings of the 8th and 13th centuries are included in the compound. I was quite fascinated by all I saw and the many quaint old carved gods.

On return to Nara we drove direct to the Public Hall in the sacred deer park, where we fed the tame deer. On our way back we visited Daibutsu-den, which is an old temple said to be the largest wooden structure in the world, being 156 ft high by 188 ft and 165 ft. It houses the colossal Daibutsu Buddha, which measures 53½ ft in height; of course the figure is seated and I should think it would have been 120 ft if erect. The middle finger is about the size of an average man and the eye is about 40 ins long. The head was damaged in an old fire and has been replaced by one which does not seem quite in keeping with the rest of the body. The whole figure is of metal.

David and Fruity both successfully squeezed through a small hole in a pillar, said to be a test of the possibility of one's getting to Heaven.

FRIDAY, 5 MAY   I got a gentleman connected with the Tourist Bureau to accompany me to Sanjokokam, one of the best sword-makers in Japan. He lives at the foot of the hill, his forge being behind the shop and I spent a fascinating time studying valuable and well-balanced blades. Eventually I chose a short sword, which I could afford, and had my name as well as that of the maker stamped on the metal of the hilt in Japanese characters. He hung up the blade and tapped it to show how true it rang. Then he fixed a wooden hilt on and gave me a wooden sheath and some preservative powder to put on. The samurai were the class privileged to carry two swords, a short and a long one, known together as the dai-sho (long-short). My sword is the 'sho' part, called wakizashi.

The Japanese, unless fighting, never draw their sword in front of a person, and treat it with the utmost reverence. When looking at the blade they usually take a piece of paper in their mouth, to prevent their moist breath from rusting the steel. Blades are usually kept stored in tightly fitting wooden sheaths to preserve them, being transferred to the ornamented sheaths and hilts only when required.

I was shown a blade made by a famous smith eight centuries ago, which had a balance quite unattainable in modern swords. The blade alone was worth 1200 yen and of course some are much more than that. The smiths only work at a certain hour in the early morning when the temperature of the air is accurately known, and may take two years tempering a blade. The man who is repairing the sword Papa got when he was out here over forty years ago is doing a rush job for me and only taking 42 days over it.[1] I found a delightful weighted garden knife for Mama, which I had marked Victoria in Japanese characters.

On return I joined up with the main party who were just off to visit the Giant Bell, which is 136 inches high and 91 inches in diameter, weighing about 50 tons. It is a contemporaneous work with the Great Buddha, being cast in the 8th century. A pole slung like a battering-ram is used to strike the bell. I did this once.

After lunch we proceeded by special tram from Nara to Osaka, arriving there after about a 50-minute run. Osaka reminds me rather of Newcastle-upon-Tyne; it is a grimy industrial town on a river by the sea.

First we went to the Castle to see the view. It is the Headquarters of the Fourth Division and we saw sixty soldiers take part in a sham bayonet fight. Next we went to the Municipal Hall for the usual exchange of addresses. After tea here we drove to the station and went in our train to Kobe. I sat on the observation platform and represented David by waving a flag to the cheering crowds at stations, etc.

At Kobe we more or less repeated the Osaka Municipal Hall stunt, eventually driving to the docks and going onboard the Japanese steamer *Teifuku Maru*, which has been placed at David's disposal for the trip on the inland sea. We changed into a dinner jacket and drove to a Japanese dinner given by the Governor of the Hyogo Prefecture. I

[1] Mountbatten secured a crop of such swords after the Japanese surrender in 1945.

regret to say that he gave us little stools to sit on, not realizing that we were thoroughly accustomed to sit on the floor in the correct style!

Before dinner we saw some geisha dancing, as there was no time for this afterwards. We also saw for the first time some dancing performances by large dolls, manipulated by three men each. These doll dances are very old and are known as Samba-so. They are given as a rule as a sort of 'curtain-raiser' to an ordinary classical play.

SATURDAY, 6 MAY   We got under way at 8.00 a.m. and proceeded along the inland sea, anchoring at 1.00 p.m. off Takamatsu, a small town on the main southern island. The scenery all round was magnificent. This was the ship's maiden trip; she will later be employed on the ferry service to Korea between Shimonoseki and Fusan.

We landed about 2.00 p.m. and were greeted ashore by the usual frock-coated officials and notables. First we drove to the public gardens, which are delightful and walked about in them. There are a number of trout in the little lake and they provided several fishing rods for us. Most of us had a try but the General and I were the only two lucky ones, catching two fairly big ones apiece. David had a great try after an extra big one but with no luck, although I followed him about with a landing net.

SUNDAY, 7 MAY   We got under way in the morning again and proceeded to the fairest of all the isles, Miyajima (the island of the temple) or, as it is also known, Itsukushima. It lies in the northern part of the Sea of Aki and is famous the world over for its beauty and for the temple or shrine lying practically in the sea.

We anchored shortly after 4.00 p.m., went ashore and got over all the official part at the pier, when we were free to go where we pleased. First we visited the hall of a thousand mats (Senjo-kaku) and here we came across a large number of flat wooden rice-spoons, known as shakushi, on which devotees had written their names and dearest wish and offered it up at the shrine in the hopes that their wish would thereby be fulfilled. One can send them through the post by writing the address on the flat part and putting stamps on and this I did, as well as buying one to keep. We saw the Horse of God near here. It is rather a measly specimen though fat, and I fear that the Gods for whom it is reserved do not give it enough exercise.

Next we went to the shrine itself which is built on the beach on short piles, so that at high tide the water comes up all round it. The

Torii or sacred arch in front of it is in this case built actually in the sea, which adds to the picturesque effect. We returned onboard for dinner. After dinner I saw one of the prettiest sights I have ever seen. At least 80,000 paper coloured lanterns on floats were let drift down on the water.

MONDAY, 8 MAY   We left the *Keifuku Maru* at 8.00 a.m. and transferred to the two Japanese escorting cruisers. We weighed and proceeded, anchoring about 9.00 a.m. in Yeta Uchi, that delightful land-locked bay appertaining to the Imperial Naval College at Etajima.

On the playing field in front of the college the 900 cadets were drawn up on parade; those in the ranks had leather belts, pouches and side arms, with rifles, while Cadet Captains wore swords. In place of gaiters blue puttees were worn.

Our party entered by the main drive, which is not quite so pretentious as Dartmouth, though made of granite, and were conducted to a waiting room. In the meanwhile the cadets had removed their equipment and had seated themselves in the main hall. On David entering they rose and made a deep bow, after which they sang the 'God Save' in English without musical accompaniment. The only word I could hear distinctly mispronounced was 'happy', which sounded 'harpy'. The Chief Cadet Captain then came forward and made a short welcoming speech in surprisingly good English. He referred to the early days of Etajima when a staff of British Naval Officers and men trained the Japanese cadets. David made a short but rather good reply, followed by a tour of inspection.

The dormitories are not unlike those at Dartmouth, but the beds are made up in box-like affairs somewhat similar to the old-fashioned 'bunk'. The sea chests are of the same pattern as our old ones, though smaller and painted brown. The whole building has an indefinable air of Dartmouth about it, though not very like it in many respects. Before we left we watched a fascinating game played by the cadets called 'Bōtaoshi' (Putting the Pole Down).

About 200 cadets a side took part, and had changed into white shirts and trousers, the sides being distinguished by pieces of red and green ribbon being tied to the left arm. Two poles, 6″ in diameter and 10′ high, surmounted by a small iron flagstaff with a red or green flag, were brought out and placed some 70 or 80 yards apart. A dozen cadets on each side formed themselves round their pole, and then half a dozen clambered on their shoulders, standing with their backs to the pole. In the meanwhile each side had split up into three parties.

The strength of each party varied at the discretion of the Captain, but as far as I could see there were about 100 in the 'attacking party', which lined up, two or three deep, some fifteen yards in front of the pole, while all the rest were 'defending party'. This latter party were again split into two, about 50 round the pole and about 50 as a 'shock-absorbing party', who lined up two deep immediately in front of the pole.

The signal to charge was given by bugle and the opposing 'attacking parties' rushed for the opposite goal. Naturally there was a terrific collision when they met in the centre, and after the attack had swept on, quite half a dozen cadets were left lying on the field, knocked over by the impact but uninjured, as they scrambled up at once and re-joined their parties.

The first line of the defence on each side was soon overcome, being outnumbered by two to one, and had to fall back as best it could on the 'pole party'. The fighting now grew furious, bold spirits of the 'attacking party' taking a run and hurling themselves on to the heads of the throng round the pole. Friendly hands would push them along, whilst defenders would endeavour to pull them down. Presently one attacker crawled to within reach of the pole, only to be forced back by the half dozen standing on their comrades' shoulders. After a fierce struggle, in which everyone looked as though they were being killed, though there were no visible casualties afterwards, both 'attacking parties' reached their poles together and by catching hold of the top and pulling brought the whole affair down till the flag or what was left of it touched the ground.

The first battle was thus a draw and the whole show had to be repeated to settle who was to be final victor.

One of the rules of the game is 'no punching in the face'; pushing with the open hand is allowed and hitting is permitted on the chest, back or shoulders. All these cadets knowing ju-jitsu, they frequently used that to trip up opponents. It is a thrilling as well as an entertaining game to watch, and the players declare that they like it immensely, indeed most of them play once a week. The sides can be of any number from about 30 a side to 400 or 500 provided they are equal. Gym shoes are usually worn.

When we returned to the cruisers, the whole college did an evolution of 'away all boats' and escorted us out in 18 cutters. We sailed at 10.00 a.m. and proceeded to Kure (the Portsmouth of Japan) which is a naval port containing the largest dockyard and only naval arsenal.

We landed about 11.30 a.m. and first drove to the house of the Commander-in-Chief, with whom we lunched.

After lunch we inspected the dockyard. We saw them converting their latest battleship, which they are not allowed to complete under the Washington agreement, to an airplane carrier. She was being built in a shallow building dock instead of a slip-way. I also saw a submarine being built, about the same size as our 'K' Class and therefore about 1800 to 2000 tons displacement on the surface. The arsenal was the most interesting part, though, and especially interesting to me since I had never seen one before. We saw them rolling armour plates, shrinking outer tubes on to guns, wire-winding guns, and machining all the various parts connected with armaments.

We left at 3.00 p.m. and embarked on board *Renown*, who had come round to pick us up. We sailed at 3.30 p.m.

TUESDAY, 9 MAY   We arrived at Kagoshima, in the extreme south of Japan, at 8.30 a.m. The British community were present on the landing stage, and after greeting them David went off to a reception given by the Governor. We went out to a small dais and saw the 'Armour Procession' form up and march off to a martial song. This procession takes place in September each year, as a rule, and entails a 10-mile march out and a 10-mile march back in full armour. It is done in memory of an old battle against the Shogunate Forces and helps to keep the martial spirit alive. The people who take part are a number of men from the district, wearing the fascinating old samurai armour of lacquer and coloured thread, and some 500 small boys with short swords dressed as fighting men. Most of the best fighting men come from this part of Japan, especially for the Navy, including old Admiral Togo, who was here today, and to whom I was introduced after lunch.

On return to *Renown* a group was taken of the combined suites, British and Japanese, after which we all said 'Sayonara' to them for the last time, and they took their departure. About 4.00 p.m. we sailed.

It is rather a relief having 'Freedom of Speech' once more, one obviously couldn't always express one's true thoughts in front of the Japanese Suite, with whom we lived. Only one bad slip was made – and that by our only trained diplomat, Godfrey. In the course of a luncheon at Akasaka Palace oranges were handed him with the name 'Blue Goose' stamped on them. 'What a ridiculous name for an orange,' he declared in a loud voice with all the Japs listening. 'Far better to call it the "Yellow Peril".'

The Journey Home

WEDNESDAY, 10 MAY   It was still quite cool today. I think we are all sorry to be leaving such an interesting and picturesque place as Japan, but there can be no doubt about everyone's joy at the prospect of returning home, especially mine! The return voyage is expected to last almost exactly six weeks.

As regards Japan from the point of view of a world power – my visit has been an eye-opener to me as regards her resources, her ships, her army. All the same I fear them less now that I know them to a certain extent, though I admit that they are wonderful in their way and have had the opportunity of picking only what is best, in their opinion, from foreign civilization. Their Navy is a crib of ours, their Army bears the unmistakable stamp of Prussia, their newspapers and police are revoltingly American and their ladies copy the latest Paris fashions. Nevertheless they are losing their old stoicism and unless considerable improvement in pay and conditions of living are granted to their services, they will have a mutiny. Japan is paying the penalty of taking civilization upon her. Unrest is growing among the working classes. Strikes and May Day disturbances have already started. A war might save them, as the people are still ultra patriotic: this is the war I fear.

SATURDAY, 13 MAY   We were met at the three-mile limit by U.S. destroyers, who escorted us in to Manila, the capital of the Philippine Islands. It is situated on the large main island, Luzon. The islands were captured from the Spaniards in the war of '98, and the Admiral was out here at the time.[1]

We landed at noon in the barge and drove off in motor cars, escorted by some local cavalry to Malacañan Palace, the old Spanish House, used as a residence for the Governor-General. H.E. is a well-

---

[1] The Philippines were at that time a United States dependency.

known General in the U.S. Army and seems a charming man. He is referred to by the Yankees as 'Governor-General Wood'.[1]

SUNDAY, 14 MAY We landed for lunch, going up the river by launch direct to the palace. After lunch I slipped away with our U.S. Secret Service man, Connelly, to see one of the notorious cock fights, which are now only legal on Sundays and holidays. Connelly's special job, in ordinary times, is crime and illegal gambling so he was pretty well known in all the low haunts of the city.

We motored to the nearest cock-pit, but had to get out and walk owing to the crowd of small two-wheeled calesas, drawn by diminutive ponies, which, having brought fares to the cock-pit, were blocking up the way waiting for them to come out. The place was even better than I had expected and might have been taken straight out of one of those 'Wild West' films which the Yankees are always producing.

The building was of timber and bamboo and consisted of a large, evil-smelling house, where there were many stalls with food and appurtenances for cock-fighting on sale. At the far end of the building, a circular erection rose to the roof and hundreds of Filipinos were gathered round its base, which formed the 'cock-pit' itself, being enclosed by bars, like a cage at the zoo.

Connelly arranged for us to be let into the pit itself and we were given two small stools among the 'elect', on the floor, which was of earth. Boxes, which really looked like ordinary wooden boxes, were arranged all the way round and were crowded with spectators, including well-dressed Filipino ladies. Behind us, seats rose in tiers and these were also crammed.

Presently two men entered carrying a cock each, and taking a bundle of dirty notes they threw them down as stakes in front of the 'boss', who sat in the centre and on our left. The owners then held up their birds for inspection, finally putting them down on the ground. At once pandemonium broke loose. Everybody stood up and shouted at everybody else, gesticulating wildly. I enquired as to the cause of all this excitement and was told that the 'betting' had started! As everyone yelled at the top of his voice I fail to understand how anyone else could make out what was being said, yet I was assured that some of the regular betters would take a dozen or twenty different bets at different

---

[1] Major General Leonard Wood had won the Congressional Medal for distinguished service against the Apache Indians. He had been a candidate for the Republican nomination as President in 1920.

odds and without writing down anything pay out or take in the right amount of money at the end of a fight.

When the odds are excessive and the crowd will only back the favourite the 'boss' orders both cocks to be removed and another fight is promoted between two fresh birds. I saw this happen once or twice including this first time.

After a while, when both 'chickens' (as my guide called them) were ready the owners unwound a piece of twine holding a scabbard in place over a wicked-looking gaff or spur, from two to three inches long, fastened over the natural spur on the cock's left leg. This gaff is like a miniature blade of a scythe, with the cutting edge up, and as sharp as a razor. The birds were then held out and 'blooded' by being allowed to peck at each other so as to thoroughly rouse them. When they were set down they fairly flew at each other, as though they had been life-long enemies waiting for this chance. They would flutter up and strike with their left leg and strut round each other waiting for another opening, but they always faced each other, neck well out and neck-feathers erect.

Some fights lasted quite a while, others were finished in a few seconds, as one true stab of that gaff would kill a bird outright, while one slash would cut its head off. After I had seen the gaff I expected to be revolted by what was to follow, but one only sees feathers flying and presently one of the birds collapses or runs away. Of course it is a brutal sport, but unless one is on the look-out for horrors one doesn't see them, while the crowd and the surroundings are all so interesting that a visit is amply worth while.

I managed to buy one of the gaffs that had been brought along for use that day and was shown how it is fastened to the cock's leg. There is such an art in getting this gaff to fit in exactly the right way and at the same angle as the natural spur that special men are employed to do this alone and get at least a peso for each bird. I also bought a peg and rope, such as is used for pegging out fighting birds. These fowls are much prized by the Filipinos and even in the tram cars, I was told, they will take out their cocks and stroke them and massage them to make them strong.

Connelly bought an egg (I think a duck's egg) from an old hag and asked if I was easily 'offensive'. Not being quite sure what he meant I said 'No'. He forthwith gave the egg to a Filipino on condition that he ate it then and there, which he did, smacking his lips. The egg contained a baby bird within 24 hours of hatching, naked, boiled and horrible! It is considered a great delicacy among the natives but made me feel very 'offensive'.

MONDAY, 15 MAY We left Manila with regret as we had such an excellent time there, while the 'stunts' were reduced to a reasonable minimum. Of course the Governor-General is exceptional and has succeeded in collecting a most delightful staff, but (for a short while anyway) Americans are always amusing and refreshing to meet.

WEDNESDAY, 17 MAY About noon we anchored at Port Victoria, which is the main harbour of the small island of Labuan. Labuan is part of the Straits Settlements, though geographically spoken of as part of Borneo. There is no real pretence of civilization here, the whites on Labuan only number 17, and they consider that a lot compared to stations on the main land. Only one white man has ever crossed the centre of Borneo itself. So we are at last in a really unexplored part of the world, though it will be our fate to see only the tiny stretch of known country of course.

THURSDAY, 18 MAY David went to Jesselton[1] in the *Cairo*, leaving at 8.00 a.m. This is the seat of administration of the North Borneo Chartered Company. We drove in cars to Government House, escorted by a score of Bajau mounted spearsmen, on their quaint little ponies. There was a lunch party here, at which Raja Brooke was present, and afterwards a dozen head hunters, whom it had taken two months to collect from the interior, were brought up and gave an exhibition with their blow pipes. These 'pipes' resemble spears in that they have a spear head lashed to the side like a bayonet, the shaft being about 6 ft long and, of course, hollow. The dart is 6 or 7 ins long, very thin and sharp, fitted with a pith 'driving band'. This they insert in the rear end and then holding the blow pipe at this end with both hands touching, they raise it and blow hard and steadily. With a final 'phut' the dart leaves the tube at a high velocity and in every case these men scored an 'inner' or a 'bull' at 20 yards range on a 12-inch target! I obtained a sapok (blow pipe), kobun (quiver) and a supply of ramok (darts) from one of these men.

---

[1] It was at Jesselton that Edwina was to die in February 1960.

FRIDAY, 19 MAY   David and seven of us went in the *Cairo* at 8.30 a.m. to Sabo Point where she anchored, while we went in the steam launch up the river to Brunei, taking rifles as the river is full of crocodiles. Twenty thousand of the inhabitants of the town live in rickety little houses built on piles in the middle of the harbour and round these we steamed to examine them at leisure.

On landing David was met by a polite little gentleman in silk orange-coloured pyjamas, American boots and a gold hat. From the fact that he wore the K.C.M.G. on his pyjamas I correctly assumed him to be H.H. The Sultan of Brunei. David was now led to a large palanquin into which both he and the Sultan clambered. They were carried to the labau or audience hall, while we walked behind with the native notables. A Durbar was held here, in which honey-coloured coffee and 18-inch long native cigars wrapped in fibre were handed round, like 'itr and pan' and short addresses were exchanged.

After this we changed into khaki shorts in the Government Offices and walked about two miles up to a delightful spot by a waterfall and pool, where a picnic lunch had been arranged. I had been on the look out to buy a head hunter's shield and sword for some while but it was only five minutes before our final departure that I secured specimens from some warriors near the water front. The owner of the shield was most reluctant to give it up even for ten dollars! I also bought some delightfully vulgar 'back-firing' brass elephants and tigers. We watched some water sports as we departed including a 'tug of war' between two canoes.

Renown sailed at 8.30 p.m.

TUESDAY, 23 MAY   We left the ship officially at 10.00 a.m. The ship had had to anchor nearly 18 miles out from Penang as the channel was not deep enough so we did not reach Victoria Pier until noon, when it suddenly came on to rain.

We had lunch at the Penang Club and afterwards David played snooker. We went on to watch some sports on the Esplanade afterwards, as the rain stopped, and then returned to the Residency. We left about 7.00 p.m., David shaking hands with ex-service men on the jetty.

In the harbour I noticed how phosphorescent the bow wave was. It seemed as though the full moon or some quiet light must be shining on the foam, but as we got outside the harbour this effect almost completely disappeared.

We reached *Renown* at 9.00 p.m. and immediately sailed.

SATURDAY, 27 MAY We arrived at Trincomalee at 6.00 a.m. and spent the day on board up to 3.30 p.m. when we landed in the barge and drove up to the Fort. On the way back we visited the club, which has been taken on by the civilians since the Navy gave up Trinco as a dockyard some 15 or 20 years ago.

THURSDAY, 1 JUNE June at last! It is wonderful to think that we get back this very month. The day was uneventful. Godfrey obtained a male and a female mongoose in Ceylon and they provide a certain amount of amusement.

SUNDAY, 4 JUNE I think I showed considerable moral courage today by going to Church and hearing my banns read out for the first time. Nobody forbade them.

SATURDAY, 10 JUNE Shepheard's is really rather a delightful hotel, and as the season is not on, it is neither very crowded nor as ruinously expensive as one is led to believe. It is rather funny, all the same having to pay for one's drinks, cabs, guides, etc., having been the guests of the government in so many other places.

I think Cairo is a fascinating place. We spent most of the morning at Hatoun's shop, where I couldn't resist buying a rather fine old Persian dagger with gold damascene work on the blade. I also got a Persian helmet with chain mail, shield, gauntlet, battle-axe, mace and another dagger. We then went on to the museum, which is wonderfully interesting. Here we saw the Mummy of Rameses II, the chap who would not let the Children of Israel go. There were plenty of other mummies and relics, including those of dogs, crocodiles, cats, birds, fishes, etc.

Fruity and I motored out about midnight to Ghiza and there engaged donkeys and rode out to see the Sphinx and Pyramids by moonlight. They are wonderful and give one the same sort of feeling as Fujiyama and I believe the Taj Mahal does. The desert by moonlight is quite romantic.

SUNDAY, 11 JUNE I was rather tired after we came back from the Pyramids last night and so had breakfast in bed and only turned out in time for lunch. We had to put on uniform and lunch with Fouad, the newly created King of Egypt.

We were warned that His Majesty barked like a dog but I have also been told of a barking lizard and a barking pigeon, neither of which I ever heard barking, and therefore treated this statement with reserve. After we had all assembled and luncheon had been announced, there was an awkward silence, which was suddenly shattered by a noise, such as might have been produced by a big dog which has had its tail trodden on. This was followed by a second yelp, which just about finished me off, as there could be no doubt as to its royal origin. Pinching myself furiously I walked in to luncheon. No sooner had we sat down in dead silence than the King barked again, four times in quick succession. I struggled afresh and hardly dared look at David and the others, who appeared to be on the point of convulsions. Throughout lunch His Majesty barked at odd moments and when he was showing David round the palace, one could trace the party by the royal yappings.

MONDAY, 12 JUNE   The train reached Port Said in the small hours of the morning and we at once proceeded on board *Renown*, who had done the passage through the canal while we were in Cairo. About 8.00 a.m. the ship sailed, but most of us slept on, being quite tired out. I played poker again in the evening and lost.

TUESDAY, 13 JUNE   An uneventful though decidedly cooler day at sea. I spent most of it carrying on with the statistical records of the tour, which I am preparing. I am also doing several maps and charts, two being of the whole world showing our tracks on the tours, which are for David and myself.[1]

SUNDAY, 18 JUNE   My banns were successfully read out for the third time.

MONDAY, 19 JUNE   We reached Plymouth Harbour, with an escort of destroyers, about 5.30 p.m. Bertie and, to my surprise Georgie, came on board and remained to dinner. At 8.30 p.m. the ship proceeded up harbour alongside Devonport dockyard. We secured ahead of the *Hood*. Georgie I arranged to put up for the night in Lord Cromer's old cabin, among all the dwarf trees from Japan.

WEDNESDAY, 21 JUNE   After breakfast David addressed the men and

[1] One of these, engraved on a silver globe, provided the Prince of Wales's wedding present to the Mountbattens.

shook hands with the officers. Bertie then came onboard and we left the ship officially at about 10.00 a.m.

David received an address from the Mayor of Plymouth and we embarked in cars and drove off to North Road Station. It was a great joy to see English crowds again and indeed it was practically our first sight of an all-white population since we left home. Georgie drove in our car and came up with us in the special train, which left at 11.00 a.m.

We had lunch in the train and arrived at about 3.30 p.m. The King and Queen and the usual high officials were there and after greetings were over we entered carriages and did an official drive through London to Buckingham Palace. The King, Bertie and Harry drove with David in the first carriage. Edwina was on the balcony of Bath House to see the procession.

The crowd gave David a wonderful reception, and thanks to the efforts of the penny press they even gave me a cheer in places with suitable remarks like 'She's waiting for you'.

At Buck House the entire family in its largest sense was collected and much kissing went on. Eventually we drove on to York House, where I hurriedly changed into a monkey jacket and then, the tour being over, drove in a taxi to 3 Belgrave Place to see Edwina who was staying there.

INDEX

More often than not the Prince of Wales and Mountbatten did the same things. I have therefore made separate index entries for the latter only when he was doing something different or the occasion was of particular significance to him.

A comma instead of a semi-colon between page references indicates that both references are covered by the previous sub-heading.

Index